AFRIKAANS
V O C A B U L A R Y

FOR ENGLISH SPEAKERS

ENGLISH-
AFRIKAANS

The most useful words
To expand your lexicon and sharpen
your language skills

9000 words

Afrikaans vocabulary for English speakers - 9000 words

By Andrey Taranov

T&P Books vocabularies are intended for helping you learn, memorize and review foreign words. The dictionary is divided into themes, covering all major spheres of everyday activities, business, science, culture, etc.

The process of learning words using T&P Books' theme-based dictionaries gives you the following advantages:

- Correctly grouped source information predetermines success at subsequent stages of word memorization
- Availability of words derived from the same root allowing memorization of word units (rather than separate words)
- Small units of words facilitate the process of establishing associative links needed for consolidation of vocabulary
- Level of language knowledge can be estimated by the number of learned words

T&P Books Publishing
www.tpbooks.com

ISBN: 978-1-78716-483-3

This book is also available in E-book formats.
Please visit www.tpbooks.com or the major online bookstores.

AFRIKAANS VOCABULARY
for English speakers

T&P Books vocabularies are intended to help you learn, memorize, and review foreign words. The vocabulary contains over 9000 commonly used words arranged thematically.

- Vocabulary contains the most commonly used words
- Recommended as an addition to any language course
- Meets the needs of beginners and advanced learners of foreign languages
- Convenient for daily use, revision sessions, and self-testing activities
- Allows you to assess your vocabulary

Special features of the vocabulary

- Words are organized according to their meaning, not alphabetically
- Words are presented in three columns to facilitate the reviewing and self-testing processes
- Words in groups are divided into small blocks to facilitate the learning process
- The vocabulary offers a convenient and simple transcription of each foreign word

The vocabulary has 256 topics including:

Basic Concepts, Numbers, Colors, Months, Seasons, Units of Measurement, Clothing & Accessories, Food & Nutrition, Restaurant, Family Members, Relatives, Character, Feelings, Emotions, Diseases, City, Town, Sightseeing, Shopping, Money, House, Home, Office, Working in the Office, Import & Export, Marketing, Job Search, Sports, Education, Computer, Internet, Tools, Nature, Countries, Nationalities and more ...

T&P BOOKS' THEME-BASED DICTIONARIES

The Correct System for Memorizing Foreign Words

Acquiring vocabulary is one of the most important elements of learning a foreign language, because words allow us to express our thoughts, ask questions, and provide answers. An inadequate vocabulary can impede communication with a foreigner and make it difficult to understand a book or movie well.

The pace of activity in all spheres of modern life, including the learning of modern languages, has increased. Today, we need to memorize large amounts of information (grammar rules, foreign words, etc.) within a short period. However, this does not need to be difficult. All you need to do is to choose the right training materials, learn a few special techniques, and develop your individual training system.

Having a system is critical to the process of language learning. Many people fail to succeed in this regard; they cannot master a foreign language because they fail to follow a system comprised of selecting materials, organizing lessons, arranging new words to be learned, and so on. The lack of a system causes confusion and eventually, lowers self-confidence.

T&P Books' theme-based dictionaries can be included in the list of elements needed for creating an effective system for learning foreign words. These dictionaries were specially developed for learning purposes and are meant to help students effectively memorize words and expand their vocabulary.

Generally speaking, the process of learning words consists of three main elements:

- Reception (creation or acquisition) of a training material, such as a word list
- Work aimed at memorizing new words
- Work aimed at reviewing the learned words, such as self-testing

All three elements are equally important since they determine the quality of work and the final result. All three processes require certain skills and a well-thought-out approach.

New words are often encountered quite randomly when learning a foreign language and it may be difficult to include them all in a unified list. As a result, these words remain written on scraps of paper, in book margins, textbooks, and so on. In order to systematize such words, we have to create and continually update a "book of new words." A paper notebook, a netbook, or a tablet PC can be used for these purposes.

This "book of new words" will be your personal, unique list of words. However, it will only contain the words that you came across during the learning process. For example, you might have written down the words "Sunday," "Tuesday," and "Friday." However, there are additional words for days of the week, for example, "Saturday," that are missing, and your list of words would be incomplete. Using a theme dictionary, in addition to the "book of new words," is a reasonable solution to this problem.

The theme-based dictionary may serve as the basis for expanding your vocabulary.

It will be your big "book of new words" containing the most frequently used words of a foreign language already included. There are quite a few theme-based dictionaries available, and you should ensure that you make the right choice in order to get the maximum benefit from your purchase.

Therefore, we suggest using theme-based dictionaries from T&P Books Publishing as an aid to learning foreign words. Our books are specially developed for effective use in the sphere of vocabulary systematization, expansion and review.

Theme-based dictionaries are not a magical solution to learning new words. However, they can serve as your main database to aid foreign-language acquisition. Apart from theme dictionaries, you can have copybooks for writing down new words, flash cards, glossaries for various texts, as well as other resources; however, a good theme dictionary will always remain your primary collection of words.

T&P Books' theme-based dictionaries are specialty books that contain the most frequently used words in a language.

The main characteristic of such dictionaries is the division of words into themes. For example, the *City* theme contains the words "street," "crossroads," "square," "fountain," and so on. The *Talking* theme might contain words like "to talk," "to ask," "question," and "answer".

All the words in a theme are divided into smaller units, each comprising 3–5 words. Such an arrangement improves the perception of words and makes the learning process less tiresome. Each unit contains a selection of words with similar meanings or identical roots. This allows you to learn words in small groups and establish other associative links that have a positive effect on memorization.

The words on each page are placed in three columns: a word in your native language, its translation, and its transcription. Such positioning allows for the use of techniques for effective memorization. After closing the translation column, you can flip through and review foreign words, and vice versa. "This is an easy and convenient method of review – one that we recommend you do often."

Our theme-based dictionaries contain transcriptions for all the foreign words. Unfortunately, none of the existing transcriptions are able to convey the exact nuances of foreign pronunciation. That is why we recommend using the transcriptions only as a supplementary learning aid. Correct pronunciation can only be acquired with the help of sound. Therefore our collection includes audio theme-based dictionaries.

The process of learning words using T&P Books' theme-based dictionaries gives you the following advantages:

- You have correctly grouped source information, which predetermines your success at subsequent stages of word memorization
- Availability of words derived from the same root (lazy, lazily, lazybones), allowing you to memorize word units instead of separate words
- Small units of words facilitate the process of establishing associative links needed for consolidation of vocabulary
- You can estimate the number of learned words and hence your level of language knowledge
- The dictionary allows for the creation of an effective and high-quality revision process
- You can revise certain themes several times, modifying the revision methods and techniques
- Audio versions of the dictionaries help you to work out the pronunciation of words and develop your skills of auditory word perception

The T&P Books' theme-based dictionaries are offered in several variants differing in the number of words: 1.500, 3.000, 5.000, 7.000, and 9.000 words. There are also dictionaries containing 15,000 words for some language combinations. Your choice of dictionary will depend on your knowledge level and goals.

We sincerely believe that our dictionaries will become your trusty assistant in learning foreign languages and will allow you to easily acquire the necessary vocabulary.

TABLE OF CONTENTS

PRONUNCIATION GUIDE

T&P phonetic alphabet	Afrikaans example	English example
[a]	land	shorter than in ask
[ã]	straat	calf, palm
[æ]	hout	chess, man
[o], [ɔ]	Australië	drop, baught
[e]	metaal	elm, medal
[ɛ]	aanlê	man, bad
[ə]	filter	driver, teacher
[ɪ]	uur	big, America
[i]	billik	shorter than in feet
[ĩ]	naïef	tree, big
[o]	koppie	pod, John
[ø]	akteur	eternal, church
[œ]	fluit	German Hölle
[u]	hulle	book
[ʊ]	hout	good, booklet
[b]	bakker	baby, book
[d]	donder	day, doctor
[f]	navraag	face, food
[g]	burger	game, gold
[h]	driehoek	home, have
[j]	byvoeg	yes, New York
[k]	kamera	clock, kiss
[l]	loon	lace, people
[m]	môre	magic, milk
[n]	neef	sang, thing
[p]	pyp	pencil, private
[r]	rigting	rice, radio
[s]	oplos	city, boss
[t]	lood, tenk	tourist, trip
[v]	bewaar	very, river
[w]	oorwinnaar	vase, winter
[z]	zoem	zebra, please
[dʒ]	enjin	joke, general
[ʃ]	artisjok	machine, shark
[ŋ]	kans	English, ring

T&P phonetic alphabet	Afrikaans example	English example
[tʃ]	tjek	church, French
[ʒ]	beige	forge, pleasure
[x]	agent	as in Scots 'loch'

ABBREVIATIONS
used in the vocabulary

English abbreviations

ab.	-	about
adj	-	adjective
adv	-	adverb
anim.	-	animate
as adj	-	attributive noun used as adjective
e.g.	-	for example
etc.	-	et cetera
fam.	-	familiar
fem.	-	feminine
form.	-	formal
inanim.	-	inanimate
masc.	-	masculine
math	-	mathematics
mil.	-	military
n	-	noun
pl	-	plural
pron.	-	pronoun
sb	-	somebody
sing.	-	singular
sth	-	something
v aux	-	auxiliary verb
vi	-	intransitive verb
vi, vt	-	intransitive, transitive verb
vt	-	transitive verb

BASIC CONCEPTS

Basic concepts. Part 1

1. Pronouns

I, me	ek, my	[ɛk], [maj]
you	jy	[jaj]
he	hy	[haj]
she	sy	[saj]
it	dit	[dit]
we	ons	[ɔŋs]
you (to a group)	julle	[jullə]
you (polite, sing.)	u	[u]
you (polite, pl)	u	[u]
they	hulle	[hullə]

2. Greetings. Salutations. Farewells

Hello! (fam.)	Hallo!	[hallo!]
Hello! (form.)	Hallo!	[hallo!]
Good morning!	Goeie môre!	[χuje mɔrə!]
Good afternoon!	Goeiemiddag!	[χuje·middaχ!]
Good evening!	Goeienaand!	[χuje·nānt!]
to say hello	dagsê	[daχsɛ:]
Hi! (hello)	Hallo!	[hallo!]
greeting (n)	groet	[χrut]
to greet (vt)	groet	[χrut]
How are you?	Hoe gaan dit?	[hu χān dit?]
What's new?	Hoe gaan dit?	[hu χān dit?]
Goodbye!	Totsiens!	[totsiŋs!]
Bye!	Koebaai!	[kubāi!]
See you soon!	Totsiens!	[totsiŋs!]
Farewell!	Totsiens!	[totsiŋs!]
Farewell! (to a friend)	Mooi loop!	[moj loəp!]
Farewell! (form.)	Vaarwel!	[fārwel!]
to say goodbye	afskeid neem	[afskæjt neəm]
So long!	Koebaai!	[kubāi!]

Thank you!	Dankie!	[danki!]
Thank you very much!	Baie dankie!	[baje danki!]
You're welcome	Plesier	[plesir]
Don't mention it!	Plesier!	[plesir!]
It was nothing	Plesier	[plesir]

Excuse me! (fam.)	Ekskuus!	[ɛkskɪs!]
Excuse me! (form.)	Verskoon my!	[ferskoən maj!]
to excuse (forgive)	verskoon	[ferskoən]

to apologize (vi)	verskoning vra	[ferskoniŋ fra]
My apologies	Verskoning	[ferskoniŋ]
I'm sorry!	Ek is jammer!	[ɛk is jammər!]

to forgive (vt)	vergewe	[ferχevə]
It's okay! (that's all right)	Maak nie saak nie!	[māk ni sāk ni!]
please (adv)	asseblief	[asseblif]

Don't forget!	Vergeet dit nie!	[ferχeet dit ni!]
Certainly!	Beslis!	[beslis!]
Of course not!	Natuurlik nie!	[natɪrlik ni!]
Okay! (I agree)	OK!	[okej!]
That's enough!	Dis genoeg!	[dis χenuχ!]

3. How to address

Excuse me, ...	Verskoon my, ...	[ferskoən maj, ...]
mister, sir	meneer	[meneər]
ma'am	mevrou	[mefræʊ]
miss	juffrou	[juffræʊ]

young man	jongman	[joŋman]
young man (little boy, kid)	boet	[but]
miss (little girl)	sussie	[sussi]

4. Cardinal numbers. Part 1

0 zero	nul	[nul]
1 one	een	[eən]
2 two	twee	[tweə]
3 three	drie	[dri]
4 four	vier	[fir]

5 five	vyf	[fajf]
6 six	ses	[ses]
7 seven	sewe	[sevə]
8 eight	ag	[aχ]
9 nine	nege	[neχə]

10 ten	**tien**	[tin]
11 eleven	**elf**	[εlf]
12 twelve	**twaalf**	[twãlf]
13 thirteen	**dertien**	[dertin]
14 fourteen	**veertien**	[feərtin]

15 fifteen	**vyftien**	[fajftin]
16 sixteen	**sestien**	[sestin]
17 seventeen	**sewetien**	[sevətin]
18 eighteen	**agtien**	[aχtin]
19 nineteen	**negetien**	[neχetin]

20 twenty	**twintig**	[twintəχ]
21 twenty-one	**een-en-twintig**	[eən-en-twintəχ]
22 twenty-two	**twee-en-twintig**	[tweə-en-twintəχ]
23 twenty-three	**drie-en-twintig**	[dri-en-twintəχ]

30 thirty	**dertig**	[dertəχ]
31 thirty-one	**een-en-dertig**	[eən-en-dertəχ]
32 thirty-two	**twee-en-dertig**	[tweə-en-dertəχ]
33 thirty-three	**drie-en-dertig**	[dri-en-dertəχ]

40 forty	**veertig**	[feərtəχ]
41 forty-one	**een-en-veertig**	[eən-en-feərtəχ]
42 forty-two	**twee-en-veertig**	[tweə-en-feərtəχ]
43 forty-three	**vier-en-veertig**	[fir-en-feərtəχ]

50 fifty	**vyftig**	[fajftəχ]
51 fifty-one	**een-en-vyftig**	[eən-en-fajftəχ]
52 fifty-two	**twee-en-vyftig**	[tweə-en-fajftəχ]
53 fifty-three	**drie-en-vyftig**	[dri-en-fajftəχ]

60 sixty	**sestig**	[sestəχ]
61 sixty-one	**een-en-sestig**	[eən-en-sestəχ]
62 sixty-two	**twee-en-sestig**	[tweə-en-sestəχ]
63 sixty-three	**drie-en-sestig**	[dri-en-sestəχ]

70 seventy	**sewentig**	[seventəχ]
71 seventy-one	**een-en-sewentig**	[eən-en-seventəχ]
72 seventy-two	**twee-en-sewentig**	[tweə-en-seventəχ]
73 seventy-three	**drie-en-sewentig**	[dri-en-seventəχ]

80 eighty	**tagtig**	[taχtəχ]
81 eighty-one	**een-en-tagtig**	[eən-en-taχtəχ]
82 eighty-two	**twee-en-tagtig**	[tweə-en-taχtəχ]
83 eighty-three	**drie-en-tagtig**	[dri-en-taχtəχ]

90 ninety	**negentig**	[neχentəχ]
91 ninety-one	**een-en-negentig**	[eən-en-neχentəχ]
92 ninety-two	**twee-en-negentig**	[tweə-en-neχentəχ]
93 ninety-three	**drie-en-negentig**	[dri-en-neχentəχ]

5. Cardinal numbers. Part 2

100 one hundred	**honderd**	[hondərt]
200 two hundred	**tweehonderd**	[twee·hondərt]
300 three hundred	**driehonderd**	[dri·hondərt]
400 four hundred	**vierhonderd**	[fir·hondərt]
500 five hundred	**vyfhonderd**	[fajf·hondərt]
600 six hundred	**seshonderd**	[ses·hondərt]
700 seven hundred	**sewehonderd**	[sevə·hondərt]
800 eight hundred	**aghonderd**	[aχ·hondərt]
900 nine hundred	**negehonderd**	[neχə·hondərt]
1000 one thousand	**duisend**	[dœisent]
2000 two thousand	**tweeduisend**	[twee·dœisent]
3000 three thousand	**drieduisend**	[dri·dœisent]
10000 ten thousand	**tienduisend**	[tin·dœisent]
one hundred thousand	**honderdduisend**	[hondərt·dajsent]
million	**miljoen**	[miljun]
billion	**miljard**	[miljart]

6. Ordinal numbers

first (adj)	**eerste**	[eərstə]
second (adj)	**tweede**	[tweedə]
third (adj)	**derde**	[derdə]
fourth (adj)	**vierde**	[firdə]
fifth (adj)	**vyfde**	[fajfdə]
sixth (adj)	**sesde**	[sesdə]
seventh (adj)	**sewende**	[sevendə]
eighth (adj)	**agste**	[aχstə]
ninth (adj)	**negende**	[neχendə]
tenth (adj)	**tiende**	[tində]

7. Numbers. Fractions

fraction	**breuk**	[brøək]
one half	**helfte**	[hɛlftə]
one third	**derde**	[derdə]
one quarter	**kwart**	[kwart]
one eighth	**agste**	[aχstə]
one tenth	**tiende**	[tində]
two thirds	**twee derde**	[tweə derdə]
three quarters	**driekwart**	[drikwart]

8. Numbers. Basic operations

subtraction	aftrekking	[aftrɛkkiŋ]
to subtract (vi, vt)	aftrek	[aftrek]
division	deling	[deliŋ]
to divide (vt)	deel	[deəl]
addition	optelling	[optɛlliŋ]
to add up (vt)	optel	[optəl]
to add (vi, vt)	optel	[optəl]
multiplication	vermenigvuldiging	[fermeniχ·fuldəχiŋ]
to multiply (vt)	vermenigvuldig	[fermeniχ·fuldəχ]

9. Numbers. Miscellaneous

digit, figure	syfer	[sajfər]
number	nommer	[nommər]
numeral	telwoord	[tɛlwoərt]
minus sign	minusteken	[minus·tekən]
plus sign	plusteken	[plus·tekən]
formula	formule	[formulə]
calculation	berekening	[berekeniŋ]
to count (vi, vt)	tel	[təl]
to count up	optel	[optəl]
to compare (vt)	vergelyk	[ferχəlajk]
How much?	Hoeveel?	[hufeəl?]
How many?	Hoeveel?	[hufeəl?]
sum, total	som, totaal	[som], [totāl]
result	resultaat	[resultāt]
remainder	oorskot	[oərskot]
little (I had ~ time)	min	[min]
few (I have ~ friends)	min	[min]
the rest	die res	[di res]
dozen	dosyn	[dosajn]
in half (adv)	middeldeur	[middəldøər]
equally (evenly)	gelyk	[χelajk]
half	helfte	[hɛlftə]
time (three ~s)	maal	[māl]

10. The most important verbs. Part 1

to advise (vt)	aanraai	[ānrāi]
to agree (say yes)	saamstem	[sāmstem]

to answer (vi, vt)	antwoord	[antwoərt]
to apologize (vi)	verskoning vra	[ferskoniŋ fra]
to arrive (vi)	aankom	[ānkom]

to ask (~ oneself)	vra	[fra]
to ask (~ sb to do sth)	vra	[fra]
to be (vi)	wees	[veəs]

to be afraid	bang wees	[baŋ veəs]
to be hungry	honger wees	[hoŋər veəs]
to be interested in ...	belangstel in ...	[belaŋstəl in ...]
to be needed	nodig wees	[nodəχ veəs]
to be surprised	verbaas wees	[ferbās veəs]

to be thirsty	dors wees	[dors veəs]
to begin (vt)	begin	[beχin]
to belong to ...	behoort aan ...	[behoərt ān ...]
to boast (vi)	spog	[spoχ]
to break (split into pieces)	breek	[breək]

to call (~ for help)	roep	[rup]
can (v aux)	kan	[kan]
to catch (vt)	vang	[faŋ]
to change (vt)	verander	[ferandər]
to choose (select)	kies	[kis]

to come down (the stairs)	afkom	[afkom]
to compare (vt)	vergelyk	[ferχəlajk]
to complain (vi, vt)	kla	[kla]
to confuse (mix up)	verwar	[ferwar]
to continue (vt)	aangaan	[ānχān]
to control (vt)	kontroleer	[kontroleər]

to cook (dinner)	kook	[koək]
to cost (vt)	kos	[kos]
to count (add up)	tel	[təl]
to count on ...	reken op ...	[reken op ...]
to create (vt)	skep	[skep]
to cry (weep)	huil	[hœil]

11. The most important verbs. Part 2

to deceive (vi, vt)	bedrieg	[bedrəχ]
to decorate (tree, street)	versier	[fersir]
to defend (a country, etc.)	verdedig	[ferdedəχ]
to demand (request firmly)	eis	[æjs]
to dig (vt)	grawe	[χravə]

| to discuss (vt) | bespreek | [bespreək] |
| to do (vt) | doen | [dun] |

to doubt (have doubts)	twyfel	[twajfəl]
to drop (let fall)	laat val	[lāt fal]
to enter (room, house, etc.)	binnegaan	[binnəχān]

to excuse (forgive)	verskoon	[ferskoən]
to exist (vi)	bestaan	[bestān]
to expect (foresee)	voorsien	[foərsin]
to explain (vt)	verduidelik	[ferdœeidəlik]
to fall (vi)	val	[fal]

to find (vt)	vind	[fint]
to finish (vt)	klaarmaak	[klārmāk]
to fly (vi)	vlieg	[fliχ]
to follow ... (come after)	volg ...	[folχ ...]
to forget (vi, vt)	vergeet	[ferχeət]

to forgive (vt)	vergewe	[ferχevə]
to give (vt)	gee	[χeə]
to go (on foot)	gaan	[χān]

to go for a swim	gaan swem	[χān swem]
to go out (for dinner, etc.)	uitgaan	[œitχān]
to guess (the answer)	raai	[rāi]

to have (vt)	hê	[hɛ:]
to have breakfast	ontbyt	[ontbajt]
to have dinner	aandete gebruik	[āndetə χebrœik]
to have lunch	gaan eet	[χān eət]
to hear (vt)	hoor	[hoər]

to help (vt)	help	[hɛlp]
to hide (vt)	wegsteek	[veχsteək]
to hope (vi, vt)	hoop	[hoəp]
to hunt (vi, vt)	jag	[jaχ]
to hurry (vi)	opskud	[opskut]

12. The most important verbs. Part 3

to inform (vt)	in kennis stel	[in kɛnnis stəl]
to insist (vi, vt)	aandring	[āndriŋ]
to insult (vt)	beledig	[beledəχ]
to invite (vt)	uitnooi	[œitnoj]
to joke (vi)	grappies maak	[χrappis māk]

to keep (vt)	bewaar	[bevār]
to keep silent	stilbly	[stilblaj]
to kill (vt)	doodmaak	[doədmāk]
to know (sb)	ken	[ken]
to know (sth)	weet	[veət]

to laugh (vi)	lag	[laχ]
to liberate (city, etc.)	bevry	[befraj]
to like (I like ...)	hou van	[hæʊ fan]
to look for ... (search)	soek ...	[suk ...]
to love (sb)	liefhê	[lifhɛ:]

to manage, to run	beheer	[beheər]
to mean (signify)	beteken	[betekən]
to mention (talk about)	verwys na	[ferwajs na]
to miss (school, etc.)	bank	[bank]
to notice (see)	raaksien	[rāksin]

to object (vi, vt)	beswaar maak	[beswār māk]
to observe (see)	waarneem	[vārneəm]
to open (vt)	oopmaak	[oəpmāk]
to order (meal, etc.)	bestel	[bestəl]
to order (mil.)	beveel	[befeəl]
to own (possess)	besit	[besit]

to participate (vi)	deelneem	[deəlneəm]
to pay (vi, vt)	betaal	[betāl]
to permit (vt)	toestaan	[tustān]
to plan (vt)	beplan	[beplan]
to play (children)	speel	[speəl]

to pray (vi, vt)	bid	[bit]
to prefer (vt)	verkies	[ferkis]
to promise (vt)	beloof	[beloəf]
to pronounce (vt)	uitspreek	[œitspreək]
to propose (vt)	voorstel	[foərstəl]
to punish (vt)	straf	[straf]

13. The most important verbs. Part 4

to read (vi, vt)	lees	[leəs]
to recommend (vt)	aanbeveel	[ānbefeəl]
to refuse (vi, vt)	weier	[væjer]
to regret (be sorry)	jammer wees	[jammər veəs]
to rent (sth from sb)	huur	[hɪr]

to repeat (say again)	herhaal	[herhāl]
to reserve, to book	bespreek	[bespreək]
to run (vi)	hardloop	[hardloəp]
to save (rescue)	red	[ret]
to say (~ thank you)	sê	[sɛ:]

to scold (vt)	uitvaar teen	[œitfār teən]
to see (vt)	sien	[sin]
to sell (vt)	verkoop	[ferkoəp]
to send (vt)	stuur	[stɪr]

to shoot (vi)	skiet	[skit]
to shout (vi)	skreeu	[skriʊ]
to show (vt)	wys	[vajs]
to sign (document)	teken	[tekən]
to sit down (vi)	gaan sit	[χān sit]

to smile (vi)	glimlag	[χlimlaχ]
to speak (vi, vt)	praat	[prāt]
to steal (money, etc.)	steel	[steəl]
to stop (for pause, etc.)	stilhou	[stilhæʊ]
to stop	ophou	[ophæʊ]
(please ~ calling me)		

to study (vt)	studeer	[studeər]
to swim (vi)	swem	[swem]
to take (vt)	vat	[fat]
to think (vi, vt)	dink	[dink]
to threaten (vt)	dreig	[dræjχ]

to touch (with hands)	aanraak	[ānrāk]
to translate (vt)	vertaal	[fertāl]
to trust (vt)	vertrou	[fertræʊ]
to try (attempt)	probeer	[probeər]
to turn (e.g., ~ left)	draai	[drāi]

to underestimate (vt)	onderskat	[ondərskat]
to understand (vt)	verstaan	[ferstān]
to unite (vt)	verenig	[ferenəχ]
to wait (vt)	wag	[vaχ]

to want (wish, desire)	wil	[vil]
to warn (vt)	waarsku	[vārsku]
to work (vi)	werk	[verk]
to write (vt)	skryf	[skrajf]
to write down	opskryf	[opskrajf]

14. Colors

color	kleur	[kløər]
shade (tint)	skakering	[skakeriŋ]
hue	tint	[tint]
rainbow	reënboog	[reɛn·boəχ]

white (adj)	wit	[vit]
black (adj)	swart	[swart]
gray (adj)	grys	[χrajs]

green (adj)	groen	[χrun]
yellow (adj)	geel	[χeəl]
red (adj)	rooi	[roj]

blue (adj)	blou	[blæʊ]
light blue (adj)	ligblou	[liχ·blæʊ]
pink (adj)	pienk	[pink]
orange (adj)	oranje	[oranje]
violet (adj)	pers	[pers]
brown (adj)	bruin	[brœin]
golden (adj)	goue	[χæʊə]
silvery (adj)	silweragtig	[silweraχtəχ]
beige (adj)	beige	[bɛ:iʒ]
cream (adj)	roomkleurig	[roəm·kløərəχ]
turquoise (adj)	turkoois	[turkojs]
cherry red (adj)	kersierooi	[kersi·roj]
lilac (adj)	lila	[lila]
crimson (adj)	karmosyn	[karmosajn]
light (adj)	lig	[liχ]
dark (adj)	donker	[donkər]
bright, vivid (adj)	helder	[hɛldər]
colored (pencils)	kleurig	[kløərəχ]
color (e.g., ~ film)	kleur	[kløər]
black-and-white (adj)	swart-wit	[swart-wit]
plain (one-colored)	effe	[ɛffə]
multicolored (adj)	veelkleurig	[feəlkløərəχ]

15. Questions

Who?	Wie?	[vi?]
What?	Wat?	[vat?]
Where? (at, in)	Waar?	[vār?]
Where (to)?	Waarheen?	[vārheən?]
From where?	Waarvandaan?	[vārfandān?]
When?	Wanneer?	[vanneər?]
Why? (What for?)	Hoekom?	[hukom?]
Why? (~ are you crying?)	Hoekom?	[hukom?]
What for?	Vir wat?	[fir vat?]
How? (in what way)	Hoe?	[hu?]
What? (What kind of ...?)	Watter?	[vattər?]
Which?	Watter een?	[vattər eən?]
To whom?	Vir wie?	[fir vi?]
About whom?	Oor wie?	[oər vi?]
About what?	Oor wat?	[oər vat?]
With whom?	Met wie?	[met vi?]
How many? How much?	Hoeveel?	[hufeəl?]

16. Prepositions

with (accompanied by)	met	[met]
without	sonder	[sondər]
to (indicating direction)	na	[na]
about (talking ~ ...)	oor	[oər]
before (in time)	voor	[foər]
in front of ...	voor ...	[foər ...]
under (beneath, below)	onder	[ondər]
above (over)	oor	[oər]
on (atop)	op	[op]
from (off, out of)	uit	[œit]
of (made from)	van	[fan]
in (e.g., ~ ten minutes)	oor	[oər]
over (across the top of)	oor	[oər]

17. Function words. Adverbs. Part 1

Where? (at, in)	**Waar?**	[vãr?]
here (adv)	**hier**	[hir]
there (adv)	**daar**	[dãr]
somewhere (to be)	**êrens**	[ærɛŋs]
nowhere (not anywhere)	**nêrens**	[nærɛŋs]
by (near, beside)	**by**	[baj]
by the window	**by**	[baj]
Where (to)?	**Waarheen?**	[vãrheən?]
here (e.g., come ~!)	**hier**	[hir]
there (e.g., to go ~)	**soontoe**	[soentu]
from here (adv)	**hiervandaan**	[hirfandãn]
from there (adv)	**daarvandaan**	[dãrfandãn]
close (adv)	**naby**	[nabaj]
far (adv)	**ver**	[fer]
near (e.g., ~ Paris)	**naby**	[nabaj]
nearby (adv)	**naby**	[nabaj]
not far (adv)	**nie ver nie**	[ni fər ni]
left (adj)	**linker-**	[linkər-]
on the left	**op linkerhand**	[op linkərhant]
to the left	**na links**	[na links]
right (adj)	**regter**	[reχtər]
on the right	**op regterhand**	[op reχtərhant]

to the right	na regs	[na reχs]
in front (adv)	voor	[foər]
front (as adj)	voorste	[foərstə]
ahead (the kids ran ~)	vooruit	[foərœit]

behind (adv)	agter	[aχtər]
from behind	van agter	[fan aχtər]
back (towards the rear)	agtertoe	[aχtərtu]

| middle | middel | [middəl] |
| in the middle | in die middel | [in di middəl] |

at the side	op die sykant	[op di sajkant]
everywhere (adv)	orals	[orals]
around (in all directions)	orals rond	[orals ront]

from inside	van binne	[fan binnə]
somewhere (to go)	êrens	[ærɛŋs]
straight (directly)	reguit	[reχœit]
back (e.g., come ~)	terug	[teruχ]

| from anywhere | êrens vandaan | [ærɛŋs fandān] |
| from somewhere | êrens vandaan | [ærɛŋs fandān] |

firstly (adv)	in die eerste plek	[in di eərstə plek]
secondly (adv)	in die tweede plek	[in di tweədə plek]
thirdly (adv)	in die derde plek	[in di derdə plek]

suddenly (adv)	skielik	[skilik]
at first (in the beginning)	aan die begin	[ān di beχin]
for the first time	vir die eerste keer	[fir di eərstə keər]
long before ...	lank voordat ...	[lank foərdat ...]
anew (over again)	opnuut	[opnɪt]
for good (adv)	vir goed	[fir χut]

never (adv)	nooit	[nojt]
again (adv)	weer	[veər]
now (adv)	nou	[næʋ]
often (adv)	dikwels	[dikwɛls]
then (adv)	toe	[tu]
urgently (quickly)	dringend	[driŋəŋ]
usually (adv)	gewoonlik	[χevoənlik]

by the way, ...	terloops, ...	[terloəps], [...]
possible (that is ~)	moontlik	[moentlik]
probably (adv)	waarskynlik	[vārskajnlik]
maybe (adv)	dalk	[dalk]
besides ...	trouens...	[træʋɛŋs...]
that's why ...	dis hoekom ...	[dis hukom ...]
in spite of ...	ondanks ...	[ondanks ...]
thanks to ...	danksy ...	[danksaj ...]
what (pron.)	wat	[vat]

that (conj.)	dat	[dat]
something	iets	[its]
anything (something)	iets	[its]
nothing	niks	[niks]

who (pron.)	wie	[vi]
someone	iemand	[imant]
somebody	iemand	[imant]

nobody	niemand	[nimant]
nowhere (a voyage to ~)	nêrens	[næʀɛŋs]
nobody's	niemand se	[nimant sə]
somebody's	iemand se	[imant sə]

so (I'm ~ glad)	so	[so]
also (as well)	ook	[oək]
too (as well)	ook	[oək]

18. Function words. Adverbs. Part 2

| Why? | Waarom? | [vãrom?] |
| because ... | omdat ... | [omdat ...] |

and	en	[ɛn]
or	of	[of]
but	maar	[mãr]
for (e.g., ~ me)	vir	[fir]

too (~ many people)	te	[te]
only (exclusively)	net	[net]
exactly (adv)	presies	[presis]
about (more or less)	ongeveer	[onχəfeər]

approximately (adv)	ongeveer	[onχəfeər]
approximate (adj)	geraamde	[χerãmdə]
almost (adv)	amper	[ampər]
the rest	die res	[di res]

the other (second)	die ander	[di andər]
other (different)	ander	[andər]
each (adj)	elke	[ɛlkə]
any (no matter which)	enige	[ɛniχə]
many (adv)	baie	[bajɛ]
much (adv)	baie	[bajɛ]
many people	baie mense	[bajɛ mɛŋsə]
all (everyone)	almal	[almal]

in return for ...	in ruil vir...	[in rœil fir...]
in exchange (adv)	as vergoeding	[as ferχudiŋ]
by hand (made)	met die hand	[met di hant]

hardly (negative opinion)	**skaars**	[skārs]
probably (adv)	**waarskynlik**	[vārskajnlik]
on purpose (intentionally)	**opsetlik**	[opsetlik]
by accident (adv)	**toevallig**	[tufalləx]
very (adv)	**baie**	[baje]
for example (adv)	**byvoorbeeld**	[bajfoərbeəlt]
between	**tussen**	[tussən]
among	**tussen**	[tussən]
so much (such a lot)	**so baie**	[so baje]
especially (adv)	**veral**	[feral]

Basic concepts. Part 2

19. Weekdays

Monday	**Maandag**	[mãndaχ]
Tuesday	**Dinsdag**	[dinsdaχ]
Wednesday	**Woensdag**	[voɛŋsdaχ]
Thursday	**Donderdag**	[dondərdaχ]
Friday	**Vrydag**	[frajdaχ]
Saturday	**Saterdag**	[satərdaχ]
Sunday	**Sondag**	[sondaχ]
today (adv)	**vandag**	[fandaχ]
tomorrow (adv)	**môre**	[mɔrə]
the day after tomorrow	**oormôre**	[oərmɔrə]
yesterday (adv)	**gister**	[χistər]
the day before yesterday	**eergister**	[eərχistər]
day	**dag**	[daχ]
working day	**werksdag**	[verks·daχ]
public holiday	**openbare vakansiedag**	[openbarə fakaŋsi·daχ]
day off	**verlofdag**	[ferlofdaχ]
weekend	**naweek**	[naveək]
all day long	**die hele dag**	[di helə daχ]
the next day (adv)	**die volgende dag**	[di folχendə daχ]
two days ago	**twee dae gelede**	[tweə daə χeledə]
the day before	**die dag voor**	[di daχ foər]
daily (adj)	**daeliks**	[daəliks]
every day (adv)	**elke dag**	[ɛlkə daχ]
week	**week**	[veək]
last week (adv)	**laas week**	[lãs veək]
next week (adv)	**volgende week**	[folχendə veək]
weekly (adj)	**weekliks**	[veəkliks]
every week (adv)	**weekliks**	[veəkliks]
every Tuesday	**elke Dinsdag**	[ɛlkə dinsdaχ]

20. Hours. Day and night

morning	**oggend**	[oχent]
in the morning	**soggens**	[soχɛŋs]
noon, midday	**middag**	[middaχ]
in the afternoon	**in die namiddag**	[in di namiddaχ]

evening	aand	[ānt]
in the evening	saans	[sāŋs]
night	nag	[naχ]
at night	snags	[snaχs]
midnight	middernag	[middərnaχ]

second	sekonde	[sekondə]
minute	minuut	[minɪt]
hour	uur	[ɪr]
half an hour	n halfuur	[n halfɪr]
fifteen minutes	vyftien minute	[fajftin minutə]
24 hours	24 ure	[fir-en-twintəχ urə]

sunrise	sonop	[son·op]
dawn	daeraad	[daerāt]
early morning	elke oggend	[ɛlkə oχent]
sunset	sononder	[son·ondər]

early in the morning	vroegdag	[fruχdaχ]
this morning	vanmôre	[fanmɔrə]
tomorrow morning	môreoggend	[mɔrə·oχent]

this afternoon	vanmiddag	[fanmiddaχ]
in the afternoon	in die namiddag	[in di namiddaχ]
tomorrow afternoon	môremiddag	[mɔrə·middaχ]

tonight (this evening)	vanaand	[fanānt]
tomorrow night	môreaand	[mɔrə·ānt]

at 3 o'clock sharp	klokslag 3 uur	[klokslaχ dri ɪr]
about 4 o'clock	omstreeks 4 uur	[omstreəks fir ɪr]
by 12 o'clock	teen 12 uur	[teən twalf ɪr]

in 20 minutes	oor twintig minute	[oər twintəχ minutə]
on time (adv)	betyds	[betajds]

a quarter of ...	kwart voor ...	[kwart foər ...]
every 15 minutes	elke 15 minute	[ɛlkə fajftin minutə]
round the clock	24 uur per dag	[fir-en-twintəχ pər daχ]

21. Months. Seasons

January	Januarie	[januari]
February	Februarie	[februari]
March	Maart	[mārt]
April	April	[april]
May	Mei	[mæj]
June	Junie	[juni]
July	Julie	[juli]
August	Augustus	[ɔuχustus]

September	September	[septembər]
October	Oktober	[oktobər]
November	November	[nofembər]
December	Desember	[desembər]

spring	lente	[lentə]
in spring	in die lente	[in di lentə]
spring (as adj)	lente-	[lentə-]

summer	somer	[somər]
in summer	in die somer	[in di somər]
summer (as adj)	somerse	[somersə]

fall	herfs	[herfs]
in fall	in die herfs	[in di herfs]
fall (as adj)	herfsagtige	[herfsaχtiχə]

winter	winter	[vintər]
in winter	in die winter	[in di vintər]
winter (as adj)	winter-	[vintər-]

month	maand	[mānt]
this month	hierdie maand	[hirdi mānt]
next month	volgende maand	[folχendə mānt]
last month	laasmaand	[lāsmānt]
in 2 months (2 months later)	oor twe maande	[oər twə māndə]
the whole month	die hele maand	[di helə mānt]

monthly (~ magazine)	maandeliks	[māndəliks]
monthly (adv)	maandeliks	[māndəliks]
every month	elke maand	[ɛlkə mānt]

year	jaar	[jār]
this year	hierdie jaar	[hirdi jār]
next year	volgende jaar	[folχendə jār]
last year	laasjaar	[lāʃār]

in two years	binne twee jaar	[binnə tweə jār]
the whole year	die hele jaar	[di helə jār]

every year	elke jaar	[ɛlkə jār]
annual (adj)	jaarliks	[jārliks]
annually (adv)	jaarliks	[jārliks]
4 times a year	4 keer per jaar	[fir keər pər jār]

date (e.g., today's ~)	datum	[datum]
date (e.g., ~ of birth)	datum	[datum]
calendar	kalender	[kalendər]
six months	ses maande	[ses māndə]
season (summer, etc.)	seisoen	[sæjsun]
century	eeu	[iʊ]

22. Time. Miscellaneous

time	**tyd**	[tajt]
moment	**moment**	[moment]
instant (n)	**oomblik**	[oəmblik]
instant (adj)	**oombliklik**	[oəmbliklik]
lapse (of time)	**tydbestek**	[tajdbestək]
life	**lewe**	[levə]
eternity	**ewigheid**	[ɛviχæjt]

epoch	**tydperk**	[tajtperk]
era	**tydperk**	[tajtperk]
cycle	**siklus**	[siklus]
period	**periode**	[periodə]
term (short-~)	**termyn**	[termajn]

the future	**die toekoms**	[di tukoms]
future (as adj)	**toekomstig**	[tukomstəχ]
next time	**die volgende keer**	[di folχendə keər]
the past	**die verlede**	[di ferledə]
past (recent)	**laas-**	[lās-]
last time	**die vorige keer**	[di foriχə keər]

later (adv)	**later**	[latər]
after (prep.)	**na**	[na]
nowadays (adv)	**deesdae**	[deəsdaə]
now (adv)	**nou**	[næʊ]
immediately (adv)	**onmiddellik**	[onmiddɛllik]
soon (adv)	**gou**	[χæʊ]
in advance (beforehand)	**by voorbaat**	[baj foərbāt]

a long time ago	**lank gelede**	[lank χeledə]
recently (adv)	**onlangs**	[onlaŋs]
destiny	**noodlot**	[noədlot]
memories (childhood ~)	**herinneringe**	[herinneriŋə]
archives	**argiewe**	[arχivə]

during …	**gedurende …**	[χedurendə …]
long, a long time (adv)	**lank**	[lank]
not long (adv)	**nie lank nie**	[ni lank ni]
early (in the morning)	**vroeg**	[fruχ]
late (not early)	**laat**	[lāt]

forever (for good)	**vir altyd**	[fir altajt]
to start (begin)	**begin**	[beχin]
to postpone (vt)	**uitstel**	[œitstəl]

at the same time	**tegelykertyd**	[teχelajkertajt]
permanently (adv)	**permanent**	[permanent]
constant (noise, pain)	**voortdurend**	[foərtdurent]
temporary (adj)	**tydelik**	[tajdelik]

sometimes (adv)	soms	[soms]
rarely (adv)	selde	[sɛldə]
often (adv)	dikwels	[dikwɛls]

23. Opposites

| rich (adj) | ryk | [rajk] |
| poor (adj) | arm | [arm] |

| ill, sick (adj) | siek | [sik] |
| well (not sick) | gesond | [χesont] |

| big (adj) | groot | [χroət] |
| small (adj) | klein | [klæjn] |

| quickly (adv) | vinnig | [finnəχ] |
| slowly (adv) | stadig | [stadəχ] |

| fast (adj) | vinnig | [finnəχ] |
| slow (adj) | stadig | [stadəχ] |

| glad (adj) | bly | [blaj] |
| sad (adj) | droewig | [druvəχ] |

| together (adv) | saam | [sãm] |
| separately (adv) | afsonderlik | [afsondərlik] |

| aloud (to read) | hardop | [hardop] |
| silently (to oneself) | stil | [stil] |

| tall (adj) | groot | [χroət] |
| low (adj) | laag | [lãχ] |

| deep (adj) | diep | [dip] |
| shallow (adj) | vlak | [flak] |

| yes | ja | [ja] |
| no | nee | [neə] |

| distant (in space) | ver | [fer] |
| nearby (adj) | naby | [nabaj] |

| far (adv) | ver | [fer] |
| nearby (adv) | naby | [nabaj] |

| long (adj) | lang | [laŋ] |
| short (adj) | kort | [kort] |

| good (kindhearted) | vriendelik | [frindəlik] |
| evil (adj) | boos | [boəs] |

married (adj)	getroud	[ҳetræʊt]
single (adj)	ongetroud	[onҳətræʊt]
to forbid (vt)	verbied	[ferbit]
to permit (vt)	toestaan	[tustān]
end	einde	[æjndə]
beginning	begin	[beҳin]
left (adj)	linker-	[linkər-]
right (adj)	regter	[reҳtər]
first (adj)	eerste	[eərstə]
last (adj)	laaste	[lāstə]
crime	misdaad	[misdāt]
punishment	straf	[straf]
to order (vt)	beveel	[befeəl]
to obey (vi, vt)	gehoorsaam	[ҳehoərsām]
straight (adj)	reguit	[reҳœit]
curved (adj)	krom	[krom]
paradise	paradys	[paradajs]
hell	hel	[həl]
to be born	gebore word	[ҳeborə vort]
to die (vi)	doodgaan	[doədҳān]
strong (adj)	sterk	[sterk]
weak (adj)	swak	[swak]
old (adj)	oud	[æʊt]
young (adj)	jong	[joŋ]
old (adj)	ou	[æʊ]
new (adj)	nuwe	[nuvə]
hard (adj)	hard	[hart]
soft (adj)	sag	[saҳ]
warm (tepid)	warm	[varm]
cold (adj)	koud	[kæʊt]
fat (adj)	vet	[fet]
thin (adj)	dun	[dun]
narrow (adj)	smal	[smal]
wide (adj)	wyd	[vajt]
good (adj)	goed	[ҳut]
bad (adj)	sleg	[sleҳ]

brave (adj)	dapper	[dappər]
cowardly (adj)	lafhartig	[lafhartəχ]

24. Lines and shapes

square	vierkant	[firkant]
square (as adj)	vierkantig	[firkantəχ]
circle	sirkel	[sirkəl]
round (adj)	rond	[ront]
triangle	driehoek	[drihuk]
triangular (adj)	driehoekig	[drihukəχ]

oval	ovaal	[ofāl]
oval (as adj)	ovaal	[ofāl]
rectangle	reghoek	[reχhuk]
rectangular (adj)	reghoekig	[reχhukəχ]

pyramid	piramide	[piramidə]
rhombus	ruit	[rœit]
trapezoid	trapesoïed	[trapesoïət]
cube	kubus	[kubus]
prism	prisma	[prisma]

circumference	omtrek	[omtrək]
sphere	sfeer	[sfeər]
ball (solid sphere)	bal	[bal]
diameter	diameter	[diametər]
radius	straal	[strāl]
perimeter (circle's ~)	omtrek	[omtrək]
center	sentrum	[sentrum]

horizontal (adj)	horisontaal	[horisontāl]
vertical (adj)	vertikaal	[fertikāl]
parallel (n)	parallel	[paralləl]
parallel (as adj)	parallel	[paralləl]

line	lyn	[lajn]
stroke	haal	[hāl]
straight line	regte lyn	[reχtə lajn]
curve (curved line)	krom	[krom]

thin (line, etc.)	dun	[dun]
contour (outline)	omtrek	[omtrək]

intersection	snypunt	[snaj·punt]
right angle	regte hoek	[reχtə huk]
segment	segment	[seχment]
sector	sektor	[sektor]
side (of triangle)	sy	[saj]
angle	hoek	[huk]

25. Units of measurement

weight	gewig	[χevəχ]
length	lengte	[leŋtə]
width	breedte	[breədtə]
height	hoogte	[hoəχtə]
depth	diepte	[diptə]
volume	volume	[folumə]
area	area	[area]
gram	gram	[χram]
milligram	milligram	[milliχram]
kilogram	kilogram	[kiloχram]
ton	ton	[ton]
pound	pond	[pont]
ounce	ons	[ɔŋs]
meter	meter	[metər]
millimeter	millimeter	[millimetər]
centimeter	sentimeter	[sentimetər]
kilometer	kilometer	[kilometər]
mile	myl	[majl]
inch	duim	[dœim]
foot	voet	[fut]
yard	jaart	[jãrt]
square meter	vierkante meter	[firkantə metər]
hectare	hektaar	[hektãr]
liter	liter	[litər]
degree	graad	[χrãt]
volt	volt	[folt]
ampere	ampère	[ampɛ:r]
horsepower	perdekrag	[perdə·kraχ]
quantity	hoeveelheid	[hufeəlhæjt]
half	helfte	[hɛlftə]
dozen	dosyn	[dosajn]
piece (item)	stuk	[stuk]
size	grootte	[χroəttə]
scale (map ~)	skaal	[skãl]
minimal (adj)	minimaal	[minimãl]
the smallest (adj)	die kleinste	[di klæjnstə]
medium (adj)	medium	[medium]
maximal (adj)	maksimaal	[maksimãl]
the largest (adj)	die grootste	[di χroətstə]

26. Containers

canning jar (glass ~)	**glaspot**	[χlas·pot]
can	**blikkie**	[blikki]
bucket	**emmer**	[ɛmmər]
barrel	**drom**	[drom]
wash basin (e.g., plastic ~)	**wasbak**	[vas·bak]
tank (100L water ~)	**tenk**	[tɛnk]
hip flask	**heupfles**	[høəp·fles]
jerrycan	**petrolblik**	[petrol·blik]
tank (e.g., tank car)	**tenk**	[tɛnk]
mug	**beker**	[bekər]
cup (of coffee, etc.)	**koppie**	[koppi]
saucer	**piering**	[piriŋ]
glass (tumbler)	**glas**	[χlas]
wine glass	**wynglas**	[vajn·χlas]
stock pot (soup pot)	**soppot**	[sop·pot]
bottle (~ of wine)	**bottel**	[bottəl]
neck (of the bottle, etc.)	**nek**	[nek]
carafe (decanter)	**kraffie**	[kraffi]
pitcher	**kruik**	[krœik]
vessel (container)	**houer**	[hæʊər]
pot (crock, stoneware ~)	**pot**	[pot]
vase	**vaas**	[fãs]
bottle (perfume ~)	**bottel**	[bottəl]
vial, small bottle	**botteltjie**	[bottɛlki]
tube (of toothpaste)	**buisie**	[bœisi]
sack (bag)	**sak**	[sak]
bag (paper ~, plastic ~)	**sak**	[sak]
pack (of cigarettes, etc.)	**pakkie**	[pakki]
box (e.g., shoebox)	**kartondoos**	[karton·doəs]
crate	**krat**	[krat]
basket	**mandjie**	[mandʒi]

27. Materials

material	**boustof**	[bæʊstof]
wood (n)	**hout**	[hæʊt]
wood-, wooden (adj)	**hout-**	[hæʊt-]
glass (n)	**glas**	[χlas]
glass (as adj)	**glas-**	[χlas-]

| stone (n) | klip | [klip] |
| stone (as adj) | klip- | [klip-] |

| plastic (n) | plastiek | [plastik] |
| plastic (as adj) | plastiek- | [plastik-] |

| rubber (n) | rubber | [rubbər] |
| rubber (as adj) | rubber- | [rubbər-] |

| cloth, fabric (n) | materiaal | [materiāl] |
| fabric (as adj) | materiaal- | [materiāl-] |

| paper (n) | papier | [papir] |
| paper (as adj) | papier- | [papir-] |

| cardboard (n) | karton | [karton] |
| cardboard (as adj) | karton- | [karton-] |

polyethylene	politeen	[politeən]
cellophane	sellofaan	[sɛllofān]
linoleum	linoleum	[linoløəm]
plywood	laaghout	[lāχhæʊt]

porcelain (n)	porselein	[porselæjn]
porcelain (as adj)	porselein-	[porselæjn-]
clay (n)	klei	[klæj]
clay (as adj)	klei-	[klæj-]
ceramic (n)	keramiek	[keramik]
ceramic (as adj)	keramiek-	[keramik-]

28. Metals

metal (n)	metaal	[metāl]
metal (as adj)	metaal-	[metāl-]
alloy (n)	allooi	[alloj]

gold (n)	goud	[χæʊt]
gold, golden (adj)	goue	[χæʊə]
silver (n)	silwer	[silwər]
silver (as adj)	silwer-	[silwər-]

iron (n)	yster	[ajstər]
iron-, made of iron (adj)	yster-	[ajstər-]
steel (n)	staal	[stāl]
steel (as adj)	staal-	[stāl-]
copper (n)	koper	[kopər]
copper (as adj)	koper-	[kopər-]

| aluminum (n) | aluminium | [aluminium] |
| aluminum (as adj) | aluminium- | [aluminium-] |

| bronze (n) | brons | [brɔŋs] |
| bronze (as adj) | brons- | [brɔŋs-] |

brass	geelkoper	[χeəl·kopər]
nickel	nikkel	[nikkəl]
platinum	platinum	[platinum]
mercury	kwik	[kwik]
tin	tin	[tin]
lead	lood	[loət]
zinc	sink	[sink]

HUMAN BEING

Human being. The body

29. Humans. Basic concepts

human being	**mens**	[mɛŋs]
man (adult male)	**man**	[man]
woman	**vrou**	[fræʊ]
child	**kind**	[kint]
girl	**meisie**	[mæjsi]
boy	**seun**	[søən]
teenager	**tiener**	[tinər]
old man	**ou man**	[æʊ man]
old woman	**ou vrou**	[æʊ fræʊ]

30. Human anatomy

organism (body)	**organisme**	[orχanismə]
heart	**hart**	[hart]
blood	**bloed**	[blut]
artery	**slagaar**	[slaχār]
vein	**aar**	[ār]
brain	**brein**	[bræjn]
nerve	**senuwee**	[senuveə]
nerves	**senuwees**	[senuveəs]
vertebra	**rugwerwels**	[ruχ·werwɛls]
spine (backbone)	**ruggraat**	[ruχ·χrāt]
stomach (organ)	**maag**	[māχ]
intestines, bowels	**ingewande**	[inχewandə]
intestine (e.g., large ~)	**derm**	[derm]
liver	**lewer**	[levər]
kidney	**nier**	[nir]
bone	**been**	[beən]
skeleton	**geraamte**	[χerāmtə]
rib	**rib**	[rip]
skull	**skedel**	[skedəl]
muscle	**spier**	[spir]
biceps	**biseps**	[biseps]

triceps	triseps	[triseps]
tendon	sening	[seniŋ]
joint	gewrig	[χevrəχ]
lungs	longe	[loŋə]
genitals	geslagsorgane	[χeslaχs·orχanə]
skin	vel	[fəl]

31. Head

head	kop	[kop]
face	gesig	[χesəχ]
nose	neus	[nøəs]
mouth	mond	[mont]

eye	oog	[oəχ]
eyes	oë	[oɛ]
pupil	pupil	[pupil]
eyebrow	wenkbrou	[vɛnk·bræʊ]
eyelash	ooghaar	[oəχ·hār]
eyelid	ooglid	[oəχ·lit]

tongue	tong	[toŋ]
tooth	tand	[tant]
lips	lippe	[lippə]
cheekbones	wangbene	[vaŋ·benə]
gum	tandvleis	[tand·flæjs]
palate	verhemelte	[fer·hemɛltə]

nostrils	neusgate	[nøəsχatə]
chin	ken	[ken]
jaw	kakebeen	[kakebeən]
cheek	wang	[vaŋ]

forehead	voorhoof	[foərhoəf]
temple	slaap	[slāp]
ear	oor	[oər]
back of the head	agterkop	[aχtərkop]
neck	nek	[nek]
throat	keel	[keəl]

hair	haar	[hār]
hairstyle	kapsel	[kapsəl]
haircut	haarstyl	[hārstajl]
wig	pruik	[prœik]

mustache	snor	[snor]
beard	baard	[bārt]
to have (a beard, etc.)	dra	[dra]
braid	vlegsel	[fleχsəl]
sideburns	bakkebaarde	[bakkəbārdə]

red-haired (adj)	rooiharig	[roj·harəχ]
gray (hair)	grys	[χrajs]
bald (adj)	kaal	[kãl]
bald patch	kaal plek	[kãl plek]

| ponytail | poniestert | [poni·stert] |
| bangs | gordyntjiekapsel | [χordajnki·kapsəl] |

32. Human body

hand	hand	[hant]
arm	arm	[arm]
finger	vinger	[fiŋər]
toe	toon	[toən]
thumb	duim	[dœim]
little finger	pinkie	[pinki]
nail	nael	[naəl]

fist	vuis	[fœis]
palm	palm	[palm]
wrist	pols	[pols]
forearm	voorarm	[foərarm]
elbow	elmboog	[ɛlmboəχ]
shoulder	skouer	[skæʊər]

leg	been	[beən]
foot	voet	[fut]
knee	knie	[kni]
calf (part of leg)	kuit	[kœit]
hip	heup	[høəp]
heel	hakskeen	[hak·skeən]

body	liggaam	[liχχãm]
stomach	maag	[mãχ]
chest	bors	[bors]
breast	bors	[bors]
flank	sy	[saj]
back	rug	[ruχ]
lower back	lae rug	[laə ruχ]
waist	middel	[middəl]

navel (belly button)	naeltjie	[naɛlki]
buttocks	boude	[bæʊdə]
bottom	sitvlak	[sitflak]

beauty mark	moesie	[musi]
birthmark (café au lait spot)	moedervlek	[mudər·flek]
tattoo	tatoe	[tatu]
scar	litteken	[littekən]

Clothing & Accessories

33. Outerwear. Coats

clothes	klere	[klerə]
outerwear	oorklere	[oərklerə]
winter clothing	winterklere	[vintər·klerə]
coat (overcoat)	jas	[jas]
fur coat	pelsjas	[pelʃas]
fur jacket	kort pelsjas	[kort pelʃas]
down coat	donsjas	[donʃas]
jacket (e.g., leather ~)	baadjie	[bādʒi]
raincoat (trenchcoat, etc.)	reënjas	[recnjas]
waterproof (adj)	waterdig	[vatərdex]

34. Men's & women's clothing

shirt (button shirt)	hemp	[hemp]
pants	broek	[bruk]
jeans	denimbroek	[denim·bruk]
suit jacket	baadjie	[bādʒi]
suit	pak	[pak]
dress (frock)	rok	[rok]
skirt	romp	[romp]
blouse	bloes	[blus]
knitted jacket (cardigan, etc.)	gebreide baadjie	[xebræjdə bādʒi]
jacket (of woman's suit)	baadjie	[bādʒi]
T-shirt	T-hemp	[te-hemp]
shorts (short trousers)	kortbroek	[kort·bruk]
tracksuit	sweetpak	[sweet·pak]
bathrobe	badjas	[batjas]
pajamas	pajama	[pajama]
sweater	trui	[trœi]
pullover	trui	[trœi]
vest	onderbaadjie	[ondər·bādʒi]
tailcoat	swaelstertbaadjie	[swaɛlstert·bādʒi]
tuxedo	aandpak	[āntpak]

uniform	**uniform**	[uniform]
workwear	**werksklere**	[verks·klerə]
overalls	**oorpak**	[oərpak]
coat (e.g., doctor's smock)	**jas**	[jas]

35. Clothing. Underwear

underwear	**onderklere**	[ondərklerə]
boxers, briefs	**onderbroek**	[ondərbruk]
panties	**onderbroek**	[ondərbruk]
undershirt (A-shirt)	**frokkie**	[frokki]
socks	**sokkies**	[sokkis]

nightgown	**nagrok**	[naχrok]
bra	**bra**	[bra]
knee highs (knee-high socks)	**kniekouse**	[kni·kæʊsə]
pantyhose	**kousbroek**	[kæʊsbruk]
stockings (thigh highs)	**kouse**	[kæʊsə]
bathing suit	**baaikostuum**	[bāj·kostɪm]

36. Headwear

hat	**hoed**	[hut]
fedora	**hoed**	[hut]
baseball cap	**bofbalpet**	[bofbal·pet]
flatcap	**pet**	[pet]

beret	**mus**	[mus]
hood	**kap**	[kap]
panama hat	**panamahoed**	[panama·hut]
knit cap (knitted hat)	**gebreide mus**	[χebræjdə mus]

headscarf	**kopdoek**	[kopduk]
women's hat	**dameshoed**	[dames·hut]
hard hat	**veiligheidshelm**	[fæjliχæjts·hɛlm]
garrison cap	**mus**	[mus]
helmet	**helmet**	[hɛlmet]

derby	**bolhoed**	[bolhut]
top hat	**hoëhoed**	[hoɛhut]

37. Footwear

footwear	**skoeisel**	[skuisəl]
shoes (men's shoes)	**mansskoene**	[maɳs·skunə]

shoes (women's shoes)	damesskoene	[dames·skunə]
boots (e.g., cowboy ~)	laarse	[lārsə]
slippers	pantoffels	[pantoffəls]

tennis shoes (e.g., Nike ~)	tennisskoene	[tɛnnis·skunə]
sneakers	tekkies	[tɛkkis]
(e.g., Converse ~)		
sandals	sandale	[sandalə]

cobbler (shoe repairer)	skoenmaker	[skun·makər]
heel	hak	[hak]
pair (of shoes)	paar	[pār]

shoestring	skoenveter	[skun·fetər]
to lace (vt)	ryg	[rajχ]
shoehorn	skoenlepel	[skun·lepəl]
shoe polish	skoenpolitoer	[skun·politur]

38. Textile. Fabrics

cotton (n)	katoen	[katun]
cotton (as adj)	katoen-	[katun-]
flax (n)	vlas	[flas]
flax (as adj)	vlas-	[flas-]

silk (n)	sy	[saj]
silk (as adj)	sy-	[saj-]
wool (n)	wol	[vol]
wool (as adj)	wol-	[vol-]

velvet	fluweel	[fluveəl]
suede	suède	[suɛdə]
corduroy	ferweel	[ferweəl]

nylon (n)	nylon	[najlon]
nylon (as adj)	nylon-	[najlon-]
polyester (n)	poliëster	[poliɛstər]
polyester (as adj)	poliëster-	[poliɛstər-]

leather (n)	leer	[leər]
leather (as adj)	leer-	[leər-]
fur (n)	bont	[bont]
fur (e.g., ~ coat)	bont-	[bont-]

39. Personal accessories

gloves	handskoene	[handskunə]
mittens	duimhandskoene	[dœim·handskunə]

scarf (muffler)	serp	[serp]
glasses (eyeglasses)	bril	[bril]
frame (eyeglass ~)	raam	[rãm]
umbrella	sambreel	[sambreəl]
walking stick	wandelstok	[vandəl·stok]
hairbrush	haarborsel	[hãr·borsəl]
fan	waaier	[vãjer]

tie (necktie)	das	[das]
bow tie	strikkie	[strikki]
suspenders	kruisbande	[krœis·bandə]
handkerchief	sakdoek	[sakduk]

comb	kam	[kam]
barrette	haarspeld	[hãrs·pɛlt]
hairpin	haarpen	[hãr·pen]
buckle	gespe	[χespə]

| belt | belt | [bɛlt] |
| shoulder strap | skouerband | [skæʊer·bant] |

bag (handbag)	handsak	[hand·sak]
purse	beursie	[bøørsi]
backpack	rugsak	[ruχsak]

40. Clothing. Miscellaneous

fashion	mode	[modə]
in vogue (adj)	in die mode	[in di modə]
fashion designer	modeontwerper	[modə·ontwerpər]

collar	kraag	[krãχ]
pocket	sak	[sak]
pocket (as adj)	sak-	[sak-]
sleeve	mou	[mæʊ]
hanging loop	lussie	[lussi]
fly (on trousers)	gulp	[χulp]

zipper (fastener)	ritssluiter	[rits·slœiter]
fastener	vasmaker	[fasmakər]
button	knoop	[knoəp]
buttonhole	knoopsgat	[knoəps·χat]
to come off (ab. button)	loskom	[loskom]

to sew (vi, vt)	naai	[nãi]
to embroider (vi, vt)	borduur	[bordɪr]
embroidery	borduurwerk	[bordɪr·werk]
sewing needle	naald	[nãlt]
thread	garing	[χariŋ]
seam	soom	[soəm]

to get dirty (vi)	**vuil word**	[fœil vort]
stain (mark, spot)	**vlek**	[flek]
to crease, crumple (vi)	**kreukel**	[krøəkəl]
to tear, to rip (vt)	**skeur**	[skøər]
clothes moth	**mot**	[mot]

41. Personal care. Cosmetics

toothpaste	**tandepasta**	[tandə·pasta]
toothbrush	**tandeborsel**	[tandə·borsəl]
to brush one's teeth	**tande borsel**	[tandə borsəl]
razor	**skeermes**	[skeər·mes]
shaving cream	**skeerroom**	[skeər·roəm]
to shave (vi)	**skeer**	[skeər]
soap	**seep**	[seəp]
shampoo	**sjampoe**	[ʃampu]
scissors	**skêr**	[skær]
nail file	**naelvyl**	[naɛl·fajl]
nail clippers	**naelknipper**	[naɛl·knippər]
tweezers	**haartangetjie**	[hãrtaŋəki]
cosmetics	**kosmetika**	[kosmetika]
face mask	**gesigmasker**	[xesiχ·maskər]
manicure	**manikuur**	[manikɪr]
to have a manicure	**laat manikuur**	[lãt manikɪr]
pedicure	**voetbehandeling**	[fut·behandeliŋ]
make-up bag	**kosmetika tassie**	[kosmetika tassi]
face powder	**gesigpoeier**	[xesiχ·pujer]
powder compact	**poeierdosie**	[pujer·dosi]
blusher	**blosser**	[blossər]
perfume (bottled)	**parfuum**	[parfɪm]
toilet water (lotion)	**reukwater**	[røək·vatər]
lotion	**vloeiroom**	[flui·roəm]
cologne	**reukwater**	[røək·vatər]
eyeshadow	**oogskadu**	[oəχ·skadu]
eyeliner	**oogomlyner**	[oəχ·omlajnər]
mascara	**maskara**	[maskara]
lipstick	**lipstiffie**	[lip·stiffi]
nail polish, enamel	**naellak**	[naɛl·lak]
hair spray	**haarsproei**	[hãrs·prui]
deodorant	**reukweermiddel**	[røək·veərmiddəl]
cream	**room**	[roəm]
face cream	**gesigroom**	[xesiχ·roəm]

hand cream	**handroom**	[hand·roəm]
anti-wrinkle cream	**antirimpelroom**	[antirimpəl·roəm]
day cream	**dagroom**	[daχ·roəm]
night cream	**nagroom**	[naχ·roəm]
day (as adj)	**dag-**	[daχ-]
night (as adj)	**nag-**	[naχ-]
tampon	**tampon**	[tampon]
toilet paper (toilet roll)	**toiletpapier**	[tojlet·papir]
hair dryer	**haardroër**	[hãr·droɛr]

42. Jewelry

jewelry	**juweliersware**	[juvelirs·warə]
precious (e.g., ~ stone)	**edel-**	[ɛdəl-]
hallmark stamp	**waarmerk**	[vãrmerk]
ring	**ring**	[riŋ]
wedding ring	**trouring**	[træʊriŋ]
bracelet	**armband**	[armbant]
earrings	**oorbelle**	[oər·bɛllə]
necklace (~ of pearls)	**halssnoer**	[hals·snur]
crown	**kroon**	[kroən]
bead necklace	**kraalsnoer**	[krãl·snur]
diamond	**diamant**	[diamant]
emerald	**smarag**	[smaraχ]
ruby	**robyn**	[robajn]
sapphire	**saffier**	[saffir]
pearl	**pêrel**	[pærəl]
amber	**amber**	[ambər]

43. Watches. Clocks

watch (wristwatch)	**polshorlosie**	[pols·horlosi]
dial	**wyserplaat**	[vajsər·plãt]
hand (of clock, watch)	**wyster**	[vajstər]
metal watch band	**metaal horlosiebandjie**	[metãl horlosi·bandʒi]
watch strap	**horlosiebandjie**	[horlosi·bandʒi]
battery	**battery**	[battəraj]
to be dead (battery)	**pap wees**	[pap veəs]
to run fast	**voorloop**	[foərloəp]
to run slow	**agterloop**	[aχtərloəp]
wall clock	**muurhorlosie**	[mɪr·horlosi]
hourglass	**uurglas**	[ɪr·χlas]

sundial	**sonwyser**	[son·wajsər]
alarm clock	**wekker**	[vɛkkər]
watchmaker	**horlosiemaker**	[horlosi·makər]
to repair (vt)	**herstel**	[herstəl]

Food. Nutricion

44. Food

meat	vleis	[flæjs]
chicken	hoender	[hundər]
Rock Cornish hen (poussin)	braaikuiken	[brāj·kœiken]
duck	eend	[eent]
goose	gans	[χaŋs]
game	wild	[vilt]
turkey	kalkoen	[kalkun]
pork	varkvleis	[fark·flæjs]
veal	kalfsvleis	[kalfs·flæjs]
lamb	lamsvleis	[lams·flæjs]
beef	beesvleis	[bees·flæjs]
rabbit	konynvleis	[konajn·flæjs]
sausage (bologna, pepperoni, etc.)	wors	[vors]
vienna sausage (frankfurter)	Weense worsie	[veɛŋsə vorsi]
bacon	spek	[spek]
ham	ham	[ham]
gammon	gerookte ham	[χeroəktə ham]
pâté	patee	[pateə]
liver	lewer	[levər]
hamburger (ground beef)	maalvleis	[māl·flæjs]
tongue	tong	[toŋ]
egg	eier	[æjer]
eggs	eiers	[æjers]
egg white	eierwit	[æjer·wit]
egg yolk	dooier	[dojer]
fish	vis	[fis]
seafood	seekos	[see·kos]
crustaceans	skaaldiere	[skāldirə]
caviar	kaviaar	[kafiār]
crab	krab	[krap]
shrimp	garnaal	[χarnāl]
oyster	oester	[ustər]
spiny lobster	seekreef	[see·kreəf]

| octopus | seekat | [seə·kat] |
| squid | pylinkvis | [pajl·inkfis] |

sturgeon	steur	[støər]
salmon	salm	[salm]
halibut	heilbot	[hæjlbot]

cod	kabeljou	[kabeljæʊ]
mackerel	makriel	[makril]
tuna	tuna	[tuna]
eel	paling	[paliŋ]

trout	forel	[forəl]
sardine	sardyn	[sardajn]
pike	varswatersnoek	[farswatər·snuk]
herring	haring	[hariŋ]

bread	brood	[broət]
cheese	kaas	[kãs]
sugar	suiker	[sœikər]
salt	sout	[sæʊt]

rice	rys	[rajs]
pasta (macaroni)	pasta	[pasta]
noodles	noedels	[nudɛls]

butter	botter	[bottər]
vegetable oil	plantaardige olie	[plantãrdiɣə oli]
sunflower oil	sonblomolie	[sonblom·oli]
margarine	margarien	[marχarin]

| olives | olywe | [olajvə] |
| olive oil | olyfolie | [olajf·oli] |

milk	melk	[melk]
condensed milk	kondensmelk	[kondɛns·melk]
yogurt	jogurt	[joχurt]

| sour cream | suurroom | [sɪr·roəm] |
| cream (of milk) | room | [roəm] |

| mayonnaise | mayonnaise | [majonɛs] |
| buttercream | crème | [krɛm] |

cereal grains (wheat, etc.)	ontbytgraan	[ontbajt·χrãn]
flour	meelblom	[meəl·blom]
canned food	blikkieskos	[blikkis·kos]

cornflakes	mielievlokkies	[mili·flokkis]
honey	heuning	[høəniŋ]
jam	konfyt	[konfajt]
chewing gum	kougom	[kæʊχom]

45. Drinks

water	water	[vatər]
drinking water	drinkwater	[drink·vatər]
mineral water	mineraalwater	[minerāl·vatər]

still (adj)	sonder gas	[sondər χas]
carbonated (adj)	soda-	[soda-]
sparkling (adj)	bruis-	[brœis-]
ice	ys	[ajs]
with ice	met ys	[met ajs]

non-alcoholic (adj)	nie-alkoholies	[ni-alkoholis]
soft drink	koeldrank	[kul·drank]
refreshing drink	verfrissende drank	[fərfrissəndə drank]
lemonade	limonade	[limonadə]

liquors	likeure	[likøərə]
wine	wyn	[vajn]
white wine	witwyn	[vit·vajn]
red wine	rooiwyn	[roj·vajn]

liqueur	likeur	[likøər]
champagne	sjampanje	[ʃampanje]
vermouth	vermoet	[fermut]

whiskey	whisky	[vhiskaj]
vodka	vodka	[fodka]
gin	jenever	[jenefər]
cognac	brandewyn	[brandə·vajn]
rum	rum	[rum]

coffee	koffie	[koffi]
black coffee	swart koffie	[swart koffi]
coffee with milk	koffie met melk	[koffi met melk]
cappuccino	capuccino	[kaputʃino]
instant coffee	poeierkoffie	[pujer·koffi]

milk	melk	[melk]
cocktail	mengeldrankie	[menχəl·dranki]
milkshake	melkskommel	[melk·skomməl]

juice	sap	[sap]
tomato juice	tamatiesap	[tamati·sap]
orange juice	lemoensap	[lemoən·sap]
freshly squeezed juice	vars geparste sap	[fars χeparstə sap]

beer	bier	[bir]
light beer	ligte bier	[liχtə bir]
dark beer	donker bier	[donkər bir]
tea	tee	[teə]

black tea	swart tee	[swart teə]
green tea	groen tee	[χrun teə]

46. Vegetables

vegetables	groente	[χruntə]
greens	groente	[χruntə]

tomato	tamatie	[tamati]
cucumber	komkommer	[komkommər]
carrot	wortel	[vortəl]
potato	aartappel	[ārtappəl]
onion	ui	[œi]
garlic	knoffel	[knoffəl]

cabbage	kool	[koəl]
cauliflower	blomkool	[blom·koəl]
Brussels sprouts	Brusselspruite	[brussɛl·sprœitə]
broccoli	broccoli	[brokoli]

beetroot	beet	[beət]
eggplant	eiervrug	[æjerfruχ]
zucchini	vingerskorsie	[fiŋər·skorsi]
pumpkin	pampoen	[pampun]
turnip	raap	[rāp]

parsley	pietersielie	[pitərsili]
dill	dille	[dillə]
lettuce	slaai	[slāi]
celery	seldery	[selderaj]
asparagus	aspersie	[aspersi]
spinach	spinasie	[spinasi]

pea	ertjie	[ɛrki]
beans	boontjies	[boənkis]
corn (maize)	mielie	[mili]
kidney bean	nierboontjie	[nir·boənki]

bell pepper	paprika	[paprika]
radish	radys	[radajs]
artichoke	artisjok	[artiʃok]

47. Fruits. Nuts

fruit	vrugte	[fruχtə]
apple	appel	[appəl]
pear	peer	[peər]
lemon	suurlemoen	[sɪr·lemun]

orange	**lemoen**	[lemun]
strawberry (garden ~)	**aarbei**	[ārbæj]
mandarin	**nartjie**	[narki]
plum	**pruim**	[prœim]
peach	**perske**	[perskə]
apricot	**appelkoos**	[appɛlkoəs]
raspberry	**framboos**	[framboəs]
pineapple	**pynappel**	[pajnappəl]
banana	**piesang**	[pisaŋ]
watermelon	**waatlemoen**	[vātlemun]
grape	**druif**	[drœif]
cherry	**kersie**	[kersi]
sour cherry	**suurkersie**	[sɪr·kersi]
sweet cherry	**soetkersie**	[sut·kersi]
melon	**spanspek**	[spaŋspek]
grapefruit	**pomelo**	[pomelo]
avocado	**avokado**	[afokado]
papaya	**papaja**	[papaja]
mango	**mango**	[manχo]
pomegranate	**granaat**	[χranāt]
redcurrant	**rooi aalbessie**	[roj ālbɛssi]
blackcurrant	**swartbessie**	[swartbɛssi]
gooseberry	**appelliefie**	[appɛllifi]
bilberry	**bosbessie**	[bosbɛssi]
blackberry	**braambessie**	[brāmbɛssi]
raisin	**rosyntjie**	[rosajnki]
fig	**vy**	[faj]
date	**dadel**	[dadəl]
peanut	**grondboontjie**	[χront·boənki]
almond	**amandel**	[amandəl]
walnut	**okkerneut**	[okkər·nøət]
hazelnut	**haselneut**	[hasɛl·nøət]
coconut	**klapper**	[klappər]
pistachios	**pistachio**	[pistatʃio]

48. Bread. Candy

bakers' confectionery (pastry)	**soet gebak**	[sut χebak]
bread	**brood**	[broət]
cookies	**koekies**	[kukis]
chocolate (n)	**sjokolade**	[ʃokoladə]
chocolate (as adj)	**sjokolade**	[ʃokoladə]

candy (wrapped)	**lekkers**	[lɛkkərs]
cake (e.g., cupcake)	**koek**	[kuk]
cake (e.g., birthday ~)	**koek**	[kuk]

pie (e.g., apple ~)	**pastei**	[pastæj]
filling (for cake, pie)	**vulsel**	[fulsəl]

jam (whole fruit jam)	**konfyt**	[konfajt]
marmalade	**marmelade**	[marmeladə]
waffles	**wafels**	[vafɛls]
ice-cream	**roomys**	[roəm·ajs]
pudding	**poeding**	[pudiŋ]

49. Cooked dishes

course, dish	**gereg**	[χerəχ]
cuisine	**kookkuns**	[koək·kuns]
recipe	**resep**	[resep]
portion	**porsie**	[porsi]

salad	**slaai**	[slāi]
soup	**sop**	[sop]

clear soup (broth)	**helder sop**	[hɛldər sop]
sandwich (bread)	**toebroodjie**	[tubroədʒi]
fried eggs	**gabakte eiers**	[χabaktə æjers]

hamburger (beefburger)	**hamburger**	[hamburχər]
beefsteak	**biefstuk**	[bifstuk]

side dish	**sygereg**	[saj·χerəχ]
spaghetti	**spaghetti**	[spaχɛtti]
mashed potatoes	**kapokaartappels**	[kapok·ārtappəls]
pizza	**pizza**	[pizza]
porridge (oatmeal, etc.)	**pap**	[pap]
omelet	**omelet**	[oməlet]

boiled (e.g., ~ beef)	**gekook**	[χekoək]
smoked (adj)	**gerook**	[χeroək]
fried (adj)	**gebak**	[χebak]
dried (adj)	**gedroog**	[χedroəχ]
frozen (adj)	**gevries**	[χefris]
pickled (adj)	**gepiekel**	[χepikəl]

sweet (sugary)	**soet**	[sut]
salty (adj)	**sout**	[sæʊt]
cold (adj)	**koud**	[kæʊt]
hot (adj)	**warm**	[varm]
bitter (adj)	**bitter**	[bittər]
tasty (adj)	**smaaklik**	[smāklik]

to cook in boiling water	kook in water	[koǝk in vatǝr]
to cook (dinner)	kook	[koǝk]
to fry (vt)	braai	[braj]
to heat up (food)	opwarm	[opwarm]

to salt (vt)	sout	[sæʊt]
to pepper (vt)	peper	[pepǝr]
to grate (vt)	rasp	[rasp]
peel (n)	skil	[skil]
to peel (vt)	skil	[skil]

50. Spices

salt	sout	[sæʊt]
salty (adj)	sout	[sæʊt]
to salt (vt)	sout	[sæʊt]

black pepper	swart peper	[swart pepǝr]
red pepper (milled ~)	rooi peper	[roj pepǝr]
mustard	mosterd	[mostert]
horseradish	peperwortel	[peper·wortǝl]

condiment	smaakmiddel	[smāk·middǝl]
spice	spesery	[spesǝraj]
sauce	sous	[sæʊs]
vinegar	asyn	[asajn]

anise	anys	[anajs]
basil	basilikum	[basilikum]
cloves	naeltjies	[naɛlkis]
ginger	gemmer	[χɛmmǝr]
coriander	koljander	[koljandǝr]
cinnamon	kaneel	[kaneǝl]

sesame	sesamsaad	[sesam·sāt]
bay leaf	lourierblaar	[læʊrir·blār]
paprika	paprika	[paprika]
caraway	komynsaad	[komajnsāt]
saffron	saffraan	[saffrān]

51. Meals

food	kos	[kos]
to eat (vi, vt)	eet	[eǝt]

breakfast	ontbyt	[ontbajt]
to have breakfast	ontbyt	[ontbajt]
lunch	middagete	[middaχ·etǝ]

to have lunch	gaan eet	[χān eət]
dinner	aandete	[āndetə]
to have dinner	aandete gebruik	[āndetə χebrœik]

| appetite | aptyt | [aptajt] |
| Enjoy your meal! | Smaaklike ete! | [smāklikə etə!] |

to open (~ a bottle)	oopmaak	[oəpmāk]
to spill (liquid)	mors	[mors]
to spill out (vi)	mors	[mors]

to boil (vi)	kook	[koək]
to boil (vt)	kook	[koək]
boiled (~ water)	gekook	[χekoək]

| to chill, cool down (vt) | laat afkoel | [lāt afkul] |
| to chill (vi) | afkoel | [afkul] |

| taste, flavor | smaak | [smāk] |
| aftertaste | nasmaak | [nasmāk] |

to slim down (lose weight)	vermaer	[fermaər]
diet	dieet	[diət]
vitamin	vitamien	[fitamin]
calorie	kalorie	[kalori]

| vegetarian (n) | vegetariër | [feχetariɛr] |
| vegetarian (adj) | vegetaries | [feχetaris] |

fats (nutrient)	vette	[fɛttə]
proteins	proteïen	[proteïen]
carbohydrates	koolhidrate	[koəlhidratə]

slice (of lemon, ham)	snytjie	[snajki]
piece (of cake, pie)	stuk	[stuk]
crumb	krummel	[krumməl]
(of bread, cake, etc.)		

52. Table setting

spoon	lepel	[lepəl]
knife	mes	[mes]
fork	vurk	[furk]

| cup (e.g., coffee ~) | koppie | [koppi] |
| plate (dinner ~) | bord | [bort] |

saucer	piering	[piriŋ]
napkin (on table)	servet	[serfət]
toothpick	tandestokkie	[tandə·stokki]

53. Restaurant

restaurant	**restaurant**	[restɔurant]
coffee house	**koffiekroeg**	[koffi·kruχ]
pub, bar	**kroeg**	[kruχ]
tearoom	**teekamer**	[teə·kamər]
waiter	**kelner**	[kɛlnər]
waitress	**kelnerin**	[kɛlnərin]
bartender	**kroegman**	[kruχman]
menu	**spyskaart**	[spajs·kārt]
wine list	**wyn**	[vajn]
to book a table	**wynkaart**	[vajn·kārt]
course, dish	**gereg**	[χerəχ]
to order (meal)	**bestel**	[bestəl]
to make an order	**bestel**	[bestəl]
aperitif	**drankie**	[dranki]
appetizer	**voorgereg**	[foərχerəχ]
dessert	**nagereg**	[naχerəχ]
check	**rekening**	[rekəniŋ]
to pay the check	**die rekening betaal**	[di rekəniŋ betāl]
to give change	**kleingeld gee**	[klæjn·χɛlt χeə]
tip	**fooitjie**	[fojki]

Family, relatives and friends

54. Personal information. Forms

name (first name)	**voornaam**	[foərnãm]
surname (last name)	**van**	[fan]
date of birth	**geboortedatum**	[χeboərtə·datum]
place of birth	**geboorteplek**	[χeboərtə·plek]
nationality	**nasionaliteit**	[naʃionalitæjt]
place of residence	**woonplek**	[voən·plek]
country	**land**	[lant]
profession (occupation)	**beroep**	[berup]
gender, sex	**geslag**	[χeslaχ]
height	**lengte**	[leŋtə]
weight	**gewig**	[χevəχ]

55. Family members. Relatives

mother	**moeder**	[mudər]
father	**vader**	[fadər]
son	**seun**	[søən]
daughter	**dogter**	[doχtər]
younger daughter	**jonger dogter**	[joŋər doχtər]
younger son	**jonger seun**	[joŋər søən]
eldest daughter	**oudste dogter**	[æʊdstə doχtər]
eldest son	**oudste seun**	[æʊdstə søən]
brother	**broer**	[brur]
elder brother	**ouer broer**	[æʊer brur]
younger brother	**jonger broer**	[joŋər brur]
sister	**suster**	[sustər]
elder sister	**ouer suster**	[æʊer sustər]
younger sister	**jonger suster**	[joŋər sustər]
cousin (masc.)	**neef**	[neəf]
cousin (fem.)	**neef**	[neəf]
mom, mommy	**ma**	[ma]
dad, daddy	**pa**	[pa]
parents	**ouers**	[æʊers]
child	**kind**	[kint]
children	**kinders**	[kindərs]

grandmother	**ouma**	[æʊma]
grandfather	**oupa**	[æʊpa]
grandson	**kleinseun**	[klæjn·søøn]
granddaughter	**kleindogter**	[klæjn·doχtər]
grandchildren	**kleinkinders**	[klæjn·kindərs]

uncle	**oom**	[oəm]
aunt	**tante**	[tantə]
nephew	**neef**	[neəf]
niece	**nig**	[niχ]

mother-in-law (wife's mother)	**skoonma**	[skoən·ma]
father-in-law (husband's father)	**skoonpa**	[skoən·pa]
son-in-law (daughter's husband)	**skoonseun**	[skoən·søøn]
stepmother	**stiefma**	[stifma]
stepfather	**stiefpa**	[stifpa]
infant	**baba**	[baba]
baby (infant)	**baba**	[baba]
little boy, kid	**seuntjie**	[søənki]

wife	**vrou**	[fræʊ]
husband	**man**	[man]
spouse (husband)	**eggenoot**	[ɛχχenoət]
spouse (wife)	**eggenote**	[ɛχχenotə]

married (masc.)	**getroud**	[χetræʊt]
married (fem.)	**getroud**	[χetræʊt]
single (unmarried)	**ongetroud**	[onχətræʊt]
bachelor	**vrygesel**	[frajχesəl]
divorced (masc.)	**geskei**	[χeskæj]
widow	**weduwee**	[veduveə]
widower	**wedunaar**	[vedunãr]

relative	**familielid**	[famililit]
close relative	**na familie**	[na famili]
distant relative	**ver familie**	[fer famili]
relatives	**familielede**	[famililedə]

orphan (boy or girl)	**weeskind**	[veəskint]
guardian (of a minor)	**voog**	[foəχ]
to adopt (a boy)	**aanneem**	[ãnneəm]
to adopt (a girl)	**aanneem**	[ãnneəm]

56. Friends. Coworkers

friend (masc.)	**vriend**	[frint]
friend (fem.)	**vriendin**	[frindin]

friendship	vriendskap	[frindskap]
to be friends	bevriend wees	[befrint vees]

buddy (masc.)	maat	[mãt]
buddy (fem.)	vriendin	[frindin]
partner	maat	[mãt]

chief (boss)	baas	[bãs]
superior (n)	baas	[bãs]
owner, proprietor	eienaar	[æjenãr]
subordinate (n)	ondergeskikte	[ondərχeskiktə]
colleague	kollega	[kolleχa]

acquaintance (person)	kennis	[kɛnnis]
fellow traveler	medereisiger	[medə·ræjsiχər]
classmate	klasmaat	[klas·mãt]

neighbor (masc.)	buurman	[bɪrman]
neighbor (fem.)	buurvrou	[bɪrfræʊ]
neighbors	bure	[burə]

57. Man. Woman

woman	vrou	[fræʊ]
girl (young woman)	meisie	[mæjsi]
bride	bruid	[brœit]

beautiful (adj)	mooi	[moj]
tall (adj)	groot	[χroət]
slender (adj)	slank	[slank]
short (adj)	kort	[kort]

blonde (n)	blondine	[blondinə]
brunette (n)	brunet	[brunet]

ladies' (adj)	dames-	[dames-]
virgin (girl)	maagd	[mãχt]
pregnant (adj)	swanger	[swaŋər]

man (adult male)	man	[man]
blond (n)	blond	[blont]
brunet (n)	brunet	[brunet]
tall (adj)	groot	[χroət]
short (adj)	kort	[kort]

rude (rough)	onbeskof	[onbeskof]
stocky (adj)	frisgebou	[frisχebæʊ]
robust (adj)	frisgebou	[frisχebæʊ]
strong (adj)	sterk	[sterk]
strength	sterkte	[sterktə]

stout, fat (adj)	**vet**	[fet]
swarthy (adj)	**blas**	[blas]
slender (well-built)	**slank**	[slank]
elegant (adj)	**elegant**	[ɛleχant]

58. Age

age	**ouderdom**	[æʊderdom]
youth (young age)	**jeug**	[jøøχ]
young (adj)	**jong**	[joŋ]

| younger (adj) | **jonger** | [joŋər] |
| older (adj) | **ouer** | [æʊer] |

young man	**jongman**	[joŋman]
teenager	**tiener**	[tinər]
guy, fellow	**ou**	[æʊ]

| old man | **ou man** | [æʊ man] |
| old woman | **ou vrou** | [æʊ fræʊ] |

adult (adj)	**volwasse**	[folwassə]
middle-aged (adj)	**middeljarig**	[middəl·jarəχ]
elderly (adj)	**bejaard**	[bejãrt]
old (adj)	**oud**	[æʊt]

retirement	**pensioen**	[pɛnsiun]
to retire (from job)	**met pensioen gaan**	[met pɛnsiun χãn]
retiree	**pensioenaris**	[pɛnsiunaris]

59. Children

child	**kind**	[kint]
children	**kinders**	[kindərs]
twins	**tweeling**	[tweəliŋ]

cradle	**wiegie**	[viχi]
rattle	**rammelaar**	[rammelãr]
diaper	**luier**	[lœiər]

pacifier	**fopspeen**	[fopspeən]
baby carriage	**kinderwaentjie**	[kindər·waenki]
kindergarten	**kindertuin**	[kindər·tœin]
babysitter	**babasitter**	[babasittər]

childhood	**kinderdae**	[kindərdaə]
doll	**pop**	[pop]
toy	**speelgoed**	[speəl·χut]

construction set (toy)	boudoos	[bæʊ·doəs]
well-bred (adj)	goed opgevoed	[χut opχəfut]
ill-bred (adj)	sleg opgevoed	[sleχ opχəfut]
spoiled (adj)	bederf	[bederf]

to be naughty	stout wees	[stæʊt veəs]
mischievous (adj)	ondeuend	[ondøent]
mischievousness	ondeuendheid	[ondøenthæjt]
mischievous child	rakker	[rakkər]

obedient (adj)	gehoorsaam	[χehoərsãm]
disobedient (adj)	ongehoorsaam	[onχəhoərsãm]

docile (adj)	soet	[sut]
clever (smart)	slim	[slim]
child prodigy	wonderkind	[vondərkint]

60. Married couples. Family life

to kiss (vt)	soen	[sun]
to kiss (vi)	mekaar soen	[mekãr sun]
family (n)	familie	[famili]
family (as adj)	gesins-	[χesins-]
couple	paartjie	[pãrki]
marriage (state)	huwelik	[huvelik]
hearth (home)	tuiste	[tœistə]
dynasty	dinastie	[dinasti]

date	datum	[datum]
kiss	soen	[sun]

love (for sb)	liefde	[lifdə]
to love (sb)	liefhë	[lifhɛ:]
beloved	geliefde	[χelifdə]

tenderness	teerheid	[teərhæjt]
tender (affectionate)	teer	[teər]
faithfulness	trou	[træʊ]
faithful (adj)	trou	[træʊ]
care (attention)	sorg	[sorχ]
caring (~ father)	sorgsaam	[sorχsãm]

newlyweds	pasgetroudes	[pas·χetræʊdes]
honeymoon	wittebroodsdae	[vittebroəds·daə]
to get married (ab. woman)	trou	[træʊ]
to get married (ab. man)	trou	[træʊ]

wedding	bruilof	[brœilof]
golden wedding	goue bruilof	[χæʊə brœilof]

anniversary	verjaardag	[ferjār·daχ]
lover (masc.)	minnaar	[minnār]
mistress (lover)	minnares	[minnares]

adultery	owerspel	[overspəl]
to cheat on ... (commit adultery)	owerspel pleeg	[overspəl pleeχ]
jealous (adj)	jaloers	[jalurs]
to be jealous	jaloers wees	[jalurs veəs]
divorce	egskeiding	[ɛχskæjdiŋ]
to divorce (vi)	skei	[skæj]

to quarrel (vi)	baklei	[baklæj]
to be reconciled (after an argument)	versoen	[fersun]
together (adv)	saam	[sām]
sex	seks	[seks]

happiness	geluk	[χeluk]
happy (adj)	gelukkig	[χelukkəχ]
misfortune (accident)	ongeluk	[onχəluk]
unhappy (adj)	ongelukkig	[onχəlukkəχ]

Character. Feelings. Emotions

61. Feelings. Emotions

feeling (emotion)	gevoel	[χeful]
feelings	gevoelens	[χefulɛŋs]
to feel (vt)	voel	[ful]

hunger	honger	[hoŋər]
to be hungry	honger wees	[hoŋər veəs]
thirst	dors	[dors]
to be thirsty	dors wees	[dors veəs]
sleepiness	slaperigheid	[slaperiχæjt]
to feel sleepy	vaak voel	[fāk ful]

tiredness	moegheid	[muχæjt]
tired (adj)	moeg	[muχ]
to get tired	moeg word	[muχ vort]

mood (humor)	stemming	[stɛmmiŋ]
boredom	verveling	[ferfeliŋ]
to be bored	verveeld wees	[ferveəlt veəs]
seclusion	afsondering	[afsondəriŋ]
to seclude oneself	jou afsonder	[jæʊ afsondər]

to worry (make anxious)	bekommerd maak	[bekommərt māk]
to be worried	bekommerd wees	[bekommərt veəs]
worrying (n)	kommerwekkend	[kommər·wɛkkent]
anxiety	vrees	[freəs]
preoccupied (adj)	behep	[behep]
to be nervous	senuweeagtig wees	[senuveə·aχtəχ veəs]
to panic (vi)	paniekerig raak	[panikerəχ rāk]

hope	hoop	[hoəp]
to hope (vi, vt)	hoop	[hoəp]

certainty	sekerheid	[sekərhæjt]
certain, sure (adj)	seker	[sekər]
uncertainty	onsekerheid	[ɔŋsekərhæjt]
uncertain (adj)	onseker	[ɔŋsekər]

drunk (adj)	dronk	[dronk]
sober (adj)	nugter	[nuχtər]
weak (adj)	swak	[swak]
happy (adj)	gelukkig	[χelukkəχ]
to scare (vt)	bang maak	[baŋ māk]

| fury (madness) | kwaadheid | [kwãdhæjt] |
| rage (fury) | woede | [vudə] |

depression	depressie	[deprɛssi]
discomfort (unease)	ongemak	[onχəmak]
comfort	gemak	[χemak]
to regret (be sorry)	jammer wees	[jammər veəs]
regret	spyt	[spajt]
bad luck	teëspoed	[teɛsput]
sadness	droefheid	[drufhæjt]

shame (remorse)	skaamte	[skãmtə]
gladness	vreugde	[frøəχdə]
enthusiasm, zeal	entoesiasme	[ɛntusiasmə]
enthusiast	entoesiasties	[ɛntusiastis]
to show enthusiasm	begeestering toon	[beχeəsteriŋ toən]

62. Character. Personality

character	karakter	[karaktər]
character flaw	karakterfout	[karaktər·fæʊt]
mind	verstand	[ferstant]
reason	verstand	[ferstant]

conscience	gewete	[χevetə]
habit (custom)	gewoonte	[χevoentə]
ability (talent)	talent	[talent]
can (e.g., ~ swim)	kan	[kan]

patient (adj)	geduldig	[χeduldəχ]
impatient (adj)	ongeduldig	[onχeduldəχ]
curious (inquisitive)	nuuskierig	[nɪskirəχ]
curiosity	nuuskierigheid	[nɪskiriχæjt]

modesty	beskeidenheid	[beskæjdenhæjt]
modest (adj)	beskeie	[beskæje]
immodest (adj)	onbeskeie	[onbeskæje]

laziness	luiheid	[lœihæjt]
lazy (adj)	lui	[lœi]
lazy person (masc.)	luiaard	[lœiãrt]

cunning (n)	sluheid	[sluhæjt]
cunning (as adj)	slu	[slu]
distrust	wantroue	[vantræʊə]
distrustful (adj)	agterdogtig	[aχtərdoχtəχ]

generosity	gulheid	[χulhæjt]
generous (adj)	gulhartig	[χulhartəχ]
talented (adj)	talentvol	[talentfol]

talent	talent	[talent]
courageous (adj)	moedig	[mudəχ]
courage	moed	[mut]
honest (adj)	eerlik	[eərlik]
honesty	eerlikheid	[eərlikhæjt]

careful (cautious)	versigtig	[fersiχtəχ]
brave (courageous)	dapper	[dappər]
serious (adj)	ernstig	[ɛrnstəχ]
strict (severe, stern)	streng	[streŋ]

decisive (adj)	vasberade	[fasberadə]
indecisive (adj)	besluiteloos	[beslœiteloes]
shy, timid (adj)	skaam	[skãm]
shyness, timidity	skaamheid	[skãmhæjt]

confidence (trust)	vertroue	[fertræʊə]
to believe (trust)	vertrou	[fertræʊ]
trusting (credulous)	goedgelowig	[χudχəloveχ]

sincerely (adv)	opreg	[opreχ]
sincere (adj)	opregte	[opreχtə]
sincerity	opregtheid	[opreχthæjt]
open (person)	oop	[oəp]

calm (adj)	kalm	[kalm]
frank (sincere)	openhartig	[openhartəχ]
naïve (adj)	naïef	[naïef]
absent-minded (adj)	verstrooid	[ferstrojt]
funny (odd)	snaaks	[snãks]

greed	hebsug	[hebsuχ]
greedy (adj)	hebsugtig	[hebsuχtəχ]
stingy (adj)	gierig	[χirəχ]
evil (adj)	boos	[boes]
stubborn (adj)	hardnekkig	[hardnɛkkəχ]
unpleasant (adj)	onaangenaam	[onãnχənãm]

selfish person (masc.)	selfsugtig	[sɛlfsuχtəχ]
selfish (adj)	selfsugtig	[sɛlfsuχtəχ]
coward	laffaard	[laffãrt]
cowardly (adj)	lafhartig	[lafhartəχ]

63. Sleep. Dreams

to sleep (vi)	slaap	[slãp]
sleep, sleeping	slaap	[slãp]
dream	droom	[droəm]
to dream (in sleep)	droom	[droəm]
sleepy (adj)	vaak	[fãk]

bed	bed	[bet]
mattress	matras	[matras]
blanket (comforter)	kombers	[kombers]
pillow	kussing	[kussiŋ]
sheet	laken	[laken]

insomnia	slaaploosheid	[slāploeshæjt]
sleepless (adj)	slaaploos	[slāploes]
sleeping pill	slaappil	[slāp·pil]

to feel sleepy	vaak voel	[fāk ful]
to yawn (vi)	gaap	[χāp]
to go to bed	gaan slaap	[χān slāp]
to make up the bed	die bed opmaak	[di bet opmāk]
to fall asleep	aan die slaap raak	[ān di slāp rāk]

nightmare	nagmerrie	[naχmerri]
snore, snoring	gesnork	[χesnork]
to snore (vi)	snork	[snork]

alarm clock	wekker	[vɛkkər]
to wake (vt)	wakker maak	[vakkər māk]
to wake up	wakker word	[vakkər vort]
to get up (vi)	opstaan	[opstān]
to wash up (wash face)	jou was	[jæʊ vas]

64. Humour. Laughter. Gladness

humor (wit, fun)	humor	[humor]
sense of humor	humorsin	[humorsin]
to enjoy oneself	jouself geniet	[jæʊsɛlf χenit]
cheerful (merry)	vrolik	[frolik]
merriment (gaiety)	pret	[pret]

smile	glimlag	[χlimlaχ]
to smile (vi)	glimlag	[χlimlaχ]

to start laughing	begin lag	[beχin laχ]
to laugh (vi)	lag	[laχ]
laugh, laughter	lag	[laχ]

anecdote	anekdote	[anekdotə]
funny (anecdote, etc.)	snaaks	[snāks]
funny (odd)	snaaks	[snāks]

to joke (vi)	grappies maak	[χrappis māk]
joke (verbal)	grappie	[χrappi]
joy (emotion)	vreugde	[frøəχdə]
to rejoice (vi)	bly wees	[blaj vees]
joyful (adj)	bly	[blaj]

65. Discussion, conversation. Part 1

communication	**kommunikasie**	[kommunikasi]
to communicate	**kommunikeer**	[kommunikeər]
conversation	**gesprek**	[χesprek]
dialog	**dialoog**	[dialoəχ]
discussion (discourse)	**diskussie**	[diskussi]
dispute (debate)	**dispuut**	[dispɪt]
to dispute	**debatteer**	[debatteər]
interlocutor	**gespreksgenoot**	[χespreks·χenoət]
topic (theme)	**onderwerp**	[ondərwerp]
point of view	**standpunt**	[stand·punt]
opinion (point of view)	**opinie**	[opini]
speech (talk)	**toespraak**	[tusprāk]
discussion (of report, etc.)	**bespreking**	[besprekiŋ]
to discuss (vt)	**bespreek**	[bespreək]
talk (conversation)	**gesprek**	[χesprek]
to talk (to chat)	**gesels**	[χesɛls]
meeting	**ontmoeting**	[ontmutiŋ]
to meet (vi, vt)	**ontmoet**	[ontmut]
proverb	**spreekwoord**	[spreək·woərt]
saying	**gesegde**	[χeseχdə]
riddle (poser)	**raaisel**	[rājsəl]
password	**wagwoord**	[vaχ·woərt]
secret	**geheim**	[χəhæjm]
oath (vow)	**eed**	[eət]
to swear (an oath)	**sweer**	[sweər]
promise	**belofte**	[beloftə]
to promise (vt)	**beloof**	[beloəf]
advice (counsel)	**raad**	[rāt]
to advise (vt)	**aanraai**	[ānrāi]
to follow one's advice	**raad volg**	[rāt folχ]
to listen to ... (obey)	**luister na**	[lœistər na]
news	**nuus**	[nɪs]
sensation (news)	**sensasie**	[sɛŋsasi]
information (data)	**inligting**	[inliχtiŋ]
conclusion (decision)	**slotsom**	[slotsom]
voice	**stem**	[stem]
compliment	**kompliment**	[kompliment]
kind (nice)	**gaaf**	[χāf]
word	**woord**	[voərt]
phrase	**frase**	[frasə]
answer	**antwoord**	[antwoərt]

truth	waarheid	[vārhæjt]
lie	leuen	[løəen]

thought	gedagte	[χedaχtə]
idea (inspiration)	idee	[ideə]
fantasy	verbeelding	[ferbeəldiŋ]

66. Discussion, conversation. Part 2

respected (adj)	gerespekteer	[χerespekteər]
to respect (vt)	respekteer	[respekteər]
respect	respek	[respek]
Dear ... (letter)	Geagte ...	[χeaχtə ...]

to introduce (sb to sb)	voorstel	[foərstəl]
to make acquaintance	kennismaak	[kɛnnismāk]

intention	voorneme	[foərnemə]
to intend (have in mind)	voornemens wees	[foərnemɛŋs veəs]
wish	wens	[vɛŋs]
to wish (~ good luck)	wens	[vɛŋs]

surprise (astonishment)	verrassing	[ferrassiŋ]
to surprise (amaze)	verras	[ferras]
to be surprised	verbaas wees	[ferbās veəs]

to give (vt)	gee	[χeə]
to take (get hold of)	vat	[fat]
to give back	teruggee	[teruχeə]
to return (give back)	terugvat	[teruχfat]

to apologize (vi)	verskoning vra	[ferskoniŋ fra]
apology	verskoning	[ferskoniŋ]
to forgive (vt)	vergewe	[ferχevə]

to talk (speak)	praat	[prāt]
to listen (vi)	luister	[lœistər]
to hear out	aanhoor	[ānhoər]
to understand (vt)	verstaan	[ferstān]

to show (to display)	wys	[vajs]
to look at ...	kyk na ...	[kajk na ...]
to call (yell for sb)	roep	[rup]
to distract (disturb)	aflei	[aflæj]
to disturb (vt)	steur	[støər]
to pass (to hand sth)	deurgee	[døərχeə]

demand (request)	versoek	[fersuk]
to request (ask)	versoek	[fersuk]
demand (firm request)	eis	[æjs]

to demand (request firmly)	eis	[æjs]
to tease (call names)	terg	[terχ]
to mock (make fun of)	terg	[terχ]
mockery, derision	spot	[spot]
nickname	bynaam	[bajnām]

insinuation	sinspeling	[sinspeliŋ]
to insinuate (imply)	sinspeel	[sinspeəl]
to mean (vt)	impliseer	[impliseər]

description	beskrywing	[beskrajviŋ]
to describe (vt)	beskryf	[beskrajf]
praise (compliments)	lof	[lof]
to praise (vt)	loof	[loəf]

disappointment	teleurstelling	[teløərstɛlliŋ]
to disappoint (vt)	teleurstel	[teløərstəl]
to be disappointed	teleurgestel	[teløərχestəl]

supposition	veronderstelling	[feronderstɛlliŋ]
to suppose (assume)	veronderstel	[feronderstəl]
warning (caution)	waarskuwing	[vārskuviŋ]
to warn (vt)	waarsku	[vārsku]

67. Discussion, conversation. Part 3

| to talk into (convince) | ompraat | [omprāt] |
| to calm down (vt) | kalmeer | [kalmeər] |

silence (~ is golden)	stilte	[stiltə]
to be silent (not speaking)	stilbly	[stilblaj]
to whisper (vi, vt)	fluister	[flœistər]
whisper	gefluister	[χeflœistər]

| frankly, sincerely (adv) | openlik | [openlik] |
| in my opinion ... | volgens my ... | [folχɛŋs maj ...] |

detail (of the story)	besonderhede	[besondərhedə]
detailed (adj)	gedetailleerd	[χedetajlleərt]
in detail (adv)	in detail	[in detajl]
hint, clue	wenk	[vɛnk]

look (glance)	kykie	[kajki]
to have a look	kyk	[kajk]
fixed (look)	strak	[strak]
to blink (vi)	knipper	[knippər]
to wink (vi)	knipoog	[knipoəχ]
to nod (in assent)	knik	[knik]
sigh	sug	[suχ]
to sigh (vi)	sug	[suχ]

to shudder (vi)	huiwer	[hœivər]
gesture	gebaar	[χebãr]
to touch (one's arm, etc.)	aanraak	[ãnrãk]
to seize	vat	[fat]
(e.g., ~ by the arm)		
to tap (on the shoulder)	op die skouer tik	[op di skæʊər tik]

Look out!	Oppas!	[oppas!]
Really?	Regtig?	[reχtəχ?]
Are you sure?	Is jy seker?	[is jaj sekər?]
Good luck!	Voorspoed!	[foərspud!]
I see!	Ek sien!	[ɛk sin!]
What a pity!	Jammer!	[jammər!]

68. Agreement. Refusal

consent	toelating	[tulatiŋ]
to consent (vi)	toelaat	[tulãt]
approval	goedkeuring	[χudkøøriŋ]
to approve (vt)	goedkeur	[χudkøər]

| refusal | weiering | [væejeriŋ] |
| to refuse (vi, vt) | weier | [væejer] |

Great!	Wonderlik!	[vondərlik!]
All right!	Goed!	[χud!]
Okay! (I agree)	OK!	[okej!]

forbidden (adj)	verbode	[ferbodə]
it's forbidden	dit is verbode	[dit is ferbodə]
it's impossible	dis onmoontlik	[dis onmoentlik]
incorrect (adj)	onjuis	[onjœis]

to reject (~ a demand)	verwerp	[ferwerp]
to support (cause, idea)	steun	[støøn]
to accept (~ an apology)	aanvaar	[ãnfãr]

to confirm (vt)	bevestig	[befestəχ]
confirmation	bevestiging	[befestəχiŋ]
permission	toelating	[tulatiŋ]
to permit (vt)	toelaat	[tulãt]

decision	besluit	[beslœit]
to say nothing	stilbly	[stilblaj]
(hold one's tongue)		

condition (term)	voorwaarde	[foərwãrdə]
excuse (pretext)	verskoning	[ferskoniŋ]
praise (compliments)	lof	[lof]
to praise (vt)	loof	[loəf]

69. Success. Good luck. Failure

success	**sukses**	[suksɛs]
successfully (adv)	**suksesvol**	[suksɛsfol]
successful (adj)	**suksesvol**	[suksɛsfol]
luck (good luck)	**geluk**	[χeluk]
Good luck!	**Voorspoed!**	[foərspud!]
lucky (e.g., ~ day)	**geluks-**	[χeluks-]
lucky (fortunate)	**gelukkig**	[χelukkəχ]
failure	**mislukking**	[mislukkiŋ]
misfortune	**teëspoed**	[teɛsput]
bad luck	**teëspoed**	[teɛsput]
unsuccessful (adj)	**onsuksesvol**	[oŋsuksɛsfol]
catastrophe	**katastrofe**	[katastrofə]
pride	**trots**	[trots]
proud (adj)	**trots**	[trots]
to be proud	**trots wees**	[trots veəs]
winner	**wenner**	[vɛnnər]
to win (vi)	**wen**	[ven]
to lose (not win)	**verloor**	[ferloər]
try	**probeerslag**	[probeərslaχ]
to try (vi)	**probeer**	[probeər]
chance (opportunity)	**kans**	[kaŋs]

70. Quarrels. Negative emotions

shout (scream)	**skreeu**	[skriʊ]
to shout (vi)	**skreeu**	[skriʊ]
to start to cry out	**begin skreeu**	[beχin skriʊ]
quarrel	**rusie**	[rusi]
to quarrel (vi)	**baklei**	[baklæj]
fight (squabble)	**stryery**	[strajeraj]
to make a scene	**spektakel maak**	[spektakəl māk]
conflict	**konflik**	[konflik]
misunderstanding	**misverstand**	[misferstant]
insult	**belediging**	[beledəχiŋ]
to insult (vt)	**beledig**	[beledəχ]
insulted (adj)	**beledig**	[beledəχ]
resentment	**gekrenktheid**	[χekrɛnkthæjt]
to offend (vt)	**beledig**	[beledəχ]
to take offense	**gekrenk voel**	[χekrɛnk ful]
indignation	**verontwaardiging**	[ferontwārdəχiŋ]
to be indignant	**verontwaardig wees**	[ferontwārdəχ veəs]

| complaint | klag | [klaχ] |
| to complain (vi, vt) | kla | [kla] |

apology	verskoning	[ferskoniŋ]
to apologize (vi)	verskoning vra	[ferskoniŋ fra]
to beg pardon	om verskoning vra	[om ferskoniŋ fra]

criticism	kritiek	[kritik]
to criticize (vt)	kritiseer	[kritiseər]
accusation	beskuldiging	[beskuldəχiŋ]
to accuse (vt)	beskuldig	[beskuldəχ]

revenge	wraak	[vrāk]
to avenge (get revenge)	wreek	[vreək]
to pay back	wraak neem	[vrāk neəm]

disdain	minagting	[minaχtiŋ]
to despise (vt)	minag	[minaχ]
hatred, hate	haat	[hāt]
to hate (vt)	haat	[hāt]

nervous (adj)	senuweeagtig	[senuveə·aχtəχ]
to be nervous	senuweeagtig wees	[senuveə·aχtəχ veəs]
angry (mad)	kwaad	[kwāt]
to make angry	kwaad maak	[kwāt māk]

humiliation	vernedering	[fernedəriŋ]
to humiliate (vt)	verneder	[fernedər]
to humiliate oneself	jouself verneder	[jæʋsɛlf fernedər]

| shock | skok | [skok] |
| to shock (vt) | skok | [skok] |

| trouble (e.g., serious ~) | probleme | [probləmə] |
| unpleasant (adj) | onaangenaam | [onānχənām] |

fear (dread)	vrees	[freəs]
terrible (storm, heat)	verskriklik	[ferskriklik]
scary (e.g., ~ story)	vreesaanjaend	[freəsānjaent]
horror	afgryse	[afχrajsə]
awful (crime, news)	vreeslik	[freəslik]

to begin to tremble	begin beef	[beχin beəf]
to cry (weep)	huil	[hœil]
to start crying	begin huil	[beχin hœil]
tear	traan	[trān]

fault	skuld	[skult]
guilt (feeling)	skuldgevoel	[skultχəful]
dishonor (disgrace)	skande	[skandə]
protest	protes	[protes]
stress	stres	[stres]

to disturb (vt)	**steur**	[støər]
to be furious	**woedend wees**	[vudent veəs]
mad, angry (adj)	**kwaad**	[kwāt]
to end (~ a relationship)	**beëindig**	[beɛindəχ]
to swear (at sb)	**sweer**	[sweər]
to scare (become afraid)	**skrik**	[skrik]
to hit (strike with hand)	**slaan**	[slān]
to fight (street fight, etc.)	**baklei**	[baklæj]
to settle (a conflict)	**besleg**	[besleχ]
discontented (adj)	**ontevrede**	[ontefredə]
furious (adj)	**woedend**	[vudent]
It's not good!	**Dis nie goed nie!**	[dis ni χut ni!]
It's bad!	**Dis sleg!**	[dis sleχ!]

Medicine

71. Diseases

sickness	**siekte**	[siktə]
to be sick	**siek wees**	[sik veəs]
health	**gesondheid**	[χesonthæjt]
runny nose (coryza)	**loopneus**	[loəpnøəs]
tonsillitis	**keelontsteking**	[keəl·ontstekiŋ]
cold (illness)	**verkoue**	[ferkæʋə]
bronchitis	**bronchitis**	[bronχitis]
pneumonia	**longontsteking**	[loŋ·ontstekiŋ]
flu, influenza	**griep**	[χrip]
nearsighted (adj)	**bysiende**	[bajsində]
farsighted (adj)	**versiende**	[fersində]
strabismus (crossed eyes)	**skeelheid**	[skeəlhæjt]
cross-eyed (adj)	**skeel**	[skeəl]
cataract	**katarak**	[katarak]
glaucoma	**gloukoom**	[χlæʋkoəm]
stroke	**beroerte**	[berurtə]
heart attack	**hartaanval**	[hart·ānfal]
myocardial infarction	**hartinfark**	[hart·infark]
paralysis	**verlamming**	[ferlammiŋ]
to paralyze (vt)	**verlam**	[ferlam]
allergy	**allergie**	[allerχi]
asthma	**asma**	[asma]
diabetes	**suikersiekte**	[sœikər·siktə]
toothache	**tandpyn**	[tand·pajn]
caries	**tandbederf**	[tand·bederf]
diarrhea	**diarree**	[diarreə]
constipation	**hardlywigheid**	[hardlajviχæjt]
stomach upset	**maagongesteldheid**	[māχ·oŋəstɛldhæjt]
food poisoning	**voedselvergiftiging**	[fudsəl·ferχiftəχiŋ]
to get food poisoning	**voedselvergiftiging kry**	[fudsəl·ferχiftəχiŋ kraj]
arthritis	**artritis**	[artritis]
rickets	**Engelse siekte**	[ɛŋəlsə siktə]
rheumatism	**reumatiek**	[røəmatik]
atherosclerosis	**artrosklerose**	[artrosklerosə]

gastritis	maagontsteking	[mãχ·ontstekiŋ]
appendicitis	blindedermontsteking	[blindəderm·ontstekiŋ]
cholecystitis	galblaasontsteking	[χalblãs·ontstekiŋ]
ulcer	maagsweer	[mãχsweər]

measles	masels	[masɛls]
rubella (German measles)	Duitse masels	[dœitsə masɛls]
jaundice	geelsug	[χeəlsuχ]
hepatitis	hepatitis	[hepatitis]

schizophrenia	skisofrenie	[skisofreni]
rabies (hydrophobia)	hondsdolheid	[hondsdolhæjt]
neurosis	neurose	[nøørosə]
concussion	harsingskudding	[harsiŋ·skuddiŋ]

cancer	kanker	[kankər]
sclerosis	sklerose	[sklerosə]
multiple sclerosis	veelvuldige sklerose	[feəlfuldiχə sklerosə]

alcoholism	alkoholisme	[alkoholismə]
alcoholic (n)	alkoholikus	[alkoholikus]
syphilis	sifilis	[sifilis]
AIDS	VIGS	[vigs]

tumor	tumor	[tumor]
malignant (adj)	kwaadaardig	[kwãdãrdəχ]
benign (adj)	goedaardig	[χudãrdəχ]

fever	koors	[koərs]
malaria	malaria	[malaria]
gangrene	gangreen	[χanχreən]
seasickness	seesiekte	[seə·siktə]
epilepsy	epilepsie	[ɛpilepsi]

epidemic	epidemie	[ɛpidemi]
typhus	tifus	[tifus]
tuberculosis	tuberkulose	[tuberkulosə]
cholera	cholera	[χolera]
plague (bubonic ~)	pes	[pes]

72. Symptoms. Treatments. Part 1

symptom	simptoom	[simptoəm]
temperature	temperatuur	[temperatɪr]
high temperature (fever)	koors	[koərs]
pulse	polsslag	[pols·slaχ]

dizziness (vertigo)	duiseligheid	[dœiseliχæjt]
hot (adj)	warm	[varm]
shivering	koue rillings	[kæʊə rilliŋs]

pale (e.g., ~ face)	bleek	[bleǝk]
cough	hoes	[hus]
to cough (vi)	hoes	[hus]
to sneeze (vi)	nies	[nis]
faint	floute	[flæutǝ]
to faint (vi)	flou word	[flæu vort]

bruise (hématome)	blou kol	[blæu kol]
bump (lump)	knop	[knop]
to bang (bump)	stamp	[stamp]
contusion (bruise)	besering	[beseriŋ]

to limp (vi)	hink	[hink]
dislocation	ontwrigting	[ontwriχtiŋ]
to dislocate (vt)	ontwrig	[ontwrǝχ]
fracture	breuk	[brøǝk]
to have a fracture	n breuk hê	[n brøǝk hɛ:]

cut (e.g., paper ~)	sny	[snaj]
to cut oneself	jouself sny	[jæusɛlf snaj]
bleeding	bloeding	[bludiŋ]

burn (injury)	brandwond	[brant·vont]
to get burned	jouself brand	[jæusɛlf brant]

to prick (vt)	prik	[prik]
to prick oneself	jouself prik	[jæusɛlf prik]
to injure (vt)	seermaak	[seǝrmāk]
injury	besering	[beseriŋ]
wound	wond	[vont]
trauma	trauma	[trɔuma]

to be delirious	yl	[ajl]
to stutter (vi)	stotter	[stottǝr]
sunstroke	sonsteek	[sɔŋ·steǝk]

73. Symptoms. Treatments. Part 2

pain, ache	pyn	[pajn]
splinter (in foot, etc.)	splinter	[splintǝr]

sweat (perspiration)	sweet	[sweǝt]
to sweat (perspire)	sweet	[sweǝt]
vomiting	braak	[brāk]
convulsions	stuiptrekkings	[stœip·trɛkkiŋs]

pregnant (adj)	swanger	[swaŋǝr]
to be born	gebore word	[χeborǝ vort]
delivery, labor	geboorte	[χeboǝrtǝ]
to deliver (~ a baby)	baar	[bār]

abortion	aborsie	[aborsi]
breathing, respiration	asemhaling	[asemhaliŋ]
in-breath (inhalation)	inaseming	[inasemiŋ]
out-breath (exhalation)	uitaseming	[œitasemiŋ]
to exhale (breathe out)	uitasem	[œitasem]
to inhale (vi)	inasem	[inasem]

disabled person	invalide	[infalidə]
cripple	kreupel	[krøəpəl]
drug addict	dwelmslaaf	[dwɛlm·slāf]

deaf (adj)	doof	[doəf]
mute (adj)	stom	[stom]
deaf mute (adj)	doofstom	[doəf·stom]

mad, insane (adj)	swaksinnig	[swaksinnəχ]
madman (demented person)	kranksinnige	[kranksinniχə]
madwoman	kranksinnige	[kranksinniχə]
to go insane	kranksinnig word	[kranksinnəχ vort]

gene	geen	[χeən]
immunity	immuniteit	[immunitæjt]
hereditary (adj)	erflik	[ɛrflik]
congenital (adj)	aangebore	[ānχəborə]

virus	virus	[firus]
microbe	mikrobe	[mikrobə]
bacterium	bakterie	[bakteri]
infection	infeksie	[infeksi]

74. Symptoms. Treatments. Part 3

hospital	hospitaal	[hospitāl]
patient	pasiënt	[pasiɛnt]

diagnosis	diagnose	[diaχnosə]
cure	genesing	[χenesiŋ]
medical treatment	mediese behandeling	[medisə behandəliŋ]
to get treatment	behandeling kry	[behandəliŋ kraj]
to treat (~ a patient)	behandel	[behandəl]
to nurse (look after)	versorg	[fersorχ]
care (nursing ~)	versorging	[fersorχin]

operation, surgery	operasie	[operasi]
to bandage (head, limb)	verbind	[ferbint]
bandaging	verband	[ferbant]

vaccination	inenting	[inɛntiŋ]
to vaccinate (vt)	inent	[inɛnt]

injection, shot	inspuiting	[inspœitiŋ]
attack	aanval	[ānfal]
amputation	amputasie	[amputasi]
to amputate (vt)	amputeer	[amputeer]
coma	koma	[koma]
intensive care	intensiewe sorg	[intɛnsivə sorχ]

to recover (~ from flu)	herstel	[herstəl]
condition (patient's ~)	kondisie	[kondisi]
consciousness	bewussyn	[bevussajn]
memory (faculty)	geheue	[χəhøə]

to pull out (tooth)	trek	[trek]
filling	vulsel	[fulsəl]
to fill (a tooth)	vul	[ful]

| hypnosis | hipnose | [hipnosə] |
| to hypnotize (vt) | hipnotiseer | [hipnotiseer] |

75. Doctors

doctor	dokter	[doktər]
nurse	verpleegster	[ferpleəχ·stər]
personal doctor	lyfarts	[lajf·arts]

dentist	tandarts	[tand·arts]
eye doctor	oogarts	[oəχ·arts]
internist	internis	[internis]
surgeon	chirurg	[ʃirurχ]

psychiatrist	psigiater	[psiχiatər]
pediatrician	kinderdokter	[kindər·doktər]
psychologist	sielkundige	[silkundiχə]
gynecologist	ginekoloog	[χinekoloəχ]
cardiologist	kardioloog	[kardioloəχ]

76. Medicine. Drugs. Accessories

medicine, drug	medisyn	[medisajn]
remedy	geneesmiddel	[χeneəs·middəl]
to prescribe (vt)	voorskryf	[foərskrajf]
prescription	voorskrif	[foərskrif]

tablet, pill	pil	[pil]
ointment	salf	[salf]
ampule	ampul	[ampul]
mixture	mengsel	[meŋsəl]
syrup	stroop	[stroəp]

pill	pil	[pil]
powder	poeier	[pujer]

gauze bandage	verband	[ferbant]
cotton wool	watte	[vattə]
iodine	iodium	[iodium]

Band-Aid	pleister	[plæjstər]
eyedropper	oogdrupper	[oəχ·druppər]
thermometer	termometer	[termometər]
syringe	spuitnaald	[spœit·nãlt]

wheelchair	rolstoel	[rol·stul]
crutches	krukke	[krukkə]

painkiller	pynstiller	[pajn·stillər]
laxative	lakseermiddel	[lakseər·middəl]
spirits (ethanol)	spiritus	[spiritus]
medicinal herbs	geneeskragtige kruie	[χeneəs·kraχtiχə krœiə]
herbal (~ tea)	kruie-	[krœie-]

77. Smoking. Tobacco products

tobacco	tabak	[tabak]
cigarette	sigaret	[siχaret]
cigar	sigaar	[siχār]
pipe	pyp	[pajp]
pack (of cigarettes)	pakkie	[pakki]

matches	vuurhoutjies	[fɪrhæʊkis]
matchbox	vuurhoutjiedosie	[fɪrhæʊki·dosi]
lighter	aansteker	[āŋstekər]
ashtray	asbak	[asbak]
cigarette case	sigarethouer	[siχaret·hæʊər]

cigarette holder	sigaretpypie	[siχaret·pajpi]
filter (cigarette tip)	filter	[filtər]

to smoke (vi, vt)	rook	[roək]
to light a cigarette	aansteek	[āŋsteək]
smoking	rook	[roək]
smoker	roker	[rokər]

stub, butt (of cigarette)	stompie	[stompi]
smoke, fumes	rook	[roək]
ash	as	[as]

HUMAN HABITAT

City

78. City. Life in the city

city, town	**stad**	[stat]
capital city	**hoofstad**	[hoəf·stat]
village	**dorp**	[dorp]
city map	**stadskaart**	[stats·kārt]
downtown	**sentrum**	[sentrum]
suburb	**voorstad**	[foərstat]
suburban (adj)	**voorstedelik**	[foərstedelik]
outskirts	**buitewyke**	[bœitəvajkə]
environs (suburbs)	**omgewing**	[omχeviŋ]
city block	**stadswyk**	[stats·wajk]
residential block (area)	**woonbuurt**	[voənbɪrt]
traffic	**verkeer**	[ferkeər]
traffic lights	**robot**	[robot]
public transportation	**openbare vervoer**	[openbarə ferfur]
intersection	**kruispunt**	[krœis·punt]
crosswalk	**sebraoorgang**	[sebra·oərχaŋ]
pedestrian underpass	**voetgangertonnel**	[futχaŋər·tonnəl]
to cross (~ the street)	**oorsteek**	[oərsteək]
pedestrian	**voetganger**	[futχaŋər]
sidewalk	**sypaadjie**	[saj·pādʒi]
bridge	**brug**	[bruχ]
embankment (river walk)	**wal**	[val]
fountain	**fontein**	[fontæjn]
allée (garden walkway)	**laning**	[laniŋ]
park	**park**	[park]
boulevard	**boulevard**	[bulefar]
square	**plein**	[plæjn]
avenue (wide street)	**laan**	[lān]
street	**straat**	[strāt]
side street	**systraat**	[saj·strāt]
dead end	**doodloopstraat**	[doədloəp·strāt]
house	**huis**	[hœis]
building	**gebou**	[χebæʋ]

skyscraper	wolkekrabber	[volkə·krabbər]
facade	gewel	[xevəl]
roof	dak	[dak]
window	venster	[fɛŋstər]
arch	arkade	[arkadə]
column	kolom	[kolom]
corner	hoek	[huk]

store window	uitstalraam	[œitstalrãm]
signboard (store sign, etc.)	reklamebord	[reklamə·bort]
poster	plakkaat	[plakkãt]
advertising poster	reklameplakkaat	[reklamə·plakkãt]
billboard	aanplakbord	[ãnplakbort]

garbage, trash	vullis	[fullis]
trashcan (public ~)	vullisbak	[fullis·bak]
to litter (vi)	rommel strooi	[romməl stroj]
garbage dump	vullishoop	[fullis·hoəp]

phone booth	telefoonhokkie	[telefoən·hokki]
lamppost	lamppaal	[lamp·pãl]
bench (park ~)	bank	[bank]

police officer	polisieman	[polisi·man]
police	polisie	[polisi]
beggar	bedelaar	[bedelãr]
homeless (n)	daklose	[daklosə]

79. Urban institutions

store	winkel	[vinkəl]
drugstore, pharmacy	apteek	[apteək]
eyeglass store	optisiën	[optisiɛn]
shopping mall	winkelsentrum	[vinkəl·sentrum]
supermarket	supermark	[supermark]

bakery	bakkery	[bakkeraj]
baker	bakker	[bakkər]
pastry shop	banketbakkery	[banket·bakkeraj]
grocery store	kruidenierswinkel	[krœidenirs·vinkəl]
butcher shop	slagter	[slaxtər]

| produce store | groentewinkel | [xruntə·vinkəl] |
| market | mark | [mark] |

coffee house	koffiekroeg	[koffi·kruχ]
restaurant	restaurant	[restɔurant]
pub, bar	kroeg	[kruχ]
pizzeria	pizzeria	[pizzeria]
hair salon	haarsalon	[hãr·salon]

post office	poskantoor	[pos·kantoər]
dry cleaners	droogskoonmakers	[droəχ·skoən·makers]
photo studio	fotostudio	[foto·studio]

shoe store	skoenwinkel	[skun·vinkəl]
bookstore	boekhandel	[buk·handəl]
sporting goods store	sportwinkel	[sport·vinkəl]

clothes repair shop	klereherstelwinkel	[klerə·herstəl·vinkəl]
formal wear rental	klereverhuurwinkel	[klerə·ferhɪr·vinkəl]
video rental store	videowinkel	[video·vinkəl]

circus	sirkus	[sirkus]
zoo	dieretuin	[dirə·tœin]
movie theater	bioskoop	[bioskoəp]
museum	museum	[musøəm]
library	biblioteek	[biblioteək]

| theater | teater | [teatər] |
| opera (opera house) | opera | [opera] |

| nightclub | nagklub | [naχ·klup] |
| casino | kasino | [kasino] |

mosque	moskee	[moskeə]
synagogue	sinagoge	[sinaχoχə]
cathedral	katedraal	[katedrãl]

| temple | tempel | [tempəl] |
| church | kerk | [kerk] |

college	kollege	[kolledʒ]
university	universiteit	[unifersitæjt]
school	skool	[skoəl]

| prefecture | stadhuis | [stat·hœis] |
| city hall | stadhuis | [stat·hœis] |

| hotel | hotel | [hotəl] |
| bank | bank | [bank] |

| embassy | ambassade | [ambassadə] |
| travel agency | reisagentskap | [ræjs·aχentskap] |

| information office | inligtingskantoor | [inliχtiŋs·kantoər] |
| currency exchange | wisselkantoor | [vissəl·kantoər] |

| subway | metro | [metro] |
| hospital | hospitaal | [hospitãl] |

| gas station | petrolstasie | [petrol·stasi] |
| parking lot | parkeerterrein | [parkeər·terræjn] |

80. Signs

signboard (store sign, etc.)	**reklamebord**	[reklamə·bort]
notice (door sign, etc.)	**kennisgewing**	[kɛnnis·χeviŋ]
poster	**plakkaat**	[plakkāt]
direction sign	**rigtingwyser**	[riχtiŋ·wajsər]
arrow (sign)	**pyl**	[pajl]

caution	**waarskuwing**	[vārskuviŋ]
warning sign	**waarskuwingsbord**	[vārskuviŋs·bort]
to warn (vt)	**waarsku**	[vārsku]

rest day (weekly ~)	**rusdag**	[rusdaχ]
timetable (schedule)	**diensrooster**	[diŋs·roəstər]
opening hours	**besigheidsure**	[besiχæjts·urə]

WELCOME!	**WELKOM!**	[vɛlkom!]
ENTRANCE	**INGANG**	[inχaŋ]
EXIT	**UITGANG**	[œitχaŋ]

PUSH	**STOOT**	[stoət]
PULL	**TREK**	[trek]
OPEN	**OOP**	[oəp]
CLOSED	**GESLUIT**	[χeslœit]

WOMEN	**DAMES**	[dames]
MEN	**MANS**	[maŋs]

DISCOUNTS	**AFSLAG**	[afslaχ]
SALE	**UITVERKOPING**	[œitferkopiŋ]
NEW!	**NUUT!**	[nɪt!]
FREE	**GRATIS**	[χratis]

ATTENTION!	**PAS OP!**	[pas op!]
NO VACANCIES	**VOLBESPREEK**	[folbespreək]
RESERVED	**BESPREEK**	[bespreək]

ADMINISTRATION	**ADMINISTRASIE**	[administrasi]
STAFF ONLY	**SLEGS PERSONEEL**	[sleχs personeəl]

BEWARE OF THE DOG!	**PAS OP VIR DIE HOND!**	[pas op fir di hont!]
NO SMOKING	**ROOK VERBODE**	[roək ferbodə]
DO NOT TOUCH!	**NIE AANRAAK NIE!**	[ni ānrāk ni!]

DANGEROUS	**GEVAARLIK**	[χefārlik]
DANGER	**GEVAAR**	[χefār]
HIGH VOLTAGE	**HOOGSPANNING**	[hoəχ·spanniŋ]
NO SWIMMING!	**NIE SWEM NIE**	[ni swem ni]
OUT OF ORDER	**BUITE WERKING**	[bœitə verkiŋ]
FLAMMABLE	**ONTVLAMBAAR**	[ontflambār]
FORBIDDEN	**VERBODE**	[ferbodə]

| NO TRESPASSING! | **TOEGANG VERBODE!** | [tuxaŋ ferbode!] |
| WET PAINT | **NAT VERF** | [nat ferf] |

81. Urban transportation

bus	**bus**	[bus]
streetcar	**trem**	[trem]
trolley bus	**trembus**	[trembus]
route (of bus, etc.)	**busroete**	[bus·rutə]
number (e.g., bus ~)	**nommer**	[nommər]
to go by ...	**ry per ...**	[raj pər ...]
to get on (~ the bus)	**inklim**	[inklim]
to get off ...	**uitklim ...**	[œitklim ...]
stop (e.g., bus ~)	**halte**	[haltə]
next stop	**volgende halte**	[folxendə haltə]
terminus	**eindpunt**	[æjnd·punt]
schedule	**diensrooster**	[diŋs·roəstər]
to wait (vt)	**wag**	[vax]
ticket	**kaartjie**	[kārki]
fare	**reistarief**	[ræjs·tarif]
cashier (ticket seller)	**kaartjieverkoper**	[kārki·ferkopər]
ticket inspection	**kaartjiekontrole**	[kārki·kontrolə]
ticket inspector	**kontroleur**	[kontroləər]
to be late (for ...)	**laat wees**	[lāt veəs]
to miss (~ the train, etc.)	**mis**	[mis]
to be in a hurry	**haastig wees**	[hāstex veəs]
taxi, cab	**taxi**	[taksi]
taxi driver	**taxibestuurder**	[taksi·bestɪrdər]
by taxi	**per taxi**	[pər taksi]
taxi stand	**taxistaanplek**	[taksi·stānplek]
traffic	**verkeer**	[ferkeər]
traffic jam	**verkeersknoop**	[ferkeərs·knoəp]
rush hour	**spitsuur**	[spits·ɪr]
to park (vi)	**parkeer**	[parkeər]
to park (vt)	**parkeer**	[parkeər]
parking lot	**parkeerterrein**	[parkeər·terræjn]
subway	**metro**	[metro]
station	**stasie**	[stasi]
to take the subway	**die metro vat**	[di metro fat]
train	**trein**	[træjn]
train station	**treinstasie**	[træjn·stasi]

82. Sightseeing

monument	**monument**	[monument]
fortress	**fort**	[fort]
palace	**paleis**	[palæjs]
castle	**kasteel**	[kasteəl]
tower	**toring**	[toriŋ]
mausoleum	**mausoleum**	[mɔusoløəm]

architecture	**argitektuur**	[arχitektɪr]
medieval (adj)	**Middeleeus**	[middeliʊs]
ancient (adj)	**oud**	[æʊt]
national (adj)	**nasionaal**	[naʃionāl]
famous (monument, etc.)	**bekend**	[bekent]

tourist	**toeris**	[turis]
guide (person)	**gids**	[χids]
excursion, sightseeing tour	**uitstappie**	[œitstappi]
to show (vt)	**wys**	[vajs]
to tell (vt)	**vertel**	[fertəl]

to find (vt)	**vind**	[fint]
to get lost (lose one's way)	**verdwaal**	[ferdwāl]
map (e.g., subway ~)	**kaart**	[kārt]
map (e.g., city ~)	**kaart**	[kārt]

souvenir, gift	**aandenking**	[āndenkiŋ]
gift shop	**geskenkwinkel**	[χeskɛnk·vinkəl]
to take pictures	**fotografeer**	[fotoχrafeər]
to have one's picture taken	**jou portret laat maak**	[jæʊ portret lāt māk]

83. Shopping

to buy (purchase)	**koop**	[koəp]
purchase	**aankoop**	[ānkoəp]
to go shopping	**inkopies doen**	[inkopis dun]
shopping	**inkoop**	[inkoəp]

| to be open (ab. store) | **oop wees** | [oəp veəs] |
| to be closed | **toe wees** | [tu veəs] |

footwear, shoes	**skoeisel**	[skuisəl]
clothes, clothing	**klere**	[klerə]
cosmetics	**kosmetika**	[kosmetika]
food products	**voedingsware**	[fudiŋs·warə]
gift, present	**present**	[present]

| salesman | **verkoper** | [ferkopər] |
| saleswoman | **verkoopsdame** | [ferkoəps·damə] |

check out, cash desk	**kassier**	[kassir]
mirror	**spieël**	[spiɛl]
counter (store ~)	**toonbank**	[toən·bank]
fitting room	**paskamer**	[pas·kamər]

to try on	**aanpas**	[ānpas]
to fit (ab. dress, etc.)	**pas**	[pas]
to like (I like ...)	**hou van**	[hæʊ fan]

price	**prys**	[prajs]
price tag	**pryskaartjie**	[prajs·kārki]
to cost (vt)	**kos**	[kos]
How much?	**Hoeveel?**	[hufeəl?]
discount	**afslag**	[afslaχ]

inexpensive (adj)	**billik**	[billik]
cheap (adj)	**goedkoop**	[χudkoəp]
expensive (adj)	**duur**	[dɪr]
It's expensive	**dis duur**	[dis dɪr]

rental (n)	**verhuur**	[ferhɪr]
to rent (~ a tuxedo)	**verhuur**	[ferhɪr]
credit (trade credit)	**krediet**	[krediet]
on credit (adv)	**op krediet**	[op krediet]

84. Money

money	**geld**	[χɛlt]
currency exchange	**valutaruil**	[faluta·rœil]
exchange rate	**wisselkoers**	[vissəl·kurs]
ATM	**OTM**	[o·te·em]
coin	**muntstuk**	[muntstuk]

dollar	**dollar**	[dollar]
euro	**euro**	[øəro]

lira	**lira**	[lira]
Deutschmark	**Duitse mark**	[dœitsə mark]
franc	**frank**	[frank]
pound sterling	**pond sterling**	[pont sterliŋ]
yen	**yen**	[jɛn]

debt	**skuld**	[skult]
debtor	**skuldenaar**	[skuldenār]
to lend (money)	**uitleen**	[œitleən]
to borrow (vi, vt)	**leen**	[leən]

bank	**bank**	[bank]
account	**rekening**	[rekəniŋ]
to deposit (vt)	**deponeer**	[deponeər]

to withdraw (vt)	**trek**	[trek]
credit card	**kredietkaart**	[kredit·kãrt]
cash	**kontant**	[kontant]
check	**tjek**	[tʃek]
checkbook	**tjekboek**	[tʃek·buk]

wallet	**beursie**	[bøərsi]
change purse	**muntstukbeursie**	[muntstuk·bøərsi]
safe	**brandkas**	[brant·kas]

heir	**erfgenaam**	[ɛrfχənãm]
inheritance	**erfenis**	[ɛrfenis]
fortune (wealth)	**fortuin**	[fortœin]

lease	**huur**	[hɪr]
rent (money)	**huur**	[hɪr]
to rent (sth from sb)	**huur**	[hɪr]

price	**prys**	[prajs]
cost	**prys**	[prajs]
sum	**som**	[som]

to spend (vt)	**spandeer**	[spandeər]
expenses	**onkoste**	[onkostə]
to economize (vi, vt)	**besuinig**	[besœinəχ]
economical	**ekonomies**	[ɛkonomis]

to pay (vi, vt)	**betaal**	[betãl]
payment	**betaling**	[betaliŋ]
change (give the ~)	**wisselgeld**	[vissəl·χɛlt]

tax	**belasting**	[belastiŋ]
fine	**boete**	[butə]
to fine (vt)	**beboet**	[bebut]

85. Post. Postal service

post office	**poskantoor**	[pos·kantoər]
mail (letters, etc.)	**pos**	[pos]
mailman	**posbode**	[pos·bodə]
opening hours	**besigheidsure**	[besiχæjts·urə]

letter	**brief**	[brif]
registered letter	**geregistreerde brief**	[χereχistreərdə brif]
postcard	**poskaart**	[pos·kãrt]
telegram	**telegram**	[teleχram]
package (parcel)	**pakkie**	[pakki]
money transfer	**geldoorplasing**	[χɛld·oərplasiŋ]
to receive (vt)	**ontvang**	[ontfaŋ]
to send (vt)	**stuur**	[stɪr]

sending	**versending**	[fersendiŋ]
address	**adres**	[adres]
ZIP code	**poskode**	[pos·kodə]
sender	**sender**	[sendər]
receiver	**ontvanger**	[ontfaŋər]

| name (first name) | **voornaam** | [foərnãm] |
| surname (last name) | **van** | [fan] |

postage rate	**postarief**	[pos·tarif]
standard (adj)	**standaard**	[standãrt]
economical (adj)	**ekonomies**	[ɛkonomis]

weight	**gewig**	[χevəχ]
to weigh (~ letters)	**weeg**	[veəχ]
envelope	**koevert**	[kufert]
postage stamp	**posseël**	[pos·seɛl]

Dwelling. House. Home

86. House. Dwelling

house	huis	[hœis]
at home (adv)	tuis	[tœis]
yard	werf	[verf]
fence (iron ~)	omheining	[omhæjniŋ]
brick (n)	baksteen	[baksteən]
brick (as adj)	baksteen-	[baksteən-]
stone (n)	klip	[klip]
stone (as adj)	klip-	[klip-]
concrete (n)	beton	[beton]
concrete (as adj)	beton-	[beton-]
new (new-built)	nuut	[nɪt]
old (adj)	ou	[æʊ]
decrepit (house)	vervalle	[ferfallə]
modern (adj)	moderne	[modernə]
multistory (adj)	multiverdieping-	[multi·ferdipiŋ-]
tall (~ building)	hoë	[hoɛ]
floor, story	verdieping	[ferdipiŋ]
single-story (adj)	enkelverdieping	[ɛnkəl·ferdipiŋ]
1st floor	eerste verdieping	[eərstə ferdipiŋ]
top floor	boonste verdieping	[boəŋstə verdipiŋ]
roof	dak	[dak]
chimney	skoorsteen	[skoərsteən]
roof tiles	dakteëls	[daktecls]
tiled (adj)	geteël	[χetecl]
attic (storage place)	solder	[soldər]
window	venster	[fɛŋstər]
glass	glas	[χlas]
window ledge	vensterbank	[fɛŋstər·bank]
shutters	luik	[lœik]
wall	muur	[mɪr]
balcony	balkon	[balkon]
downspout	reënpyp	[reɛn·pajp]
upstairs (to be ~)	bo	[bo]
to go upstairs	boontoe gaan	[boentu χãn]

| to come down (the stairs) | afkom | [afkom] |
| to move (to new premises) | verhuis | [ferhœis] |

87. House. Entrance. Lift

entrance	ingang	[inχaŋ]
stairs (stairway)	trap	[trap]
steps	treetjies	[treəkis]
banister	leuning	[løəniŋ]
lobby (hotel ~)	voorportaal	[foər·portāl]

mailbox	posbus	[pos·bus]
garbage can	vullisblik	[fullis·blik]
trash chute	vullisgeut	[fullis·χøət]

elevator	hysbak	[hajsbak]
freight elevator	vraghysbak	[fraχ·hajsbak]
elevator cage	hysbak	[hajsbak]
to take the elevator	hysbak neem	[hajsbak neəm]

apartment	woonstel	[voəŋstəl]
residents (~ of a building)	bewoners	[bevoners]
neighbor (masc.)	buurman	[bɪrman]
neighbor (fem.)	buurvrou	[bɪrfræʊ]
neighbors	bure	[burə]

88. House. Electricity

electricity	krag, elektrisiteit	[kraχ], [elektrisitæjt]
light bulb	gloeilamp	[χlui·lamp]
switch	skakelaar	[skakəlār]
fuse (plug fuse)	sekering	[sekəriŋ]

cable, wire (electric ~)	kabel	[kabəl]
wiring	bedrading	[bedradiŋ]
electricity meter	kragmeter	[kraχ·metər]
readings	lesings	[lesiŋs]

89. House. Doors. Locks

door	deur	[døər]
gate (vehicle ~)	hek	[hek]
handle, doorknob	deurknop	[døər·knop]
to unlock (unbolt)	oopsluit	[oəpslœit]
to open (vt)	oopmaak	[oəpmāk]
to close (vt)	sluit	[slœit]

key	sleutel	[sløətəl]
bunch (of keys)	bos	[bos]
to creak (door, etc.)	kraak	[krāk]
creak	gekraak	[χekrāk]
hinge (door ~)	skarnier	[skarnir]
doormat	deurmat	[døər·mat]

door lock	deurslot	[døər·slot]
keyhole	sleutelgat	[sløətəl·χat]
crossbar (sliding bar)	grendel	[χrendəl]
door latch	deurknip	[døər·knip]
padlock	hangslot	[haŋslot]

to ring (~ the door bell)	lui	[lœi]
ringing (sound)	gelui	[χelœi]
doorbell	deurklokkie	[døər·klokki]
doorbell button	belknoppie	[bɛl·knoppi]
knock (at the door)	klop	[klop]
to knock (vi)	klop	[klop]

code	kode	[kodə]
combination lock	kombinasieslot	[kombinasi·slot]
intercom	interkom	[interkom]
number (on the door)	nommer	[nommər]
doorplate	naambordjie	[nām·bordʒi]
peephole	loergaatjie	[lurχāki]

90. Country house

village	dorp	[dorp]
vegetable garden	groentetuin	[χruntə·tœin]
fence	heining	[hæjniŋ]
picket fence	spitspaalheining	[spitspāl·hæjniŋ]
wicket gate	tuinhekkie	[tœin·hɛkki]

granary	graanstoorplek	[χrāŋ·stoərplek]
root cellar	wortelkelder	[vortəl·keldər]
shed (garden ~)	tuinhuisie	[tœin·hœisi]
well (water)	waterput	[vatər·put]

| stove (wood-fired ~) | houtkaggel | [hæʊt·kaχχəl] |
| to stoke the stove | die houtkaggel stook | [di hæʊt·kaχχəl stoək] |

| firewood | brandhout | [brant·hæʊt] |
| log (firewood) | stomp | [stomp] |

veranda	stoep	[stup]
deck (terrace)	dek	[dek]
stoop (front steps)	ingangstrappie	[inχaŋs·trappi]
swing (hanging seat)	swaai	[swāi]

91. Villa. Mansion

country house	**buitewoning**	[bœitə·voniŋ]
villa (seaside ~)	**landhuis**	[land·hœis]
wing (~ of a building)	**vleuel**	[fløəəl]
garden	**tuin**	[tœin]
park	**park**	[park]
tropical greenhouse	**tropiese kweekhuis**	[tropisə kweek·hœis]
to look after (garden, etc.)	**versorg**	[fersorχ]
swimming pool	**swembad**	[swem·bat]
gym (home gym)	**gim**	[χim]
tennis court	**tennisbaan**	[tɛnnis·bān]
home theater (room)	**huisteater**	[hœis·teatər]
garage	**garage**	[χaraʒə]
private property	**privaat besit**	[prifāt besit]
private land	**privaateiendom**	[prifāt·æjendom]
warning (caution)	**waarskuwing**	[vārskuviŋ]
warning sign	**waarskuwingsbord**	[vārskuviŋs·bort]
security	**sekuriteit**	[sekuritæjt]
security guard	**veiligheidswag**	[fæjliχæjts·waχ]
burglar alarm	**diefalarm**	[dif·alarm]

92. Castle. Palace

castle	**kasteel**	[kasteəl]
palace	**paleis**	[palæjs]
fortress	**fort**	[fort]
wall (round castle)	**ringmuur**	[riŋ·mɪr]
tower	**toring**	[toriŋ]
keep, donjon	**toring**	[toriŋ]
portcullis	**valhek**	[falhek]
underground passage	**tonnel**	[tonnəl]
moat	**grag**	[χraχ]
chain	**ketting**	[kɛttiŋ]
arrow loop	**skietgat**	[skitχat]
magnificent (adj)	**pragtig**	[praχtəχ]
majestic (adj)	**majestueus**	[majestuøəs]
impregnable (adj)	**onneembaar**	[onneəmbār]
medieval (adj)	**Middeleeus**	[middeliʋs]

93. Apartment

apartment	woonstel	[voəŋstəl]
room	kamer	[kamər]
bedroom	slaapkamer	[slāp·kamər]
dining room	eetkamer	[eət·kamər]
living room	sitkamer	[sit·kamər]
study (home office)	studeerkamer	[studeər·kamər]
entry room	ingangsportaal	[inχaŋs·portāl]
bathroom (room with a bath or shower)	badkamer	[bad·kamər]
half bath	toilet	[tojlet]
ceiling	plafon	[plafon]
floor	vloer	[flur]
corner	hoek	[huk]

94. Apartment. Cleaning

to clean (vi, vt)	skoonmaak	[skoənmāk]
to put away (to stow)	bère	[bærə]
dust	stof	[stof]
dusty (adj)	stoffig	[stoffəχ]
to dust (vt)	afstof	[afstof]
vacuum cleaner	stofsuier	[stof·sœiər]
to vacuum (vt)	stofsuig	[stofsœiχ]
to sweep (vi, vt)	vee	[feə]
sweepings	veegsel	[feəχsəl]
order	orde	[ordə]
disorder, mess	wanorde	[vanordə]
mop	mop	[mop]
dust cloth	stoflap	[stoflap]
short broom	kort besem	[kort besem]
dustpan	skoppie	[skoppi]

95. Furniture. Interior

furniture	meubels	[møəbɛls]
table	tafel	[tafel]
chair	stoel	[stul]
bed	bed	[bet]
couch, sofa	rusbank	[rusbank]
armchair	gemakstoel	[χemak·stul]

| bookcase | boekkas | [buk·kas] |
| shelf | rak | [rak] |

wardrobe	klerekas	[klerə·kas]
coat rack (wall-mounted ~)	kapstok	[kapstok]
coat stand	kapstok	[kapstok]

| bureau, dresser | laaikas | [lājkas] |
| coffee table | koffietafel | [koffi·tafəl] |

mirror	spieël	[spiɛl]
carpet	mat	[mat]
rug, small carpet	matjie	[maki]

fireplace	vuurherd	[fɪr·hert]
candle	kers	[kers]
candlestick	kandelaar	[kandelār]

drapes	gordyne	[χordajnə]
wallpaper	muurpapier	[mɪr·papir]
blinds (jalousie)	blindings	[blindiŋs]

table lamp	tafellamp	[tafel·lamp]
wall lamp (sconce)	muurlamp	[mɪr·lamp]
floor lamp	staanlamp	[stān·lamp]
chandelier	kroonlugter	[kroən·luχtər]

leg (of chair, table)	poot	[poət]
armrest	armleuning	[arm·løəniŋ]
back (backrest)	rugleuning	[ruχ·løəniŋ]
drawer	laai	[lāi]

96. Bedding

bedclothes	beddegoed	[beddə·χut]
pillow	kussing	[kussiŋ]
pillowcase	kussingsloop	[kussiŋ·sloəp]
duvet, comforter	duvet	[dufet]
sheet	laken	[laken]
bedspread	bedsprei	[bed·spræj]

97. Kitchen

kitchen	kombuis	[kombœis]
gas	gas	[χas]
gas stove (range)	gasstoof	[χas·stoəf]
electric stove	elektriese stoof	[elektrisə stoəf]
oven	oond	[oent]

microwave oven	**mikrogolfoond**	[mikroχolf·oent]
refrigerator	**yskas**	[ajs·kas]
freezer	**vrieskas**	[friskas]
dishwasher	**skottelgoedwasser**	[skottɛlχud·wassər]
meat grinder	**vleismeul**	[flæjs·møəl]
juicer	**versapper**	[fersappər]
toaster	**broodrooster**	[broəd·roəstər]
mixer	**menger**	[meŋər]
coffee machine	**koffiemasjien**	[koffi·maʃin]
coffee pot	**koffiepot**	[koffi·pot]
coffee grinder	**koffiemeul**	[koffi·møəl]
kettle	**fluitketel**	[flœit·ketəl]
teapot	**teepot**	[teə·pot]
lid	**deksel**	[deksəl]
tea strainer	**teesiffie**	[teə·siffi]
spoon	**lepel**	[lepəl]
teaspoon	**teelepeltjie**	[teə·lepəlki]
soup spoon	**soplepel**	[sop·lepəl]
fork	**vurk**	[furk]
knife	**mes**	[mes]
tableware (dishes)	**tafelgerei**	[tafel·χeræj]
plate (dinner ~)	**bord**	[bort]
saucer	**piering**	[piriŋ]
shot glass	**likeurglas**	[likøər·χlas]
glass (tumbler)	**glas**	[χlas]
cup	**koppie**	[koppi]
sugar bowl	**suikerpot**	[sœikər·pot]
salt shaker	**soutvaatjie**	[sæut·fāki]
pepper shaker	**pepervaatjie**	[pepər·fāki]
butter dish	**botterbakkie**	[bottər·bakki]
stock pot (soup pot)	**soppot**	[sop·pot]
frying pan (skillet)	**braaipan**	[brāj·pan]
ladle	**opskeplepel**	[opskep·lepəl]
colander	**vergiet**	[ferχit]
tray (serving ~)	**skinkbord**	[skink·bort]
bottle	**bottel**	[bottəl]
jar (glass)	**fles**	[fles]
can	**blikkie**	[blikki]
bottle opener	**botteloopmaker**	[bottəl·oəpmakər]
can opener	**blikoopmaker**	[blik·oəpmakər]
corkscrew	**kurktrekker**	[kurk·trɛkkər]
filter	**filter**	[filtər]

to filter (vt)	**filter**	[filtər]
trash, garbage (food waste, etc.)	**vullis**	[fullis]
trash can (kitchen ~)	**vullisbak**	[fullis·bak]

98. Bathroom

bathroom	**badkamer**	[bad·kamər]
water	**water**	[vatər]
faucet	**kraan**	[krān]
hot water	**warme water**	[varmə vatər]
cold water	**koue water**	[kæʊə vatər]

toothpaste	**tandepasta**	[tandə·pasta]
to brush one's teeth	**tande borsel**	[tandə borsəl]
toothbrush	**tandeborsel**	[tandə·borsəl]

to shave (vi)	**skeer**	[skeər]
shaving foam	**skeerroom**	[skeər·roəm]
razor	**skeermes**	[skeər·mes]

to wash (one's hands, etc.)	**was**	[vas]
to take a bath	**bad**	[bat]
shower	**stort**	[stort]
to take a shower	**stort**	[stort]

bathtub	**bad**	[bat]
toilet (toilet bowl)	**toilet**	[tojlet]
sink (washbasin)	**wasbak**	[vas·bak]

| soap | **seep** | [seəp] |
| soap dish | **seepbakkie** | [seəp·bakki] |

sponge	**spons**	[spoŋs]
shampoo	**sjampoe**	[ʃampu]
towel	**handdoek**	[handduk]
bathrobe	**badjas**	[batjas]

laundry (process)	**was**	[vas]
washing machine	**wasmasjien**	[vas·maʃin]
to do the laundry	**die wasgoed was**	[di vasχut vas]
laundry detergent	**waspoeier**	[vas·pujer]

99. Household appliances

TV set	**TV-stel**	[te·fe-stəl]
tape recorder	**bandspeler**	[band·spelər]
VCR (video recorder)	**videomasjien**	[video·maʃin]

radio	**radio**	[radio]
player (CD, MP3, etc.)	**speler**	[spelər]

video projector	**videoprojektor**	[video·projektor]
home movie theater	**tuisfliekteater**	[tœis·flik·teatər]
DVD player	**DVD-speler**	[de·fe·de-spelər]
amplifier	**versterker**	[fersterkər]
video game console	**videokonsole**	[video·kɔŋsolə]

video camera	**videokamera**	[video·kamera]
camera (photo)	**kamera**	[kamera]
digital camera	**digitale kamera**	[diχitalə kamera]

vacuum cleaner	**stofsuier**	[stof·sœiər]
iron (e.g., steam ~)	**strykyster**	[strajk·ajstər]
ironing board	**strykplank**	[strajk·plank]

telephone	**telefoon**	[telefoən]
cell phone	**selfoon**	[sɛlfoən]
typewriter	**tikmasjien**	[tik·maʃin]
sewing machine	**naaimasjien**	[naj·maʃin]

microphone	**mikrofoon**	[mikrofoən]
headphones	**koptelefoon**	[kop·telefoən]
remote control (TV)	**afstandsbeheer**	[afstands·beheər]

CD, compact disc	**CD**	[se·de]
cassette, tape	**kasset**	[kasset]
vinyl record	**plaat**	[plāt]

100. Repairs. Renovation

renovations	**opknapwerk**	[opknap·werk]
to renovate (vt)	**opknap**	[opknap]
to repair, to fix (vt)	**herstel**	[herstəl]
to put in order	**aan kant maak**	[ān kant māk]
to redo (do again)	**oordoen**	[oərdun]

paint	**verf**	[ferf]
to paint (~ a wall)	**verf**	[ferf]
house painter	**skilder**	[skildər]
paintbrush	**verfborsel**	[ferf·borsəl]

whitewash	**witkalk**	[vitkalk]
to whitewash (vt)	**wit**	[vit]

wallpaper	**muurpapier**	[mɪr·papir]
to wallpaper (vt)	**behang**	[behaŋ]
varnish	**vernis**	[fernis]
to varnish (vt)	**vernis**	[fernis]

101. Plumbing

water	**water**	[vatər]
hot water	**warme water**	[varmə vatər]
cold water	**koue water**	[kæʊə vatər]
faucet	**kraan**	[krãn]
drop (of water)	**druppel**	[druppəl]
to drip (vi)	**drup**	[drup]
to leak (ab. pipe)	**lek**	[lek]
leak (pipe ~)	**lekkasie**	[lɛkkasi]
puddle	**poeletjie**	[puləki]
pipe	**pyp**	[pajp]
valve (e.g., ball ~)	**kraan**	[krãn]
to be clogged up	**verstop raak**	[ferstop rãk]
tools	**gereedskap**	[χereədskap]
adjustable wrench	**skroefsleutel**	[skruf·sløətəl]
to unscrew (lid, filter, etc.)	**losskroef**	[losskruf]
to screw (tighten)	**vasskroef**	[fasskruf]
to unclog (vt)	**oopmaak**	[oəpmãk]
plumber	**loodgieter**	[loədχitər]
basement	**kelder**	[kɛldər]
sewerage (system)	**riolering**	[riolerin]

102. Fire. Conflagration

fire (accident)	**brand**	[brant]
flame	**vlam**	[flam]
spark	**vonk**	[fonk]
smoke (from fire)	**rook**	[roək]
torch (flaming stick)	**fakkel**	[fakkel]
campfire	**kampvuur**	[kampfɪr]
gas, gasoline	**petrol**	[petrol]
kerosene (type of fuel)	**kerosien**	[kerosin]
flammable (adj)	**ontvambaar**	[ontfambãr]
explosive (adj)	**ontplofbaar**	[ontplofbãr]
NO SMOKING	**ROOK VERBODE**	[roək ferbodə]
safety	**veiligheid**	[fæjliχæjt]
danger	**gevaar**	[χefãr]
dangerous (adj)	**gevaarlik**	[χefãrlik]
to catch fire	**vlam vat**	[flam fat]
explosion	**ontploffing**	[ontploffin]
to set fire	**aan die brand steek**	[ãn di brant steək]

| arsonist | brandstigter | [brant·stiӽtər] |
| arson | brandstigting | [brant·stiӽtiŋ] |

to blaze (vi)	brand	[brant]
to burn (be on fire)	brand	[brant]
to burn down	afbrand	[afbrant]

to call the fire department	die brandweer roep	[di brantveər rup]
firefighter, fireman	brandweerman	[brantveər·man]
fire truck	brandweerwa	[brantveər·wa]
fire department	brandweer	[brantveər]
fire truck ladder	brandweerwaleer	[brantveər·wa·leər]

fire hose	brandslang	[brant·slaŋ]
fire extinguisher	brandblusser	[brant·blussər]
helmet	helmet	[hɛlmet]
siren	sirene	[sirenə]

to cry (for help)	skreeu	[skriʊ]
to call for help	hulp roep	[hulp rup]
rescuer	redder	[rɛddər]
to rescue (vt)	red	[ret]

to arrive (vi)	aankom	[ānkom]
to extinguish (vt)	blus	[blus]
water	water	[vatər]
sand	sand	[sant]

ruins (destruction)	ruïnes	[ruïnes]
to collapse (building, etc.)	instort	[instort]
to fall down (vi)	val	[fal]
to cave in (ceiling, floor)	instort	[instort]

| piece of debris | brokstukke | [brokstukkə] |
| ash | as | [as] |

| to suffocate (die) | verstik | [ferstik] |
| to be killed (perish) | omkom | [omkom] |

HUMAN ACTIVITIES

Job. Business. Part 1

office (company ~)	kantoor	[kantoər]
office (of director, etc.)	kantoor	[kantoər]
reception desk	ontvangs	[ontfaŋs]
secretary	sekretaris	[sekretaris]
secretary (fem.)	sekretaresse	[sekretarɛssə]
director	direkteur	[direktøər]
manager	bestuurder	[bestɪrdər]
accountant	boekhouer	[bukhæʊər]
employee	werknemer	[verknemər]
furniture	meubels	[møəbɛls]
desk	lessenaar	[lɛssenãr]
desk chair	draaistoel	[drãj·stul]
drawer unit	laaikas	[lãjkas]
coat stand	kapstok	[kapstok]
computer	rekenaar	[rekənãr]
printer	drukker	[drukkər]
fax machine	faksmasjien	[faks·maʃin]
photocopier	fotostaatmasjien	[fotostãt·maʃin]
paper	papier	[papir]
office supplies	kantoorbenodigdhede	[kantoər·benodiχdhedə]
mouse pad	muismatjie	[mœis·maki]
sheet (of paper)	blaai	[blãi]
binder	binder	[bindər]
catalog	katalogus	[kataloχus]
phone directory	telefoongids	[telefoən·χids]
documentation	dokumentasie	[dokumentasi]
brochure	brosjure	[broʃurə]
(e.g., 12 pages ~)		
leaflet (promotional ~)	strooibiljet	[stroj·biljet]
sample	monsterkaart	[mɔnstər·kãrt]
training meeting	opleidingsvergadering	[oplæjdiŋs·ferχaderiŋ]
meeting (of managers)	vergadering	[ferχaderiŋ]
lunch time	middagpouse	[middaχ·pæʊsə]

to make multiple copies	aantal kopieë maak	[ãntal kopiɛ māk]
to call (by phone)	bel	[bəl]
to answer (vt)	antwoord	[antwoərt]
to put through	deursit	[døərsit]

to arrange, to set up	reël	[reɛl]
to demonstrate (vt)	demonstreer	[demɔŋstreər]
to be absent	afwesig wees	[afwesəχ veəs]
absence	afwesigheid	[afwesiχæjt]

104. Business processes. Part 1

| business | besigheid | [besiχæjt] |
| occupation | beroep | [berup] |

firm	firma	[firma]
company	maatskappy	[mātskappaj]
corporation	korporasie	[korporasi]
enterprise	onderneming	[ondərnemiŋ]
agency	agentskap	[aχentskap]

agreement (contract)	ooreenkoms	[oəreənkoms]
contract	kontrak	[kontrak]
deal	transaksie	[traŋsaksi]
order (to place an ~)	bestelling	[bestɛlliŋ]
terms (of the contract)	voorwaarde	[foərwārdə]

wholesale (adv)	groothandels-	[χroət·handəls-]
wholesale (adj)	groothandels-	[χroət·handəls-]
wholesale (n)	groothandel	[χroət·handəl]
retail (adj)	kleinhandels-	[klæjn·handəls-]
retail (n)	kleinhandel	[klæjn·handəl]

competitor	konkurrent	[konkurrent]
competition	konkurrensie	[konkurreŋsi]
to compete (vi)	kompeteer	[kompeteər]

| partner (associate) | vennoot | [fɛnnoət] |
| partnership | vennootskap | [fɛnnoətskap] |

crisis	krisis	[krisis]
bankruptcy	bankrotskap	[bankrotskap]
to go bankrupt	bankrot speel	[bankrot speəl]
difficulty	moeilikheid	[muilikhæjt]
problem	probleem	[probleəm]
catastrophe	katastrofe	[katastrofe]
economy	ekonomie	[ɛkonomi]
economic (~ growth)	ekonomiese	[ɛkonomisə]
economic recession	ekonomiese agteruitgang	[ɛkonomisə aχtər·œitχaŋ]

| goal (aim) | **doel** | [dul] |
| task | **opdrag** | [opdraχ] |

to trade (vi)	**handel**	[handəl]
network (distribution ~)	**netwerk**	[netwerk]
inventory (stock)	**voorraad**	[foərrāt]
range (assortment)	**reeks**	[reəks]

leader (leading company)	**leier**	[læjer]
large (~ company)	**groot**	[χroət]
monopoly	**monopolie**	[monopoli]

theory	**teorie**	[teori]
practice	**praktyk**	[praktajk]
experience (in my ~)	**ervaring**	[ɛrfariŋ]
trend (tendency)	**tendens**	[tendɛŋs]
development	**ontwikkeling**	[ontwikkeliŋ]

105. Business processes. Part 2

| profit (foregone ~) | **wins** | [vins] |
| profitable (~ deal) | **voordelig** | [foərdeləχ] |

delegation (group)	**delegasie**	[deleχasi]
salary	**salaris**	[salaris]
to correct (an error)	**korrigeer**	[korriχeər]
business trip	**sakereis**	[sakeræjs]
commission	**kommissie**	[kommissi]

to control (vt)	**kontroleer**	[kontroleər]
conference	**konferensie**	[konferɛŋsi]
license	**lisensie**	[lisɛŋsi]
reliable (~ partner)	**betroubaar**	[betræʊbār]

initiative (undertaking)	**inisiatief**	[inisiatif]
norm (standard)	**norm**	[norm]
circumstance	**omstandigheid**	[omstandiχæjt]
duty (of employee)	**taak**	[tāk]

organization (company)	**organisasie**	[orχanisasi]
organization (process)	**organisasie**	[orχanisasi]
organized (adj)	**georganiseer**	[χeorχaniseər]
cancellation	**kansellering**	[kaŋsɛlleriŋ]
to cancel (call off)	**kanselleer**	[kaŋsɛlleər]
report (official ~)	**verslag**	[ferslaχ]

patent	**patent**	[patent]
to patent (obtain patent)	**patenteer**	[patenteər]
to plan (vt)	**beplan**	[beplan]
bonus (money)	**bonus**	[bonus]

| professional (adj) | professioneel | [profɛssioneəl] |
| procedure | prosedure | [prosedurə] |

to examine (contract, etc.)	ondersoek	[ondərsuk]
calculation	berekening	[berekeniŋ]
reputation	reputasie	[reputasi]
risk	risiko	[risiko]

to manage, to run	beheer	[beheər]
information	informasie	[informasi]
property	eiendom	[æjendom]
union	unie	[uni]

life insurance	lewensversekering	[levɛŋs·fersekeriŋ]
to insure (vt)	verseker	[fersekər]
insurance	versekering	[fersekeriŋ]

auction (~ sale)	veiling	[fæjliŋ]
to notify (inform)	laat weet	[lāt veət]
management (process)	beheer	[beheər]
service (~ industry)	diens	[diŋs]

forum	forum	[forum]
to function (vi)	funksioneer	[funksioneər]
stage (phase)	stadium	[stadium]
legal (~ services)	regs-	[reχs-]
lawyer (legal advisor)	regsgeleerde	[reχs·χeleərdə]

106. Production. Works

plant	fabriek	[fabrik]
factory	fabriek	[fabrik]
workshop	werkplek	[verkplek]
works, production site	bedryf	[bedrajf]

industry (manufacturing)	industrie	[industri]
industrial (adj)	industrieel	[industriəl]
heavy industry	swaar industrie	[swār industri]
light industry	ligte industrie	[liχtə industri]

products	produkte	[produktə]
to produce (vt)	produseer	[produseər]
raw materials	grondstowwe	[χront·stowə]

foreman (construction ~)	voorman	[foərman]
workers team (crew)	werkspan	[verks·pan]
worker	werker	[verkər]

| working day | werksdag | [verks·daχ] |
| pause (rest break) | pouse | [pæusə] |

| meeting | vergadering | [ferχaderiŋ] |
| to discuss (vt) | bespreek | [bespreek] |

plan	plan	[plan]
to fulfill the plan	die plan uitvoer	[di plan œitfur]
rate of output	produksienorm	[produksi·norm]
quality	kwaliteit	[kwalitæjt]
control (checking)	kontrole	[kontrolə]
quality control	kwaliteitskontrole	[kwalitæjts·kontrolə]

workplace safety	werkplekveiligheid	[verkplek·fæjliχæjt]
discipline	dissipline	[dissiplinə]
violation	oortreding	[oərtrediŋ]
(of safety rules, etc.)		
to violate (rules)	oortree	[oərtreə]

| strike | staking | [stakiŋ] |
| striker | staker | [stakər] |

| to be on strike | staak | [stāk] |
| labor union | vakbond | [fakbont] |

to invent (machine, etc.)	uitvind	[œitfint]
invention	uitvinding	[œitfindiŋ]
research	navorsing	[naforsiŋ]
to improve (make better)	verbeter	[ferbetər]

| technology | tegnologie | [teχnoloχi] |
| technical drawing | tegniese tekening | [teχnisə tekəniŋ] |

load, cargo	vrag	[fraχ]
loader (person)	laaier	[lājer]
to load (vehicle, etc.)	laai	[lāi]
loading (process)	laai	[lāi]

| to unload (vi, vt) | uitlaai | [œitlāi] |
| unloading | uitlaai | [œitlāi] |

transportation	vervoer	[ferfur]
transportation company	vervoermaatskappy	[ferfur·mātskappaj]
to transport (vt)	vervoer	[ferfur]

freight car	trok	[trok]
tank (e.g., oil ~)	tenk	[tɛnk]
truck	vragmotor	[fraχ·motor]

| machine tool | werktuigmasjien | [verktœiχ·maʃin] |
| mechanism | meganisme | [meχanismə] |

industrial waste	industriële afval	[industriɛlə affal]
packing (process)	verpakking	[ferpakkiŋ]
to pack (vt)	verpak	[ferpak]

107. Contract. Agreement

contract	kontrak	[kontrak]
agreement	ooreenkoms	[oəreənkoms]
addendum	addendum	[addendum]
signature	handtekening	[hand·tekəniŋ]
to sign (vt)	onderteken	[ondərtekən]
seal (stamp)	stempel	[stempəl]
subject of contract	onderwerp van ooreenkoms	[ondərwerp fan oəreənkoms]
clause	klousule	[klæʊsulə]
parties (in contract)	partye	[partaje]
legal address	wetlike adres	[vetlikə adres]
to violate the contract	die kontrak verbreek	[di kontrak ferbreək]
commitment (obligation)	verpligting	[ferpliχtiŋ]
responsibility	verantwoordelikheid	[ferant·voərdelikhæjt]
force majeure	oormag	[oərmaχ]
dispute	geskil	[χeskil]
penalties	boete	[butə]

108. Import & Export

import	invoer	[infur]
importer	invoerder	[infurdər]
to import (vt)	invoer	[infur]
import (as adj.)	invoer-	[infur-]
export (exportation)	uitvoer	[œitfur]
exporter	uitvoerder	[œitfurdər]
to export (vi, vt)	uitvoer	[œitfur]
export (as adj.)	uitvoer-	[œitfur-]
goods (merchandise)	goedere	[χuderə]
consignment, lot	besending	[besendiŋ]
weight	gewig	[χevəχ]
volume	volume	[folumə]
cubic meter	kubieke meter	[kubikə metər]
manufacturer	produsent	[produsent]
transportation company	vervoermaatskappy	[ferfur·mātskappaj]
container	houer	[hæʊər]
border	grens	[χrɛŋs]
customs	doeane	[duanə]
customs duty	doeanereg	[duanə·reχ]

customs officer	doeanebeampte	[duanə·beamptə]
smuggling	smokkel	[smokkəl]
contraband (smuggled goods)	smokkelgoed	[smokkəl·χut]

109. Finances

stock (share)	aandeel	[āndeəl]
bond (certificate)	obligasie	[obliχasi]
promissory note	promesse	[promɛssə]

| stock exchange | beurs | [bøərs] |
| stock price | aandeelkoers | [āndeəl·kurs] |

| to go down (become cheaper) | daal | [dāl] |
| to go up (become more expensive) | styg | [stajχ] |

| share | aandeel | [āndeəl] |
| controlling interest | meerderheidsbelang | [meərderhæjts·belaŋ] |

investment	belegging	[beleχχiŋ]
to invest (vt)	belè	[belɛ:]
percent	persent	[persent]
interest (on investment)	rente	[rentə]

profit	wins	[vins]
profitable (adj)	voordelig	[foərdeləχ]
tax	belasting	[belastiŋ]

currency (foreign ~)	valuta	[faluta]
national (adj)	nasionaal	[naʃionāl]
exchange (currency ~)	wissel	[vissəl]

| accountant | boekhouer | [bukhæʊər] |
| accounting | boekhouding | [bukhæʊdiŋ] |

bankruptcy	bankrotskap	[bankrotskap]
collapse, crash	ineenstorting	[ineɛŋstortiŋ]
ruin	bankrotskap	[bankrotskap]
to be ruined (financially)	geruïneer wees	[χeruïneər veəs]
inflation	inflasie	[inflasi]
devaluation	devaluasie	[defaluasi]

capital	kapitaal	[kapitāl]
income	inkomste	[inkomstə]
turnover	omset	[omset]
resources	hulpbronne	[hulpbronnə]
monetary resources	monetère hulpbronne	[monetærə hulpbronnə]

| overhead | oorhoofse koste | [oərhoəfsə kostə] |
| to reduce (expenses) | verminder | [fermindər] |

110. Marketing

marketing	bemarking	[bemarkiŋ]
market	mark	[mark]
market segment	marksegment	[mark·seχment]
product	produk	[produk]
goods (merchandise)	goedere	[χuderə]

brand	merk	[merk]
trademark	handelsmerk	[handəls·merk]
logotype	logo	[loχo]
logo	logo	[loχo]

demand	vraag	[frãχ]
supply	aanbod	[ānbot]
need	behoefte	[behuftə]
consumer	verbruiker	[ferbrœikər]

analysis	analise	[analisə]
to analyze (vt)	analiseer	[analiseər]
positioning	plasing	[plasiŋ]
to position (vt)	plaas	[plãs]

price	prys	[prajs]
pricing policy	prysbeleid	[prajs·belæjt]
price formation	prysvorming	[prajs·formiŋ]

111. Advertising

advertising	reklame	[reklamə]
to advertise (vt)	adverteer	[adferteər]
budget	begroting	[beχrotiŋ]

ad, advertisement	advertensie	[adfertɛŋsi]
TV advertising	TV-advertensie	[te·fe-adfertɛŋsi]
radio advertising	radioreklame	[radio·reklamə]
outdoor advertising	buitereklame	[bœitə·reklamə]

mass media	massamedia	[massa·media]
periodical (n)	tydskrif	[tajdskrif]
image (public appearance)	imago	[imaχo]

slogan	slagspreuk	[slaχ·sprøək]
motto (maxim)	motto	[motto]
campaign	veldtog	[fɛldtoχ]

| advertising campaign | reklameveldtog | [reklamə·fɛldtoχ] |
| target group | doelgroep | [dul·χrup] |

business card	besigheidskaartjie	[besiχæjts·kārki]
leaflet (promotional ~)	strooibiljet	[stroj·biljet]
brochure	brosjure	[broʃurə]
(e.g., 12 pages ~)		
pamphlet	pamflet	[pamflet]
newsletter	nuusbrief	[nɪsbrif]

signboard (store sign, etc.)	reklamebord	[reklamə·bort]
poster	plakkaat	[plakkāt]
billboard	aanplakbord	[ānplakbort]

112. Banking

| bank | bank | [bank] |
| branch (of bank, etc.) | tak | [tak] |

| bank clerk, consultant | bankklerk | [bank·klerk] |
| manager (director) | bestuurder | [bestɪrdər] |

bank account	bankrekening	[bank·rekəniŋ]
account number	rekeningnommer	[rekəniŋ·nommər]
checking account	tjekrekening	[tʃek·rekəniŋ]
savings account	spaarrekening	[spār·rekəniŋ]

| to close the account | die rekening sluit | [di rekəniŋ slœit] |
| to withdraw (vt) | trek | [trek] |

deposit	deposito	[deposito]
wire transfer	telegrafiese oorplasing	[teleχrafisə oərplasiŋ]
to wire, to transfer	oorplaas	[oərplās]

| sum | som | [som] |
| How much? | Hoeveel? | [hufeəl?] |

| signature | handtekening | [hand·tekəniŋ] |
| to sign (vt) | onderteken | [ondərtekən] |

credit card	kredietkaart	[kredit·kārt]
code (PIN code)	kode	[kodə]
credit card number	kredietkaartnommer	[kredit·kārt·nommər]
ATM	OTM	[o·te·em]

| check | tjek | [tʃek] |
| checkbook | tjekboek | [tʃek·buk] |

| loan (bank ~) | lening | [leniŋ] |
| guarantee | waarborg | [vārborχ] |

113. Telephone. Phone conversation

telephone	**telefoon**	[telefoən]
cell phone	**selfoon**	[sɛlfoən]
answering machine	**antwoordmasjien**	[antwoərt·maʃin]
to call (by phone)	**bel**	[bəl]
phone call	**oproep**	[oprup]
Hello!	**Hallo!**	[hallo!]
to ask (vt)	**vra**	[fra]
to answer (vi, vt)	**antwoord**	[antwoərt]
to hear (vt)	**hoor**	[hoər]
well (adv)	**goed**	[χut]
not well (adv)	**nie goed nie**	[ni χut ni]
noises (interference)	**steurings**	[støəriŋs]
receiver	**gehoorstuk**	[χehoərstuk]
to pick up (~ the phone)	**optel**	[optəl]
to hang up (~ the phone)	**afskakel**	[afskakəl]
busy (engaged)	**besig**	[besəχ]
to ring (ab. phone)	**lui**	[lœi]
telephone book	**telefoongids**	[telefoən·χids]
local (adj)	**lokale**	[lokalə]
local call	**lokale oproep**	[lokalə oprup]
long distance (~ call)	**langafstand**	[lanχ·afstant]
long-distance call	**langafstand oproep**	[lanχ·afstant oprup]
international (adj)	**internasionale**	[internaʃionalə]
international call	**internasionale oproep**	[internaʃionalə oprup]

114. Cell phone

cell phone	**selfoon**	[sɛlfoən]
display	**skerm**	[skerm]
button	**knoppie**	[knoppi]
SIM card	**SIMkaart**	[sim·kārt]
battery	**battery**	[battəraj]
to be dead (battery)	**pap wees**	[pap veəs]
charger	**batterylaaier**	[battəraj·lajer]
menu	**spyskaart**	[spajs·kārt]
settings	**instellings**	[instɛlliŋs]
tune (melody)	**wysie**	[vajsi]
to select (vt)	**kies**	[kis]
calculator	**sakrekenaar**	[sakrekənār]

voice mail	stempos	[stem·pos]
alarm clock	wekker	[vɛkkər]
contacts	kontakte	[kontaktə]

| SMS (text message) | SMS | [es·em·es] |
| subscriber | intekenaar | [intekənãr] |

115. Stationery

| ballpoint pen | bolpen | [bol·pen] |
| fountain pen | vulpen | [ful·pen] |

pencil	potlood	[potloət]
highlighter	merkpen	[merk·pen]
felt-tip pen	viltpen	[filt·pen]

| notepad | notaboekie | [nota·buki] |
| agenda (diary) | dagboek | [daχ·buk] |

ruler	liniaal	[liniãl]
calculator	sakrekenaar	[sakrekənãr]
eraser	uitveër	[œitfeɛr]
thumbtack	duimspyker	[dœim·spajkər]
paper clip	skuifspeld	[skœif·spɛlt]

glue	gom	[χom]
stapler	krammasjien	[kram·maʃin]
hole punch	ponsmasjien	[pɔŋs·maʃin]
pencil sharpener	skerpmaker	[skerp·makər]

116. Various kinds of documents

account (report)	verslag	[ferslaχ]
agreement	ooreenkoms	[oəreənkoms]
application form	aansoekvorm	[ãŋsuk·form]
authentic (adj)	outentiek	[æʊtentik]
badge (identity tag)	lapelkaart	[lapəl·kãrt]
business card	besigheidskaartjie	[besiχæjts·kãrki]

certificate (~ of quality)	sertifikaat	[sertifikãt]
check (e.g., draw a ~)	tjek	[tʃek]
check (in restaurant)	rekening	[rekəniŋ]
constitution	grondwet	[χront·wet]

contract (agreement)	kontrak	[kontrak]
copy	kopie	[kopi]
copy (of contract, etc.)	kopie	[kopi]
customs declaration	doeaneverklaring	[duanə·ferklariŋ]

document	dokument	[dokument]
driver's license	bestuurslisensie	[bestɪrs·lisɛŋsi]
addendum	addendum	[addendum]
form	vorm	[form]

ID card (e.g., FBI ~)	identiteitskaart	[identitæjts·kãrt]
inquiry (request)	navraag	[nafrãχ]
invitation card	uitnodiging	[œitnodəχiŋ]
invoice	rekening	[rekəniŋ]

law	wet	[vet]
letter (mail)	brief	[brif]
letterhead	briefhoof	[brifhoəf]
list (of names, etc.)	lys	[lajs]
manuscript	manuskrip	[manuskrip]
newsletter	nuusbrief	[nɪsbrif]
note (short letter)	briefie	[brifi]

pass (for worker, visitor)	lapelkaart	[lapəl·kãrt]
passport	paspoort	[paspoərt]
permit	permit	[permit]
résumé	curriculum vitae	[kurrikulum fitaə]
debt note, IOU	skuldbekentenis	[skuld·bekentənis]
receipt (for purchase)	kwitansie	[kwitaŋsi]
sales slip, receipt	strokie	[stroki]
report (mil.)	verslag	[ferslaχ]

to show (ID, etc.)	wys	[vajs]
to sign (vt)	onderteken	[ondərtekən]
signature	handtekening	[hand·tekəniŋ]
seal (stamp)	stempel	[stempəl]
text	teks	[teks]
ticket (for entry)	kaartjie	[kãrki]

| to cross out | doodtrek | [doədtrek] |
| to fill out (~ a form) | invul | [inful] |

| waybill (shipping invoice) | vragbrief | [fraχ·brif] |
| will (testament) | testament | [testament] |

117. Kinds of business

accounting services	boekhoudienste	[bukhæʊ·diŋstə]
advertising	reklame	[reklamə]
advertising agency	reklameburo	[reklamə·buro]
air-conditioners	lugversorger	[luχfersorχər]
airline	lugredery	[luχrederaj]

| alcoholic beverages | alkoholiese dranke | [alkoholisə drankə] |
| antiques (antique dealers) | antiek | [antik] |

| art gallery (contemporary ~) | kunsgalery | [kuns·χaleraj] |
| audit services | ouditeursdienste | [æʊditøərs·diŋstə] |

banking industry	bankwese	[bankwesə]
bar	kroeg	[kruχ]
beauty parlor	skoonheidssalon	[skoənhæjts·salon]
bookstore	boekhandel	[buk·handəl]
brewery	brouery	[bræʊeraj]
business center	sakesentrum	[sakə·sentrum]
business school	besigheidsskool	[besiχæjts·skoəl]

casino	kasino	[kasino]
construction	boubedryf	[bæʊbedrajf]
consulting	advieskantoor	[adfis·kantoər]

dental clinic	tandekliniek	[tandə·klinik]
design	ontwerp	[ontwerp]
drugstore, pharmacy	apteek	[apteək]
dry cleaners	droogskoonmakers	[droəχ·skoən·makers]
employment agency	arbeidsburo	[arbæjds·buro]

financial services	finansiële dienste	[finaŋsiɛlə diŋstə]
food products	voedingsware	[fudiŋs·warə]
funeral home	begrafnisonderneming	[beχrafnis·ondərnemiŋ]
furniture (e.g., house ~)	meubels	[møəbɛls]
clothing, garment	klerasie	[klerasi]
hotel	hotel	[hotəl]

ice-cream	roomys	[roəm·ajs]
industry (manufacturing)	industrie	[industri]
insurance	versekering	[fersekeriŋ]
Internet	internet	[internet]
investments (finance)	investerings	[infesteriŋs]

jeweler	juwelier	[juvelir]
jewelry	juweliersware	[juvelirs·warə]
laundry (shop)	wassery	[vasseraj]
legal advisor	regsadviseur	[reχs·adfisøər]
light industry	ligte industrie	[liχtə industri]

magazine	tydskrif	[tajdskrif]
mail-order selling	posorderbedryf	[pos·ordər·bedrajf]
medicine	geneesmiddels	[χeneəs·middəls]
movie theater	bioskoop	[bioskoəp]
museum	museum	[musøəm]

news agency	nuusagentskap	[nɪs·aχentskap]
newspaper	koerant	[kurant]
nightclub	nagklub	[naχ·klup]
oil (petroleum)	olie	[oli]
courier services	koerierdienste	[kurir·diŋstə]

pharmaceutics	**farmasie**	[farmasi]
printing (industry)	**drukkery**	[drukkəraj]
publishing house	**uitgewery**	[œitχevəraj]
radio (~ station)	**radio**	[radio]
real estate	**eiendom**	[æjendom]
restaurant	**restaurant**	[restɔurant]
security company	**sekuriteitsfirma**	[sekuritæjts·firma]
sports	**sport**	[sport]
stock exchange	**beurs**	[bøərs]
store	**winkel**	[vinkəl]
supermarket	**supermark**	[supermark]
swimming pool (public ~)	**swembad**	[swem·bat]
tailor shop	**kleremaker**	[klerə·makər]
television	**televisie**	[telefisi]
theater	**teater**	[teatər]
trade (commerce)	**handel**	[handəl]
transportation	**vervoer**	[ferfur]
travel	**reisbedryf**	[ræjs·bedrajf]
veterinarian	**veearts**	[fee·arts]
warehouse	**pakhuis**	[pak·hœis]
waste collection	**afvalinsameling**	[affal·insameliŋ]

Job. Business. Part 2

118. Show. Exhibition

exhibition, show	**skou**	[skæʋ]
trade show	**handelsskou**	[handəls·skæʋ]
participation	**deelneming**	[deəlnemiŋ]
to participate (vi)	**deelneem**	[deəlneəm]
participant (exhibitor)	**deelnemer**	[deəlnemər]
director	**bestuurder**	[bestɪrdər]
organizers' office	**organisasiekantoor**	[orχanisasi·kantoər]
organizer	**organiseerder**	[orχaniseərdər]
to organize (vt)	**organiseer**	[orχaniseər]
participation form	**deelnemingsvorm**	[deəlnemiŋs·form]
to fill out (vt)	**invul**	[inful]
details	**besonderhede**	[besondərhedə]
information	**informasie**	[informasi]
price (cost, rate)	**prys**	[prajs]
including	**insluitend**	[inslœitent]
to include (vt)	**insluit**	[inslœit]
to pay (vi, vt)	**betaal**	[betāl]
registration fee	**registrasiefooi**	[reχistrasi·foj]
entrance	**ingang**	[inχaŋ]
pavilion, hall	**paviljoen**	[pafiljun]
to register (vt)	**registreer**	[reχistreər]
badge (identity tag)	**lapelkaart**	[lapəl·kārt]
booth, stand	**stalletjie**	[stalləki]
to reserve, to book	**bespreek**	[bespreək]
display case	**uistalkas**	[œistalkas]
spotlight	**kollig**	[kolləχ]
design	**ontwerp**	[ontwerp]
to place (put, set)	**sit**	[sit]
to be placed	**geplaas wees**	[χeplās veəs]
distributor	**verdeler**	[ferdelər]
supplier	**verskaffer**	[ferskaffər]
to supply (vt)	**verskaf**	[ferskaf]
country	**land**	[lant]
foreign (adj)	**buitelands**	[bœitəlands]

product	produk	[produk]
association	vereniging	[ferenəxiŋ]
conference hall	konferensiesaal	[konferɛŋsi·sāl]
congress	kongres	[konχres]
contest (competition)	wedstryd	[vedstrajt]

visitor (attendee)	besoeker	[besukər]
to visit (attend)	besoek	[besuk]
customer	kliënt	[kliɛnt]

119. Mass Media

newspaper	koerant	[kurant]
magazine	tydskrif	[tajdskrif]
press (printed media)	pers	[pers]
radio	radio	[radio]
radio station	omroep	[omrup]
television	televisie	[telefisi]

presenter, host	aanbieder	[ānbidər]
newscaster	nuusleser	[nɪslesər]
commentator	kommentator	[kommentator]

journalist	joernalis	[jurnalis]
correspondent (reporter)	korrespondent	[korrespondɛnt]
press photographer	persfotograaf	[pers·fotoχrāf]
reporter	verslaggewer	[ferslaχ·χevər]

| editor | redakteur | [redaktøər] |
| editor-in-chief | hoofredakteur | [hoəf·redaktøər] |

to subscribe (to …)	inteken op …	[intekən op …]
subscription	intekening	[intekəniŋ]
subscriber	intekenaar	[intekənār]
to read (vi, vt)	lees	[leəs]
reader	leser	[lesər]

circulation (of newspaper)	oplaag	[oplāχ]
monthly (adj)	maandeliks	[māndəliks]
weekly (adj)	weekliks	[veəkliks]
issue (edition)	nommer	[nommər]
new (~ issue)	nuwe	[nuvə]

headline	opskrif	[opskrif]
short article	kort artikel	[kort artikəl]
column (regular article)	kolom	[kolom]
article	artikel	[artikəl]
page	bladsy	[bladsaj]
reportage, report	veslag	[feslaχ]
event (happening)	gebeurtenis	[χebøərtenis]

sensation (news)	sensasie	[sɛŋsasi]
scandal	skandaal	[skandāl]
scandalous (adj)	skandelik	[skandəlik]
great (~ scandal)	groot	[χroət]

show (e.g., cooking ~)	program	[proχram]
interview	onderhoud	[ondərhæʊt]
live broadcast	regstreekse uitsending	[reχstreəksə œitsendiŋ]
channel	kanaal	[kanāl]

120. Agriculture

agriculture	landbou	[landbæʊ]
peasant (masc.)	boer	[bur]
peasant (fem.)	boervrou	[bur·fræʊ]
farmer	boer	[bur]

| tractor (farm ~) | trekker | [trɛkkər] |
| combine, harvester | stroper | [stropər] |

plow	ploeg	[pluχ]
to plow (vi, vt)	ploeg	[pluχ]
plowland	ploegland	[pluχlant]
furrow (in field)	voor	[foər]

to sow (vi, vt)	saai	[sāi]
seeder	saaier	[sājer]
sowing (process)	saai	[sāi]

| scythe | sens | [sɛŋs] |
| to mow, to scythe | maai | [māi] |

| spade (tool) | graaf | [χrāf] |
| to till (vt) | omspit | [omspit] |

hoe	skoffel	[skoffəl]
to hoe, to weed	skoffel	[skoffəl]
weed (plant)	onkruid	[onkrœit]

watering can	gieter	[χitər]
to water (plants)	nat gooi	[nat χoj]
watering (act)	nat gooi	[nat χoj]

| pitchfork | gaffel | [χaffəl] |
| rake | hark | [hark] |

fertilizer	misstof	[misstof]
to fertilize (vt)	bemes	[bemes]
manure (fertilizer)	misstof	[misstof]
field	veld	[fɛlt]

meadow	weiland	[væjlant]
vegetable garden	groentetuin	[χruntə·tœin]
orchard (e.g., apple ~)	boord	[boərt]
to graze (vt)	wei	[væj]
herder (herdsman)	herder	[herdər]
pasture	weiland	[væjlant]
cattle breeding	veeboerdery	[feə·burderaj]
sheep farming	skaapboerdery	[skāp·burderaj]
plantation	aanplanting	[ānplantiŋ]
row (garden bed ~s)	bedding	[beddiŋ]
hothouse	broeikas	[bruikas]
drought (lack of rain)	droogte	[droəχtə]
dry (~ summer)	droog	[droəχ]
grain	graan	[χrān]
cereal crops	graangewasse	[χrān·χəwassə]
to harvest, to gather	oes	[us]
miller (person)	meulenaar	[møələnār]
mill (e.g., gristmill)	meul	[møəl]
to grind (grain)	maal	[māl]
flour	meelblom	[meəl·blom]
straw	strooi	[stroj]

121. Building. Building process

construction site	bouperseel	[bæu·perseəl]
to build (vt)	bou	[bæu]
construction worker	bouwerker	[bæu·verkər]
project	projek	[projek]
architect	argitek	[arχitek]
worker	werker	[verkər]
foundation (of a building)	fondament	[fondament]
roof	dak	[dak]
foundation pile	heipaal	[hæjpāl]
wall	muur	[mɪr]
reinforcing bars	betonstaal	[betoŋ·stāl]
scaffolding	steiers	[stæjers]
concrete	beton	[beton]
granite	graniet	[χranit]
stone	klip	[klip]
brick	baksteen	[baksteən]

sand	**sand**	[sant]
cement	**sement**	[sement]
plaster (for walls)	**pleister**	[plæjstər]
to plaster (vt)	**pleister**	[plæjstər]

paint	**verf**	[fɛrf]
to paint (~ a wall)	**verf**	[fɛrf]
barrel	**drom**	[drom]

crane	**kraan**	[krãn]
to lift, to hoist (vt)	**optel**	[optəl]
to lower (vt)	**laat sak**	[lãt sak]

bulldozer	**stootskraper**	[stoət·skrapər]
excavator	**graafmasjien**	[χrãf·maʃin]
scoop, bucket	**bak**	[bak]
to dig (excavate)	**grawe**	[χravə]
hard hat	**helmet**	[hɛlmet]

122. Science. Research. Scientists

science	**wetenskap**	[vetɛŋskap]
scientific (adj)	**wetenskaplik**	[vetɛŋskaplik]
scientist	**wetenskaplike**	[vetɛŋskaplikə]
theory	**teorie**	[teori]

axiom	**aksioma**	[aksioma]
analysis	**analise**	[analisə]
to analyze (vt)	**analiseer**	[analiseər]
argument (strong ~)	**argument**	[arχument]
substance (matter)	**substansie**	[substaŋsi]

hypothesis	**hipotese**	[hipotesə]
dilemma	**dilemma**	[dilɛmma]
dissertation	**proefskrif**	[prufskrif]
dogma	**dogma**	[doχma]

doctrine	**doktrine**	[doktrinə]
research	**navorsing**	[naforsiŋ]
to research (vt)	**navors**	[nafors]
tests (laboratory ~)	**toetse**	[tutsə]
laboratory	**laboratorium**	[laboratorium]

method	**metode**	[metodə]
molecule	**molekule**	[molekulə]
monitoring	**monitering**	[moniteriŋ]
discovery (act, event)	**ontdekking**	[ontdɛkkiŋ]

postulate	**postulaat**	[postulãt]
principle	**beginsel**	[beχinsəl]

| forecast | **voorspelling** | [foərspɛliŋ] |
| to forecast (vt) | **voorspel** | [foərspel] |

synthesis	**sintese**	[sintesə]
trend (tendency)	**tendens**	[tendɛŋs]
theorem	**stelling**	[stɛliŋ]

teachings	**leer**	[leər]
fact	**feit**	[fæjt]
expedition	**ekspedisie**	[ɛkspedisi]
experiment	**eksperiment**	[ɛksperiment]

academician	**akademikus**	[akademikus]
bachelor (e.g., ~ of Arts)	**baccalaureus**	[bakalɔurøəs]
doctor (PhD)	**doktor**	[doktor]
Associate Professor	**medeprofessor**	[medə·profɛssor]
Master (e.g., ~ of Arts)	**Magister**	[maχistər]
professor	**professor**	[profɛssor]

Professions and occupations

123. Job search. Dismissal

job	baantjie	[bānki]
staff (work force)	personeel	[personeəl]
personnel	personeel	[personeəl]

career	loopbaan	[loəpbān]
prospects (chances)	vooruitsigte	[foərœit·siχtə]
skills (mastery)	meesterskap	[meəsterskap]

selection (screening)	seleksie	[seleksi]
employment agency	arbeidsburo	[arbæjds·buro]
résumé	curriculum vitae	[kurrikulum fitaə]
job interview	werksonderhoud	[werk·ondərhæʊt]
vacancy, opening	vakature	[fakaturə]

salary, pay	salaris	[salaris]
fixed salary	vaste salaris	[fastə salaris]
pay, compensation	loon	[loən]

position (job)	posisie	[posisi]
duty (of employee)	taak	[tāk]
range of duties	reeks opdragte	[reəks opdraχtə]
busy (I'm ~)	besig	[besəχ]

| to fire (dismiss) | afdank | [afdank] |
| dismissal | afdanking | [afdankiŋ] |

unemployment	werkloosheid	[verkloəshæjt]
unemployed (n)	werkloos	[verkloəs]
retirement	pensioen	[pɛnsiun]
to retire (from job)	met pensioen gaan	[met pɛnsiun χān]

124. Business people

director	direkteur	[direktøər]
manager (director)	bestuurder	[bestɪrdər]
boss	baas	[bās]

superior	hoof	[hoəf]
superiors	hoofde	[hoəfdə]
president	direkteur	[direktøər]

chairman	voorsitter	[foərsittər]
deputy (substitute)	adjunk	[adjunk]
assistant	assistent	[assistent]
secretary	sekretaris	[sekretaris]
personal assistant	persoonlike assistent	[persoənlikə assistent]
businessman	sakeman	[sakəman]
entrepreneur	entrepreneur	[ɛntrəprenøər]
founder	stigter	[stiχtər]
to found (vt)	stig	[stiχ]
incorporator	stigter	[stiχtər]
partner	vennoot	[fɛnnoət]
stockholder	aandeelhouer	[āndeəl·hæʊər]
millionaire	miljoenêr	[miljunær]
billionaire	miljardêr	[miljardær]
owner, proprietor	eienaar	[æjenār]
landowner	grondeienaar	[χront·æjenār]
client	kliënt	[kliɛnt]
regular client	vaste kliënt	[fastə kliɛnt]
buyer (customer)	koper	[kopər]
visitor	besoeker	[besukər]
professional (n)	professioneel	[profɛssioneəl]
expert	kenner	[kɛnnər]
specialist	spesialis	[spesialis]
banker	bankier	[bankir]
broker	makelaar	[makəlār]
cashier, teller	kassier	[kassir]
accountant	boekhouer	[bukhæʊər]
security guard	veiligheidswag	[fæjliχæjts·waχ]
investor	belegger	[beleχər]
debtor	skuldenaar	[skuldenār]
creditor	krediteur	[kreditøər]
borrower	lener	[lenər]
importer	invoerder	[infurdər]
exporter	uitvoerder	[œitfurdər]
manufacturer	produsent	[produsent]
distributor	verdeler	[ferdelər]
middleman	tussenpersoon	[tussən·persoən]
consultant	raadgewer	[rāt·χevər]
sales representative	verkoopsagent	[ferkoəps·aχent]
agent	agent	[aχent]
insurance agent	versekeringsagent	[fersəkeriŋs·aχent]

125. Service professions

cook	kok	[kok]
chef (kitchen chef)	sjef	[ʃef]
baker	bakker	[bakkər]

bartender	kroegman	[kruχman]
waiter	kelner	[kɛlnər]
waitress	kelnerin	[kɛlnərin]

lawyer, attorney	advokaat	[adfokāt]
lawyer (legal expert)	prokureur	[prokurøər]
notary	notaris	[notaris]

electrician	elektrisiën	[ɛlektrisiɛn]
plumber	loodgieter	[loədχitər]
carpenter	timmerman	[timmerman]

masseur	masseerder	[masseerdər]
masseuse	masseerster	[masseerstər]
doctor	dokter	[doktər]

taxi driver	taxibestuurder	[taksi·bestɪrdər]
driver	bestuurder	[bestɪrdər]
delivery man	koerier	[kurir]

chambermaid	kamermeisie	[kamər·mæjsi]
security guard	veiligheidswag	[fæjliχæjts·waχ]
flight attendant (fem.)	lugwaardin	[luχ·wārdin]

schoolteacher	onderwyser	[ondərwajsər]
librarian	bibliotekaris	[bibliotekaris]
translator	vertaler	[fertalər]
interpreter	tolk	[tolk]
guide	gids	[χids]

hairdresser	haarkapper	[hār·kappər]
mailman	posbode	[pos·bodə]
salesman (store staff)	verkoper	[ferkopər]

gardener	tuinman	[tœin·man]
domestic servant	bediende	[bedində]
maid (female servant)	bediende	[bedində]
cleaner (cleaning lady)	skoonmaakster	[skoən·mākstər]

126. Military professions and ranks

private	soldaat	[soldāt]
sergeant	sersant	[sersant]

| lieutenant | luitenant | [lœitənant] |
| captain | kaptein | [kaptæjn] |

major	majoor	[majoər]
colonel	kolonel	[kolonəl]
general	generaal	[χenerāl]
marshal	maarskalk	[mārskalk]
admiral	admiraal	[admirāl]

military (n)	leër	[leɛr]
soldier	soldaat	[soldāt]
officer	offisier	[offisir]
commander	kommandant	[kommandant]

border guard	grenswag	[χrɛŋs·waχ]
radio operator	radio-operateur	[radio-operatøər]
scout (searcher)	verkenner	[ferkɛnnər]
pioneer (sapper)	sappeur	[sappøər]
marksman	skutter	[skuttər]
navigator	navigator	[nafiχator]

127. Officials. Priests

| king | koning | [koniŋ] |
| queen | koningin | [koniŋin] |

| prince | prins | [prins] |
| princess | prinses | [prinsəs] |

| czar | tsaar | [tsār] |
| czarina | tsarina | [tsarina] |

president	president	[president]
Secretary (minister)	minister	[ministər]
prime minister	eerste minister	[eərstə ministər]
senator	senator	[senator]

diplomat	diplomaat	[diplomāt]
consul	konsul	[kɔŋsul]
ambassador	ambassadeur	[ambassadøər]
counsilor (diplomatic officer)	adviseur	[adfisøər]

official, functionary (civil servant)	amptenaar	[amptənar]
prefect	prefek	[prefek]
mayor	burgermeester	[burgər·meəstər]
judge	regter	[reχtər]
prosecutor (e.g., district attorney)	aanklaer	[ānklaər]

missionary	sendeling	[sendəliŋ]
monk	monnik	[monnik]
abbot	ab	[ap]
rabbi	rabbi	[rabbi]

vizier	visier	[fisir]
shah	sjah	[ʃah]
sheikh	sjeik	[ʃæjk]

128. Agricultural professions

beekeeper	byeboer	[bajebur]
herder, shepherd	herder	[herdər]
agronomist	landboukundige	[landbæʊ·kundiχə]
cattle breeder	veeteler	[feə·telər]
veterinarian	veearts	[feə·arts]

farmer	boer	[bur]
winemaker	wynmaker	[vajn·makər]
zoologist	dierkundige	[dir·kundiχə]
cowboy	cowboy	[kovboj]

129. Art professions

| actor | akteur | [aktøər] |
| actress | aktrise | [aktrisə] |

| singer (masc.) | sanger | [saŋər] |
| singer (fem.) | sangeres | [saŋəres] |

| dancer (masc.) | danser | [daŋsər] |
| dancer (fem.) | danseres | [daŋsəres] |

| performer (masc.) | verhoogkunstenaar | [ferhoəχ·kunstənãr] |
| performer (fem.) | verhoogkunstenares | [ferhoəχ·kunstənares] |

musician	musikant	[musikant]
pianist	pianis	[pianis]
guitar player	kitaarspeler	[kitãr·spelər]

conductor (orchestra ~)	dirigent	[diriχent]
composer	komponis	[komponis]
impresario	impresario	[impresario]

film director	filmregisseur	[film·reχissøər]
producer	produsent	[produsent]
scriptwriter	draaiboekskrywer	[drãjbuk·skrajvər]
critic	kritikus	[kritikus]

writer	skrywer	[skrajvər]
poet	digter	[diχtər]
sculptor	beeldhouer	[beəldhæʊər]
artist (painter)	kunstenaar	[kunstenãr]

juggler	jongleur	[jonχløər]
clown	hanswors	[haŋswors]
acrobat	akrobaat	[akrobãt]
magician	goëlaar	[χoɛlãr]

130. Various professions

doctor	dokter	[doktər]
nurse	verpleegster	[ferpleəχ·stər]
psychiatrist	psigiater	[psiχiatər]
dentist	tandarts	[tand·arts]
surgeon	chirurg	[ʃirurχ]

astronaut	astronout	[astronæʊt]
astronomer	astronoom	[astronoəm]
pilot	piloot	[piloət]

driver (of taxi, etc.)	bestuurder	[bestɪrdər]
engineer (train driver)	treindrywer	[træjn·drajvər]
mechanic	werktuigkundige	[verktœiχ·kundiχə]

miner	mynwerker	[majn·werkər]
worker	werker	[verkər]
locksmith	slotmaker	[slot·makər]
joiner (carpenter)	skrynwerker	[skrajn·werkər]
turner (lathe machine operator)	draaibankwerker	[drãjbank·werkər]
construction worker	bouwerker	[bæʊ·verkər]
welder	sweiser	[swæjsər]

professor (title)	professor	[profɛssor]
architect	argitek	[arχitek]
historian	historikus	[historikus]
scientist	wetenskaplike	[vetɛŋskaplikə]
physicist	fisikus	[fisikus]
chemist (scientist)	skeikundige	[skæjkundiχə]

archeologist	argeoloog	[arχeoloəχ]
geologist	geoloog	[χeoloəχ]
researcher (scientist)	navorser	[naforsər]

babysitter	babasitter	[babasittər]
teacher, educator	onderwyser	[ondərwajsər]
editor	redakteur	[redaktøər]
editor-in-chief	hoofredakteur	[hoəf·redaktøər]

| correspondent | korrespondent | [korrespondɛnt] |
| typist (fem.) | tikster | [tikstər] |

designer	ontwerper	[ontwerpər]
computer expert	rekenaarkenner	[rekənār·kɛnnər]
programmer	programmeur	[proχrammøər]
engineer (designer)	ingenieur	[inχeniøər]

sailor	matroos	[matroəs]
seaman	seeman	[seəman]
rescuer	redder	[rɛddər]

fireman	brandweerman	[brantveər·man]
police officer	polisieman	[polisi·man]
watchman	bewaker	[bevakər]
detective	speurder	[spøərdər]

customs officer	doeanebeampte	[duanə·beamptə]
bodyguard	lyfwag	[lajf·waχ]
prison guard	tronkbewaarder	[tronk·bevārdər]
inspector	inspekteur	[inspektøər]

sportsman	sportman	[sportman]
trainer, coach	breier	[bræjer]
butcher	slagter	[slaχtər]
cobbler (shoe repairer)	skoenmaker	[skun·makər]
merchant	handelaar	[handəlār]
loader (person)	laaier	[lājer]

| fashion designer | modeontwerper | [modə·ontwerpər] |
| model (fem.) | model | [modəl] |

131. Occupations. Social status

| schoolboy | skoolseun | [skoəl·søən] |
| student (college ~) | student | [student] |

philosopher	filosoof	[filosoəf]
economist	ekonoom	[ɛkonoəm]
inventor	uitvinder	[œitfindər]

unemployed (n)	werkloos	[verkloəs]
retiree	pensioentrekker	[pɛnsiun·trɛkkər]
spy, secret agent	spioen	[spiun]

prisoner	gevangene	[χefaŋənə]
striker	staker	[stakər]
bureaucrat	burokraat	[burokrāt]
traveler (globetrotter)	reisiger	[ræjsiχer]
gay, homosexual (n)	gay	[χaaj]

| hacker | kuberkraker | [kubər·krakər] |
| hippie | hippie | [hippi] |

bandit	bandiet	[bandit]
hit man, killer	huurmoordenaar	[hɪr·moərdenār]
drug addict	dwelmslaaf	[dwɛlm·slāf]
drug dealer	dwelmhandelaar	[dwɛlm·handelār]
prostitute (fem.)	prostituut	[prostitɪt]
pimp	pooier	[pojer]

sorcerer	towenaar	[tovenār]
sorceress (evil ~)	heks	[heks]
pirate	piraat, seerower	[pirāt], [seə·rovər]
slave	slaaf	[slāf]
samurai	samoerai	[samuraj]
savage (primitive)	wilde	[vildə]

Sports

sportsman	**sportman**	[sportman]
kind of sports	**sportsoorte**	[sport·soərtə]
basketball	**basketbal**	[basketbal]
basketball player	**basketbalspeler**	[basketbal·spelər]
baseball	**bofbal**	[bofbal]
baseball player	**bofbalspeler**	[bofbal·spelər]
soccer	**sokker**	[sokkər]
soccer player	**sokkerspeler**	[sokkər·spelər]
goalkeeper	**doelwagter**	[dul·waχtər]
hockey	**hokkie**	[hokki]
hockey player	**hokkiespeler**	[hokki·spelər]
volleyball	**vlugbal**	[fluχbal]
volleyball player	**vlugbalspeler**	[fluχbal·spelər]
boxing	**boks**	[boks]
boxer	**bokser**	[boksər]
wrestling	**stoei**	[stui]
wrestler	**stoeier**	[stujer]
karate	**karate**	[karatə]
karate fighter	**karatevegter**	[karatə·feχtər]
judo	**judo**	[judo]
judo athlete	**judoka**	[judoka]
tennis	**tennis**	[tɛnnis]
tennis player	**tennisspeler**	[tɛnnis·spelər]
swimming	**swem**	[swem]
swimmer	**swemmer**	[swemmər]
fencing	**skerm**	[skerm]
fencer	**skermer**	[skermər]
chess	**skaak**	[skāk]
chess player	**skaakspeler**	[skāk·spelər]

| alpinism | alpinisme | [alpinismə] |
| alpinist | alpinis | [alpinis] |

| running | hardloop | [hardloəp] |
| runner | hardloper | [hardlopər] |

| athletics | atletiek | [atletik] |
| athlete | atleet | [atleət] |

| horseback riding | perdry | [perdraj] |
| horse rider | ruiter | [rœitər] |

figure skating	kunsskaats	[kuns·skãts]
figure skater (masc.)	kunsskaatser	[kuns·skãtsər]
figure skater (fem.)	kunsskaatser	[kuns·skãtsər]

| powerlifting | gewigoptel | [χeviχ·optəl] |
| powerlifter | gewigopteller | [χeviχ·optɛllər] |

| car racing | motorwedren | [motor·wedrən] |
| racing driver | renjaer | [renjaər] |

| cycling | fiets | [fits] |
| cyclist | fietser | [fitsər] |

broad jump	verspring	[fer·spriŋ]
pole vault	polsstokspring	[polsstok·spriŋ]
jumper	springer	[spriŋər]

133. Kinds of sports. Miscellaneous

football	sokker	[sokkər]
badminton	pluimbal	[plœimbal]
biathlon	tweekamp	[tweəkamp]
billiards	biljart	[biljart]

bobsled	bobslee	[bobsleə]
bodybuilding	liggaamsbou	[liχχãmsbæʊ]
water polo	waterpolo	[vatər·polo]
handball	handbal	[handbal]
golf	gholf	[golf]

rowing, crew	roei	[rui]
scuba diving	duik	[dœik]
cross-country skiing	veldski	[fɛlt·ski]
table tennis (ping-pong)	tafeltennis	[tafel·tɛnnis]

sailing	seil	[sæjl]
rally racing	tydren jaag	[tajdren jãχ]
rugby	rugby	[ragbi]

| snowboarding | sneeuplankry | [sniʊ·plankraj] |
| archery | boogskiet | [boəχ·skit] |

134. Gym

| barbell | staafgewig | [stāf·χevəχ] |
| dumbbells | handgewigte | [hand·χeviχtə] |

training machine	oefenmasjien	[ufen·maʃin]
exercise bicycle	oefenfiets	[ufen·fits]
treadmill	trapmeul	[trapmøəl]

horizontal bar	rekstok	[rekstok]
parallel bars	brug	[bruχ]
vault (vaulting horse)	springperd	[spriŋ·pert]
mat (exercise ~)	oefenmat	[ufen·mat]

jump rope	springtou	[spriŋ·tæʊ]
aerobics	aërobiese oefeninge	[aɛrobisə ufeniŋə]
yoga	joga	[joga]

135. Hockey

hockey	hokkie	[hokki]
hockey player	hokkiespeler	[hokki·spelər]
to play hockey	hokkie speel	[hokki speəl]
ice	ys	[ajs]

puck	skyf	[skajf]
hockey stick	hokkiestok	[hokki·stok]
ice skates	ysskaatse	[ajs·skātsə]

| board (ice hockey rink ~) | bord | [bort] |
| shot | skoot | [skoət] |

| goaltender | doelwagter | [dul·waχtər] |
| goal (score) | doelpunt | [dulpunt] |

period	periode	[periodə]
second period	tweede periode	[tweədə periodə]
substitutes bench	plaasvervangersbank	[plās·ferfaŋərs·bank]

136. Soccer

| soccer | sokker | [sokkər] |
| soccer player | sokkerspeler | [sokkər·spelər] |

to play soccer	sokker speel	[sokkər speəl]
major league	seniorliga	[senior·liɣa]
soccer club	sokkerklub	[sokkər·klup]
coach	breier	[bræjer]
owner, proprietor	eienaar	[æjenār]

team	span	[span]
team captain	spankaptein	[spanə·kaptæjn]
player	speler	[spelər]
substitute	plaasvervanger	[plās·ferfaŋər]

forward	voorspeler	[foər·spelər]
center forward	middelvoorspeler	[middəlfoər·spelər]
scorer	doelpuntmaker	[dulpunt·makər]
defender, back	verdediger	[ferdediɣər]
midfielder, halfback	middelveldspeler	[middəlfɛld·spelər]

match	wedstryd	[vedstrajt]
to meet (vi, vt)	ontmoet	[ontmut]
final	finale	[finalə]
semi-final	semi-finale	[semi-finalə]
championship	kampioenskap	[kampiunskap]

period, half	helfte	[hɛlftə]
first period	eerste helfte	[eerstə hɛlftə]
half-time	rustyd	[rustajt]

goal	doel	[dul]
goalkeeper	doelwagter	[dul·waχtər]
goalpost	doelpale	[dul·palə]
crossbar	dwarslat	[dwars·lat]
net	net	[net]

ball	bal	[bal]
pass	deurgee	[døərχeə]
kick	skop	[skop]
to kick (~ the ball)	skop	[skop]
free kick (direct ~)	vryskop	[frajskop]
corner kick	hoekskop	[hukskop]

attack	aanval	[ānfal]
counterattack	teenaanval	[teən·ānfal]
combination	kombinasie	[kombinasi]

referee	skeidsregter	[skæjds·reχtər]
to blow the whistle	die fluitjie blaas	[di flœiki blās]
whistle (sound)	fluitsienjaal	[flœit·sinjāl]
foul, misconduct	oortreding	[oərtredin]
to send off	van die veld stuur	[fan di fɛlt stɪr]

| yellow card | geel kaart | [χeəl kārt] |
| red card | rooi kaart | [roj kārt] |

disqualification	diskwalifikasie	[diskvalifikasi]
to disqualify (vt)	diskwalifiseer	[diskwalifiseər]
penalty kick	strafskop	[strafskop]
wall	muur	[mɪr]
to score (vi, vt)	doel aanteken	[dul äntekən]
goal (score)	doelpunt	[dulpunt]

substitution	plaasvervanging	[pläs·ferfaŋiŋ]
to replace (a player)	vervang	[ferfaŋ]
rules	reëls	[reɛls]
tactics	taktiek	[taktik]

stadium	stadion	[stadion]
stand (bleachers)	tribune	[tribunə]
fan, supporter	ondersteuner	[ondərstøənər]
to shout (vi)	skreeu	[skriʊ]
scoreboard	telbord	[tɛlbort]
score	stand	[stant]

defeat	nederlaag	[nedərläχ]
to lose (not win)	verloor	[ferloər]
tie	gelykspel	[χelajkspəl]
to tie (vi)	gelykop speel	[χelajkop speəl]

victory	oorwinning	[oərwinniŋ]
to win (vi, vt)	wen	[ven]
champion	kampioen	[kampiun]
best (adj)	beste	[bestə]
to congratulate (vt)	gelukwens	[χelukwɛŋs]

commentator	kommentator	[kommentator]
to commentate (vt)	verslag lewer	[ferslaχ levər]
broadcast	uitsending	[œitsendiŋ]

137. Alpine skiing

to ski (vi)	ski	[ski]
mountain-ski resort	berg ski-oord	[berχ ski-oərt]
ski lift	skihysbak	[ski·hajsbak]
ski poles	skistokke	[ski·stokkə]
slope	helling	[hɛlliŋ]
slalom	slalom	[slalom]

138. Tennis. Golf

golf	gholf	[golf]
golf club	gholfklub	[golf·klup]
golfer	gholfspeler	[golf·spelər]

hole	putjie	[puki]
club	gholfstok	[golf·stok]
golf trolley	gholfkarretjie	[golf·karrəki]

tennis	tennis	[tɛnnis]
tennis court	tennisbaan	[tɛnnis·bān]
serve	afslaan	[afslān]
to serve (vt)	afslaan	[afslān]
racket	raket	[raket]
net	net	[net]
ball	bal	[bal]

139. Chess

chess	skaak	[skāk]
chessmen	skaakstukke	[skāk·stukkə]
chess player	skaakspeler	[skāk·spelər]
chessboard	skaakbord	[skāk·bort]
chessman	stuk	[stuk]

| White (white pieces) | wit | [vit] |
| Black (black pieces) | swart | [swart] |

pawn	pion	[pion]
bishop	loper	[lopər]
knight	ruiter	[rœitər]
rook	toring	[toriŋ]
queen	dame	[damə]
king	koning	[koniŋ]

move	skuif	[skœif]
to move (vi, vt)	skuif	[skœif]
to sacrifice (vt)	opoffer	[opoffər]
castling	rokade	[rokadə]

| check | skaak | [skāk] |
| checkmate | skaakmat | [skāk·mat] |

chess tournament	skaakwedstryd	[skāk·wedstrajt]
Grand Master	Grootmeester	[xroət·meəstər]
combination	kombinasie	[kombinasi]
game (in chess)	spel	[spel]
checkers	damspel	[dam·spəl]

140. Boxing

| boxing | boks | [boks] |
| fight (bout) | geveg | [xefex] |

| boxing match | boksgeveg | [boks·χefəχ] |
| round (in boxing) | rondte | [rondtə] |

| ring | kryt | [krajt] |
| gong | gong | [χoŋ] |

punch	hou	[hæʊ]
knockdown	uitklophou	[œitklophæʊ]
knockout	uitklophou	[œitklophæʊ]
to knock out	uitklophou plant	[œitklophæʊ plant]

| boxing glove | bokshandskoen | [boks·handskun] |
| referee | skeidsregter | [skæjds·reχtər] |

lightweight	liggegewig	[liχχə·χevəχ]
middleweight	middelgewig	[middəl·χevəχ]
heavyweight	swaargewig	[swār·χevəχ]

141. Sports. Miscellaneous

Olympic Games	Olimpiese Spele	[olimpisə spelə]
winner	oorwinnaar	[oərwinnār]
to be winning	wen	[ven]
to win (vi)	wen	[ven]

| leader | leier | [læjer] |
| to lead (vi) | lei | [læj] |

first place	eerste plek	[eərstə plek]
second place	tweede plek	[tweedə plek]
third place	derde plek	[derdə plek]

medal	medalje	[medalje]
trophy	trofee	[trofeə]
prize cup (trophy)	beker	[bekər]
prize (in game)	prys	[prajs]
main prize	hoofprys	[hoef·prajs]
record	rekord	[rekort]

| final | finale | [finalə] |
| final (adj) | finale | [finalə] |

| champion | kampioen | [kampiun] |
| championship | kampioenskap | [kampiunskap] |

stadium	stadion	[stadion]
stand (bleachers)	tribune	[tribunə]
fan, supporter	ondersteuner	[ondərstøənər]
opponent, rival	teëstander	[teɛstandər]
start (start line)	wegspringplek	[veχspriŋ·plek]

finish line	eindstreep	[æjnd·streəp]
defeat	nederlaag	[nedərlãχ]
to lose (not win)	verloor	[ferloər]

referee	skeidsregter	[skæjds·reχtər]
jury (judges)	beoordelaars	[be·oərdelãrs]
score	stand	[stant]
tie	gelykspel	[χelajkspəl]
to tie (vi)	gelykop speel	[χelajkop speəl]
point	punt	[punt]
result (final score)	puntestand	[puntəstant]

| period | periode | [periodə] |
| half-time | rustyd | [rustajt] |

doping	opkikkers	[opkikkərs]
to penalize (vt)	straf	[straf]
to disqualify (vt)	diskwalifiseer	[diskwalifiseər]

apparatus	apparaat	[apparãt]
javelin	spies	[spis]
shot (metal ball)	koeël	[kuɛl]
ball (snooker, etc.)	bal	[bal]

aim (target)	doelwit	[dulwit]
target	teiken	[tæjkən]
to shoot (vi)	skiet	[skit]
accurate (~ shot)	akkuraat	[akkurãt]

trainer, coach	breier	[bræjer]
to train (sb)	afrig	[afrəχ]
to train (vi)	oefen	[ufen]
training	oefen	[ufen]

gym	gimnastieksaal	[χimnastik·sãl]
exercise (physical)	oefening	[ufeniŋ]
warm-up (athlete ~)	opwarm	[opwarm]

Education

142. School

school	skool	[skoəl]
principal (headmaster)	prinsipaal	[prinsipāl]
pupil (boy)	leerder	[leərdər]
pupil (girl)	leerder	[leərdər]
schoolboy	skoolseun	[skoəl·søən]
schoolgirl	skooldogter	[skoəl·doχtər]
to teach (sb)	leer	[leər]
to learn (language, etc.)	leer	[leər]
to learn by heart	van buite leer	[fan bœitə leər]
to learn (~ to count, etc.)	leer	[leər]
to be in school	op skool wees	[op skoəl veəs]
to go to school	skooltoe gaan	[skoəltu χān]
alphabet	alfabet	[alfabet]
subject (at school)	vak	[fak]
classroom	klaskamer	[klas·kamər]
lesson	les	[les]
recess	pouse	[pæʊsə]
school bell	skoolbel	[skoəl·bəl]
school desk	skoolbank	[skoəl·bank]
chalkboard	bord	[bort]
grade	simbool	[simboəl]
good grade	goeie punt	[χuje punt]
bad grade	slegte punt	[sleχtə punt]
mistake, error	fout	[fæʊt]
to make mistakes	foute maak	[fæʊtə māk]
to correct (an error)	korrigeer	[korriχeər]
cheat sheet	afskryfbriefie	[afskrajf·brifi]
homework	huiswerk	[hœis·werk]
exercise (in education)	oefening	[ufeniŋ]
to be present	aanwesig wees	[ānwesəχ veəs]
to be absent	afwesig wees	[afwesəχ veəs]
to miss school	stokkies draai	[stokkis drāj]
to punish (vt)	straf	[straf]

| punishment | straf | [straf] |
| conduct (behavior) | gedrag | [χedraχ] |

report card	rapport	[rapport]
pencil	potlood	[potloət]
eraser	uitveër	[œitfeɛr]
chalk	kryt	[krajt]
pencil case	potloodsakkie	[potloət·sakki]

schoolbag	boekesak	[bukə·sak]
pen	pen	[pen]
school notebook	skryfboek	[skrajf·buk]
textbook	handboek	[hand·buk]
compasses	passer	[passər]

| to make technical drawings | tegniese tekeninge maak | [teχnisə tekənikə māk] |
| technical drawing | tegniese tekening | [teχnisə tekəniŋ] |

poem	gedig	[χedəχ]
by heart (adv)	van buite	[fan bœitə]
to learn by heart	van buite leer	[fan bœitə leər]

school vacation	skoolvakansie	[skoəl·fakaŋsi]
to be on vacation	met vakansie wees	[met fakaŋsi veəs]
to spend one's vacation	jou vakansie deurbring	[jæʊ fakaŋsi døərbriŋ]

test (written math ~)	toets	[tuts]
essay (composition)	opstel	[opstəl]
dictation	diktee	[dikteə]
exam (examination)	eksamen	[ɛksamen]
experiment (e.g., chemistry ~)	eksperiment	[ɛksperiment]

143. College. University

academy	akademie	[akademi]
university	universiteit	[unifersitæjt]
faculty (e.g., ~ of Medicine)	fakulteit	[fakultæjt]

student (masc.)	student	[student]
student (fem.)	student	[student]
lecturer (teacher)	lektor	[lektor]

lecture hall, room	lesingsaal	[lesiŋ·sāl]
graduate	gegradueerde	[χeχradueərdə]
diploma	sertifikaat	[sertifikāt]
dissertation	proefskrif	[prufskrif]
study (report)	navorsing	[naforsiŋ]

laboratory	**laboratorium**	[laboratorium]
lecture	**lesing**	[lesiŋ]
coursemate	**medestudent**	[medə·student]
scholarship	**beurs**	[bøərs]
academic degree	**akademiese graad**	[akademisə χrāt]

144. Sciences. Disciplines

mathematics	**wiskunde**	[viskundə]
algebra	**algebra**	[alχebra]
geometry	**meetkunde**	[meətkundə]

astronomy	**astronomie**	[astronomi]
biology	**biologie**	[bioloχi]
geography	**geografie**	[χeoχrafi]
geology	**geologie**	[χeoloχi]
history	**geskiedenis**	[χeskidenis]

medicine	**geneeskunde**	[χeneəs·kundə]
pedagogy	**pedagogie**	[pedaχoχi]
law	**regte**	[reχtə]

physics	**fisika**	[fisika]
chemistry	**chemie**	[χemi]
philosophy	**filosofie**	[filosofi]
psychology	**sielkunde**	[silkundə]

145. Writing system. Orthography

grammar	**grammatika**	[χrammatika]
vocabulary	**woordeskat**	[voərdeskat]
phonetics	**fonetika**	[fonetika]

| noun | **selfstandige naamwoord** | [sɛlfstandiχə nāmwoərt] |
| adjective | **byvoeglike naamwoord** | [bajfuχlikə nāmvoərt] |

| verb | **werkwoord** | [verk·woərt] |
| adverb | **bijwoord** | [bij·woərt] |

pronoun	**voornaamwoord**	[foərnām·voərt]
interjection	**tussenwerpsel**	[tussən·werpsəl]
preposition	**voorsetsel**	[foərsetsəl]

root	**stam**	[stam]
ending	**agtervoegsel**	[aχtər·fuχsəl]
prefix	**voorvoegsel**	[foər·fuχsəl]
syllable	**lettergreep**	[lɛttər·χreəp]
suffix	**agtervoegsel, suffiks**	[aχtər·fuχsəl], [suffiks]

stress mark	klemteken	[klem·tekən]
apostrophe	afkappingsteken	[afkappiŋs·tekən]
period, dot	punt	[punt]
comma	komma	[komma]
semicolon	kommapunt	[komma·punt]

colon	dubbelpunt	[dubbəl·punt]
ellipsis	beletselteken	[beletsəl·tekən]

question mark	vraagteken	[frāχ·tekən]
exclamation point	uitroepteken	[œitrup·tekən]

quotation marks	aanhalingstekens	[ānhaliŋs·tekəns]
in quotation marks	tussen aanhalingstekens	[tussən ānhaliŋs·tekəns]

parenthesis	hakies	[hakis]
in parenthesis	tussen hakies	[tussən hakis]

hyphen	koppelteken	[koppəl·tekən]
dash	strepie	[strepi]
space (between words)	spasie	[spasi]

letter	letter	[lɛttər]
capital letter	hoofletter	[hoəf·lɛttər]

vowel (n)	klinker	[klinkər]
consonant (n)	konsonant	[kɔŋsonant]

sentence	sin	[sin]
subject	onderwerp	[ondərwerp]
predicate	predikaat	[predikāt]

line	reël	[reɛl]
paragraph	paragraaf	[paraχrāf]

word	woord	[voərt]
group of words	woordgroep	[voərt·χrup]
expression	uitdrukking	[œitdrukkiŋ]

synonym	sinoniem	[sinonim]
antonym	antoniem	[antonim]

rule	reël	[reɛl]
exception	uitsondering	[œitsondəriŋ]
correct (adj)	korrek	[korrek]

conjugation	vervoeging	[fərfuχiŋ]
declension	verbuiging	[ferbœəχiŋ]
nominal case	naamval	[nāmfal]
question	vraag	[frāχ]
to underline (vt)	onderstreep	[ondərstreəp]
dotted line	stippellyn	[stippəl·lajn]

146. Foreign languages

language	**taal**	[tāl]
foreign (adj)	**vreemd**	[freəmt]
foreign language	**vreemde taal**	[freəmdə tāl]
to study (vt)	**studeer**	[studeər]
to learn (language, etc.)	**leer**	[leər]

to read (vi, vt)	**lees**	[leəs]
to speak (vi, vt)	**praat**	[prāt]
to understand (vt)	**verstaan**	[ferstān]
to write (vt)	**skryf**	[skrajf]

fast (adv)	**vinnig**	[finnəχ]
slowly (adv)	**stadig**	[stadəχ]
fluently (adv)	**vlot**	[flot]

rules	**reëls**	[rɛɛls]
grammar	**grammatika**	[χrammatika]
vocabulary	**woordeskat**	[voərdeskat]
phonetics	**fonetika**	[fonetika]

textbook	**handboek**	[hand·buk]
dictionary	**woordeboek**	[voərdə·buk]
teach-yourself book	**selfstudie boek**	[sɛlfstudi buk]
phrasebook	**taalgids**	[tāl·χids]

cassette, tape	**kasset**	[kasset]
videotape	**videoband**	[video·bant]
CD, compact disc	**CD**	[se·de]
DVD	**DVD**	[de·fe·de]

alphabet	**alfabet**	[alfabet]
to spell (vt)	**spel**	[spel]
pronunciation	**uitspraak**	[œitsprāk]
accent	**aksent**	[aksent]

word	**woord**	[voərt]
meaning	**betekenis**	[betekənis]

course (e.g., a French ~)	**kursus**	[kursus]
to sign up	**inskryf**	[inskrajf]
teacher	**onderwyser**	[ondərwajsər]

translation (process)	**vertaling**	[fertaliŋ]
translation (text, etc.)	**vertaling**	[fertaliŋ]
translator	**vertaler**	[fertalər]
interpreter	**tolk**	[tolk]

polyglot	**poliglot**	[poliχlot]
memory	**geheue**	[χəhøə]

145

147. Fairy tale characters

Santa Claus	**Kersvader**	[kers·fadər]
Cinderella	**Assepoester**	[assepustər]
mermaid	**meermin**	[meərmin]
Neptune	**Neptunus**	[neptunus]
magician, wizard	**towenaar**	[tovenãr]
fairy	**feetjie**	[feəki]
magic (adj)	**magies**	[maχis]
magic wand	**towerstaf**	[tovər·staf]
fairy tale	**sprokie**	[sproki]
miracle	**wonderwerk**	[vondərwerk]
dwarf	**dwerg**	[dwerχ]
to turn into ...	**verander in ...**	[ferandər in ...]
ghost	**gees**	[χeəs]
phantom	**spook**	[spoək]
monster	**monster**	[mɔŋstər]
dragon	**draak**	[drãk]
giant	**reus**	[røəs]

148. Zodiac Signs

Aries	**Ram**	[ram]
Taurus	**Stier**	[stir]
Gemini	**Tweelinge**	[tweəliŋə]
Cancer	**Kreef**	[kreəf]
Leo	**Leeu**	[liʊ]
Virgo	**Maagd**	[mãχt]
Libra	**Weegskaal**	[veəχskãl]
Scorpio	**Skerpioen**	[skerpiun]
Sagittarius	**Boogskutter**	[boəχskuttər]
Capricorn	**Steenbok**	[steənbok]
Aquarius	**Waterman**	[vatərman]
Pisces	**Visse**	[fissə]
character	**karakter**	[karaktər]
character traits	**karaktertrekke**	[karaktər·trɛkkə]
behavior	**gedrag**	[χedraχ]
to tell fortunes	**waarsê**	[vãrsɛ:]
fortune-teller	**waarsêer**	[vãrsɛər]
horoscope	**horoskoop**	[horoskoəp]

Arts

149. Theater

theater	teater	[teatər]
opera	opera	[opera]
operetta	operette	[operɛttə]
ballet	ballet	[ballet]
theater poster	plakkaat	[plakkāt]
troupe	teatergeselskap	[teatər·xesɛlskap]
(theatrical company)		
tour	toer	[tur]
to be on tour	op toer wees	[op tur veəs]
to rehearse (vi, vt)	repeteer	[repeteər]
rehearsal	repetisie	[repetisi]
repertoire	repertoire	[repertuarə]
performance	voorstelling	[foərstɛllin]
theatrical show	opvoering	[opfurin]
play	toneelstuk	[toneəl·stuk]
ticket	kaartjie	[kārki]
box office (ticket booth)	loket	[lokət]
lobby, foyer	voorportaal	[foər·portāl]
coat check (cloakroom)	bewaarkamer	[bevār·kamər]
coat check tag	bewaarkamerkaartjie	[bevār·kamər·kārki]
binoculars	verkyker	[ferkajkər]
usher	plekaanwyser	[plek·ānwajsər]
orchestra seats	stalles	[stalles]
balcony	balkon	[balkon]
dress circle	eerste balkon	[eərstə balkon]
box	losie	[losi]
row	ry	[raj]
seat	sitplek	[sitplek]
audience	gehoor	[xehoər]
spectator	toehoorders	[tuhoərders]
to clap (vi, vt)	klap	[klap]
applause	applous	[applæʊs]
ovation	toejuiging	[tujœəχin]
stage	verhoog	[ferhoəχ]
curtain	gordyn	[χordajn]
scenery	dekor	[dekor]

backstage	agter die verhoog	[aχtər di ferhoəχ]
scene (e.g., the last ~)	toneel	[toneəl]
act	bedryf	[bedrajf]
intermission	pouse	[pæusə]

150. Cinema

| actor | akteur | [aktøər] |
| actress | aktrise | [aktrisə] |

movies (industry)	filmbedryf	[film·bedrajf]
movie	fliek	[flik]
episode	episode	[εpisodə]

detective movie	speurfliek	[spøər·flik]
action movie	aksiefliek	[aksi·flik]
adventure movie	avontuurfliek	[afontɪr·flik]
science fiction movie	wetenskapfiksiefilm	[vetεŋskapfiksi·film]
horror movie	gruwelfliek	[χruvεl·flik]

comedy movie	komedie	[komedi]
melodrama	melodrama	[melodrama]
drama	drama	[drama]

fictional movie	rolprent	[rolprent]
documentary	dokumentêre rolprent	[dokumentεrə rolprent]
cartoon	tekenfilm	[tekən·film]
silent movies	stilprent	[stil·prent]

role (part)	rol	[rol]
leading role	hoofrol	[hoəf·rol]
to play (vi, vt)	speel	[speəl]

movie star	filmster	[film·stər]
well-known (adj)	bekend	[bekent]
famous (adj)	beroemd	[berumt]
popular (adj)	gewild	[χevilt]

script (screenplay)	draaiboek	[drājbuk]
scriptwriter	draaiboekskrywer	[drājbuk·skrajvər]
movie director	filmregisseur	[film·reχissøər]
producer	produsent	[produsent]
assistant	assistent	[assistent]
cameraman	kameraman	[kameraman]
stuntman	waaghals	[vāχhals]
double (stuntman)	dubbel	[dubbəl]

audition, screen test	filmtoets	[film·tuts]
shooting	skiet	[skit]
movie crew	filmspan	[film·span]

| movie set | rolprentstel | [rolprent·stəl] |
| camera | kamera | [kamera] |

| movie theater | bioskoop | [bioskoəp] |
| screen (e.g., big ~) | skerm | [skerm] |

soundtrack	klankbaan	[klank·bān]
special effects	spesiale effekte	[spesialə ɛffektə]
subtitles	onderskrif	[ondərskrif]
credits	erkenning	[ɛrkɛnniŋ]
translation	vertaling	[fertaliŋ]

151. Painting

art	kuns	[kuns]
fine arts	skone kunste	[skonə kunstə]
art gallery	kunsgalery	[kuns·χaleraj]
art exhibition	kunsuitstalling	[kuns·œitstalliŋ]

painting (art)	skildery	[skilderaj]
graphic art	grafiese kuns	[χrafisə kuns]
abstract art	abstrakte kuns	[abstraktə kuns]
impressionism	impressionisme	[imprɛssionismə]

picture (painting)	skildery	[skilderaj]
drawing	tekening	[tekəniŋ]
poster	plakkaat	[plakkāt]

illustration (picture)	illustrasie	[illustrasi]
miniature	miniatuur	[miniatɪr]
copy (of painting, etc.)	kopie	[kopi]
reproduction	reproduksie	[reproduksi]

mosaic	mosaiek	[mosajek]
stained glass window	gebrandskilderde venster	[χebrandskilderdə fɛŋstər]
fresco	fresko	[fresko]
engraving	gravure	[χrafurə]

bust (sculpture)	borsbeeld	[borsbeəlt]
sculpture	beeldhouwerk	[beəldhæʊverk]
statue	standbeeld	[standbeəlt]
plaster of Paris	gips	[χips]
plaster (as adj)	gips-	[χips-]

portrait	portret	[portret]
self-portrait	selfportret	[sɛlf·portret]
landscape painting	landskap	[landskap]
still life	stillewe	[stillevə]
caricature	karikatuur	[karikatɪr]

sketch	skets	[skets]
paint	verf	[ferf]
watercolor paint	waterverf	[vatər·ferf]
oil (paint)	olieverf	[oli·ferf]
pencil	potlood	[potloət]
India ink	Indiese ink	[indisə ink]
charcoal	houtskool	[hæʊts·koəl]

| to draw (vi, vt) | teken | [tekən] |
| to paint (vi, vt) | skilder | [skildər] |

to pose (vi)	poseer	[poseər]
artist's model (masc.)	naakmodel	[nākmodəl]
artist's model (fem.)	naakmodel	[nākmodəl]

artist (painter)	kunstenaar	[kunstenār]
work of art	kunswerk	[kuns·werk]
masterpiece	meesterstuk	[meestər·stuk]
studio (artist's workroom)	studio	[studio]

canvas (cloth)	doek	[duk]
easel	skildersesel	[skilders·esəl]
palette	palet	[palet]

frame (picture ~, etc.)	raam	[rām]
restoration	restourasie	[restæʊrasi]
to restore (vt)	restoureer	[restæʊreər]

152. Literature & Poetry

literature	literatuur	[literatɪr]
author (writer)	skrywer	[skrajvər]
pseudonym	skuilnaam	[skœil·nām]

book	boek	[buk]
volume	deel	[deəl]
table of contents	inhoudsopgawe	[inhæʊds·opχavə]
page	bladsy	[bladsaj]
main character	hoofkarakter	[hoəf·karaktər]
autograph	outograaf	[æʊtoχrāf]

short story	kortverhaal	[kort·ferhāl]
story (novella)	novelle	[nofɛllə]
novel	roman	[roman]
work (writing)	werk	[verk]
fable	fabel	[fabəl]
detective novel	speurroman	[spøər·roman]

| poem (verse) | gedig | [χedəχ] |
| poetry | digkuns | [diχkuns] |

| poem (epic, ballad) | epos | [ɛpos] |
| poet | digter | [diχtər] |

fiction	fiksie	[fiksi]
science fiction	wetenskapsfiksie	[vetɛŋskaps·fiksi]
adventures	avonture	[afonturə]
educational literature	opvoedkundige literatuur	[opfutkundiχə literatɪr]
children's literature	kinderliteratuur	[kindər·literatɪr]

153. Circus

circus	sirkus	[sirkus]
traveling circus	rondreisende sirkus	[rondræjsendə sirkus]
program	program	[proχram]
performance	voorstelling	[foərstɛlliŋ]

| act (circus ~) | nommer | [nommər] |
| circus ring | sirkusring | [sirkus·riŋ] |

| pantomime (act) | pantomime | [pantomimə] |
| clown | hanswors | [haŋswors] |

acrobat	akrobaat	[akrobãt]
acrobatics	akrobatiek	[akrobatik]
gymnast	gimnas	[χimnas]
gymnastics	gimnastiek	[χimnastik]
somersault	salto	[salto]

athlete (strongman)	atleet	[atleet]
tamer (e.g., lion ~)	temmer	[tɛmmər]
rider (circus horse ~)	ruiter	[rœitər]
assistant	assistent	[assistent]

stunt	waaghalsige toertjie	[vãχhalsiχə turki]
magic trick	goëltoertjie	[χoɛl·turki]
conjurer, magician	goëlaar	[χoɛlãr]

juggler	jongleur	[jonχløər]
to juggle (vi, vt)	jongleer	[jonχleər]
animal trainer	dresseerder	[drɛsseer·dər]
animal training	dressering	[drɛsseriŋ]
to train (animals)	afrig	[afrəχ]

154. Music. Pop music

| music | musiek | [musik] |
| musician | musikant | [musikant] |

musical instrument	musiekinstrument	[musik·instrument]
to play ...	speel ...	[speəl ...]
guitar	kitaar	[kitãr]
violin	viool	[fioəl]
cello	tjello	[ʧello]
double bass	kontrabas	[kontrabas]
harp	harp	[harp]
piano	piano	[piano]
grand piano	vleuelklavier	[fløɛl·klafir]
organ	orrel	[orrəl]
wind instruments	blaasinstrumente	[blãs·instrumentə]
oboe	hobo	[hobo]
saxophone	saksofoon	[saksofoən]
clarinet	klarinet	[klarinet]
flute	dwarsfluit	[dwars·flœit]
trumpet	trompet	[trompet]
accordion	trekklavier	[trɛkklafir]
drum	trommel	[tromməl]
duo	duet	[duet]
trio	trio	[trio]
quartet	kwartet	[kwartet]
choir	koor	[koər]
orchestra	orkes	[orkes]
pop music	popmusiek	[pop·musik]
rock music	rockmusiek	[rok·musik]
rock group	rockgroep	[rok·χrup]
jazz	jazz	[jazz]
idol	held	[hɛlt]
admirer, fan	bewonderaar	[bevondərãr]
concert	konsert	[kɔnsert]
symphony	simfonie	[simfoni]
composition	komposisie	[komposisi]
to compose (write)	komponeer	[komponeər]
singing (n)	sang	[saŋ]
song	lied	[lit]
tune (melody)	wysie	[vajsi]
rhythm	ritme	[ritmə]
blues	blues	[blues]
sheet music	bladmusiek	[blad·musik]
baton	dirigeerstok	[diriχeər·stok]
bow	strykstok	[strajk·stok]
string	snaar	[snãr]
case (e.g., guitar ~)	houer	[hæuər]

Rest. Entertainment. Travel

155. Trip. Travel

tourism, travel	toerisme	[turismə]
tourist	toeris	[turis]
trip, voyage	reis	[ræjs]
adventure	avontuur	[afontɪr]
trip, journey	reis	[ræjs]
vacation	vakansie	[fakaŋsi]
to be on vacation	met vakansie wees	[met fakaŋsi veəs]
rest	rus	[rus]
train	trein	[træjn]
by train	per trein	[pər træjn]
airplane	vliegtuig	[fliχtœiχ]
by airplane	per vliegtuig	[pər fliχtœiχ]
by car	per motor	[pər motor]
by ship	per skip	[pər skip]
luggage	bagasie	[baχasi]
suitcase	tas	[tas]
luggage cart	bagasiekarretjie	[baχasi·karrəki]
passport	paspoort	[paspoərt]
visa	visum	[fisum]
ticket	kaartjie	[kārki]
air ticket	lugkaartjie	[luχ·kārki]
guidebook	reisgids	[ræjsχids]
map (tourist ~)	kaart	[kārt]
area (rural ~)	gebied	[χebit]
place, site	plek	[plek]
exotica (n)	eksotiese dinge	[ɛksotisə diŋə]
exotic (adj)	eksoties	[ɛksotis]
amazing (adj)	verbasend	[ferbasent]
group	groep	[χrup]
excursion, sightseeing tour	uitstappie	[œitstappi]
guide (person)	gids	[χids]

156. Hotel

hotel	**hotel**	[hotəl]
motel	**motel**	[motəl]
three-star (~ hotel)	**drie-ster**	[dri-stər]
five-star	**vyf-ster**	[fajf-stər]
to stay (in a hotel, etc.)	**oornag**	[oərnaχ]
room	**kamer**	[kamər]
single room	**enkelkamer**	[ɛnkəl·kamər]
double room	**dubbelkamer**	[dubbəl·kamər]
half board	**met aandete, bed en ontbyt**	[met āndetə], [bet en ontbajt]
full board	**volle losies**	[follə losis]
with bath	**met bad**	[met bat]
with shower	**met stortbad**	[met stort·bat]
satellite television	**satelliet-TV**	[satɛllit-te·fe]
air-conditioner	**lugversorger**	[luχfersorχər]
towel	**handdoek**	[handduk]
key	**sleutel**	[sløətəl]
administrator	**bestuurder**	[bestɪrdər]
chambermaid	**kamermeisie**	[kamər·mæjsi]
porter, bellboy	**hoteljoggie**	[hotəl·joχi]
doorman	**portier**	[portir]
restaurant	**restaurant**	[restɔurant]
pub, bar	**kroeg**	[kruχ]
breakfast	**ontbyt**	[ontbajt]
dinner	**aandete**	[āndetə]
buffet	**buffetete**	[buffetetə]
lobby	**voorportaal**	[foər·portāl]
elevator	**hysbak**	[hajsbak]
DO NOT DISTURB	**MOENIE STEUR NIE**	[muni støər ni]
NO SMOKING	**ROOK VERBODE**	[roək ferbodə]

157. Books. Reading

book	**boek**	[buk]
author	**outeur**	[æutøər]
writer	**skrywer**	[skrajvər]
to write (~ a book)	**skryf**	[skrajf]
reader	**leser**	[lesər]
to read (vi, vt)	**lees**	[leəs]

reading (activity)	lees	[lees]
silently (to oneself)	stil	[stil]
aloud (adv)	hardop	[hardop]

to publish (vt)	uitgee	[œitχee]
publishing (process)	uitgee	[œitχee]
publisher	uitgewer	[œitχevər]
publishing house	uitgewery	[œitχeverəj]

to come out (be released)	verskyn	[ferskajn]
release (of a book)	verskyn	[ferskajn]
print run	oplaag	[oplāχ]

| bookstore | boekhandel | [buk·handəl] |
| library | biblioteek | [biblioteək] |

story (novella)	novelle	[nofɛllə]
short story	kortverhaal	[kort·ferhāl]
novel	roman	[roman]
detective novel	speurroman	[spøər·roman]

memoirs	memoires	[memuares]
legend	legende	[leχendə]
myth	mite	[mitə]

poetry, poems	poësie	[poɛsi]
autobiography	outobiografie	[æʊtobioχrafi]
selected works	bloemlesing	[blumlesiŋ]
science fiction	wetenskapsfiksie	[vetɛŋskaps·fiksi]

title	titel	[titel]
introduction	inleiding	[inlæjdiŋ]
title page	titelblad	[titel·blat]

chapter	hoofstuk	[hoəfstuk]
extract	fragment	[fraχment]
episode	episode	[ɛpisodə]

plot (storyline)	plot	[plot]
contents	inhoud	[inhæʊt]
table of contents	inhoudsopgawe	[inhæʊds·opχavə]
main character	hoofkarakter	[hoəf·karaktər]

volume	deel	[deəl]
cover	omslag	[omslaχ]
binding	band	[bant]
bookmark	bladwyser	[blat·vajsər]
page	bladsy	[bladsaj]
to page through	deurblaai	[døərblāi]
margins	marges	[marχəs]
annotation	annotasie	[annotasi]
(marginal note, etc.)		

footnote	voetnota	[fut·nota]
text	teks	[teks]
type, font	lettertipe	[lɛttər·tipə]
misprint, typo	drukfout	[druk·fæʊt]

translation	vertaling	[fertaliŋ]
to translate (vt)	vertaal	[fertãl]
original (n)	oorspronklike	[oərspronklikə]

famous (adj)	beroemd	[berumt]
unknown (not famous)	onbekend	[onbekent]
interesting (adj)	interessante	[interessantə]
bestseller	blitsverkoper	[blits·ferkopər]

dictionary	woordeboek	[voərdə·buk]
textbook	handboek	[hand·buk]
encyclopedia	ensiklopedie	[ɛŋsiklopedi]

158. Hunting. Fishing

hunting	jag	[jaχ]
to hunt (vi, vt)	jag	[jaχ]
hunter	jagter	[jaχtər]

to shoot (vi)	skiet	[skit]
rifle	geweer	[χeveər]
bullet (shell)	patroon	[patroən]
shot (lead balls)	hael	[haəl]

steel trap	slagyster	[slaχ·ajstər]
snare (for birds, etc.)	valstrik	[falstrik]
to fall into the steel trap	in die valstrik trap	[in di falstrik trap]
to lay a steel trap	n valstrik lê	[ə falstrik lɛ:]

poacher	wildstroper	[vilt·stropər]
game (in hunting)	wild	[vilt]
hound dog	jaghond	[jaχ·hont]

| safari | safari | [safari] |
| mounted animal | opgestopte dier | [opχestoptə dir] |

fisherman, angler	visterman	[fisterman]
fishing (angling)	vis vang	[fis faŋ]
to fish (vi)	vis vang	[fis faŋ]

fishing rod	visstok	[fis·stok]
fishing line	vislyn	[fis·lajn]
hook	vishoek	[fis·huk]
float, bobber	vlotter	[flottər]
bait	aas	[ãs]

to cast a line	lyngooi	[lajnχoj]
to bite (ab. fish)	byt	[bajt]
catch (of fish)	vang	[faŋ]
ice-hole	gat in die ys	[χat in di ajs]

| fishing net | visnet | [fis·net] |
| boat | boot | [boət] |

to cast[throw] the net	die net gooi	[di net χoj]
to haul the net in	die net intrek	[di net intrek]
to fall into the net	in die net val	[in di net fal]

whaler (person)	walvisvanger	[valfis·vaŋər]
whaleboat	walvisboot	[valfis·boət]
harpoon	harpoen	[harpun]

159. Games. Billiards

billiards	biljart	[biljart]
billiard room, hall	biljartkamer	[biljart·kamər]
ball (snooker, etc.)	bal	[bal]

| cue | biljartstok | [biljart·stok] |
| pocket | sakkie | [sakki] |

160. Games. Playing cards

diamonds	diamante	[diamantə]
spades	skoppens	[skoppɛns]
hearts	harte	[hartə]
clubs	klawers	[klavərs]

ace	aas	[ās]
king	koning	[koniŋ]
queen	dame	[damə]
jack, knave	boer	[bur]

| playing card | speelkaart | [speəl·kārt] |
| cards | kaarte | [kārtə] |

| trump | troefkaart | [truf·kārt] |
| deck of cards | pak kaarte | [pak kārtə] |

point	punt	[punt]
to deal (vi, vt)	uitdeel	[œitdeəl]
to shuffle (cards)	skommel	[skomməl]
lead, turn (n)	beurt	[bøərt]
cardsharp	valsspeler	[fals·spelər]

161. Casino. Roulette

casino	**kasino**	[kasino]
roulette (game)	**roulette**	[ræʊlɛt]
bet	**inset**	[inset]
to place bets	**wed**	[vet]

red	**rooi**	[roj]
black	**swart**	[swart]
to bet on red	**wed op rooi**	[vet op roj]
to bet on black	**wed op swart**	[vet op swart]

croupier (dealer)	**kroepier**	[krupir]
to spin the wheel	**die wiel draai**	[di vil drāi]
rules (of game)	**reëls**	[reɛls]
chip	**tjip**	[tʃip]

to win (vi, vt)	**wen**	[ven]
win (winnings)	**wins**	[vins]

to lose (~ 100 dollars)	**verloor**	[ferloər]
loss (losses)	**verlies**	[ferlis]

player	**speler**	[spelər]
blackjack (card game)	**blackjack**	[blɛk dʒɛk]
craps (dice game)	**dobbelspel**	[dobbəl·spəl]
dice (a pair of ~)	**dobbelsteen**	[dobbəl·steən]
slot machine	**muntoutomaat**	[munt·æʊtomāt]

162. Rest. Games. Miscellaneous

to stroll (vi, vt)	**wandel**	[vandəl]
stroll (leisurely walk)	**wandeling**	[vandəliŋ]
car ride	**motorrit**	[motor·rit]
adventure	**avontuur**	[afontɪr]
picnic	**piekniek**	[piknik]

game (chess, etc.)	**spel**	[spel]
player	**speler**	[spelər]
game (one ~ of chess)	**spel**	[spel]

collector (e.g., philatelist)	**versamelaar**	[fersamelār]
to collect (stamps, etc.)	**versamel**	[fersaməl]
collection	**versameling**	[fersameliŋ]

crossword puzzle	**blokkiesraaisel**	[blokkis·rāisəl]
racetrack	**perderesiesbaan**	[perdə·resisbān]
(horse racing venue)		
disco (discotheque)	**disko**	[disko]

sauna	sauna	[sɔuna]
lottery	lotery	[loteraj]

camping trip	kampeeruitstappie	[kampeǝr·ajtstappi]
camp	kamp	[kamp]
tent (for camping)	tent	[tɛnt]
compass	kompas	[kompas]
camper	kampeerder	[kampeǝrdǝr]

to watch (movie, etc.)	kyk	[kajk]
viewer	kyker	[kajkǝr]
TV show (TV program)	TV-program	[te·fe-proxram]

163. Photography

camera (photo)	kamera	[kamera]
photo, picture	foto	[foto]

photographer	fotograaf	[fotoxrãf]
photo studio	fotostudio	[foto·studio]
photo album	fotoalbum	[foto·album]

camera lens	kameralens	[kamera·lɛŋs]
telephoto lens	telefotolens	[telefoto·lɛŋs]
filter	filter	[filtǝr]
lens	lens	[lɛŋs]

optics (high-quality ~)	optiek	[optik]
diaphragm (aperture)	diafragma	[diafraxma]
exposure time (shutter speed)	beligtingstyd	[belixtiŋs·tajt]
viewfinder	soeker	[sukǝr]

digital camera	digitale kamera	[dixitalǝ kamera]
tripod	driepoot	[dripoǝt]
flash	flits	[flits]

to photograph (vt)	fotografeer	[fotoxrafeǝr]
to take pictures	fotografeer	[fotoxrafeǝr]
to have one's picture taken	jou portret laat maak	[jæʊ portret lãt mãk]

focus	fokus	[fokus]
to focus	fokus	[fokus]
sharp, in focus (adj)	skerp	[skerp]
sharpness	skerpheid	[skerphæjt]

contrast	kontras	[kontras]
contrast (as adj)	kontrasryk	[kontrasrajk]
picture (photo)	kiekie	[kiki]
negative (n)	negatief	[nexatif]

film (a roll of ~)	**rolfilm**	[rolfilm]
frame (still)	**raampie**	[rāmpi]
to print (photos)	**druk**	[druk]

164. Beach. Swimming

beach	**strand**	[strant]
sand	**sand**	[sant]
deserted (beach)	**verlate**	[ferlatə]

suntan	**sonbruin kleur**	[sonbrœin kløər]
to get a tan	**bruinbrand**	[brœinbrant]
tan (adj)	**bruingebrand**	[brœiŋəbrant]
sunscreen	**sonskermroom**	[sɔŋ·skerm·roəm]

bikini	**bikini**	[bikini]
bathing suit	**baaikostuum**	[bāj·kostɪm]
swim trunks	**baaibroek**	[bāj·bruk]

swimming pool	**swembad**	[swem·bat]
to swim (vi)	**swem**	[swem]
shower	**stort**	[stort]
to change (one's clothes)	**verklee**	[ferkleə]
towel	**handdoek**	[handduk]

| boat | **boot** | [boət] |
| motorboat | **motorboot** | [motor·boət] |

water ski	**waterski**	[vatər·ski]
paddle boat	**waterfiets**	[vatər·fits]
surfing	**branderplankry**	[brandərplank·raj]
surfer	**branderplankryer**	[brandərplank·rajer]

scuba set	**duiklong**	[dœiklɔŋ]
flippers (swim fins)	**paddavoet**	[padda·fut]
mask (diving ~)	**duikmasker**	[dœik·maskər]
diver	**duiker**	[dœikər]
to dive (vi)	**duik**	[dœik]
underwater (adv)	**onder water**	[ondər vatər]

beach umbrella	**strandsambreel**	[strand·sambreəl]
sunbed (lounger)	**strandstoel**	[strand·stul]
sunglasses	**sonbril**	[son·bril]
air mattress	**opblaasmatras**	[opblās·matras]

| to play (amuse oneself) | **speel** | [speəl] |
| to go for a swim | **gaan swem** | [χān swem] |

| beach ball | **strandbal** | [strand·bal] |
| to inflate (vt) | **opblaas** | [opblās] |

inflatable, air (adj)	**opblaas-**	[opblãs-]
wave	**golf**	[χolf]
buoy (line of ~s)	**boei**	[bui]
to drown (ab. person)	**verdrink**	[ferdrink]

to save, to rescue	**red**	[ret]
life vest	**reddingsbaadjie**	[rɛddiŋs·bādʒi]
to observe, to watch	**dophou**	[dophæʊ]
lifeguard	**lewensredder**	[levɛŋs·rɛddər]

TECHNICAL EQUIPMENT. TRANSPORTATION

Technical equipment

165. Computer

computer	rekenaar	[rekənār]
notebook, laptop	skootrekenaar	[skoət·rekənār]
to turn on	aanskakel	[āŋskakəl]
to turn off	afskakel	[afskakəl]
keyboard	toetsbord	[tuts·bort]
key	toets	[tuts]
mouse	muis	[mœis]
mouse pad	muismatjie	[mœis·maki]
button	knop	[knop]
cursor	loper	[lopər]
monitor	monitor	[monitor]
screen	skerm	[skerm]
hard disk	harde skyf	[hardə skajf]
hard disk capacity	harde skyf se vermoë	[hardə skajf sə fermoɛ]
memory	geheue	[χəhøəə]
random access memory	RAM-geheue	[ram-χehøəə]
file	lêer	[lɛər]
folder	gids	[χids]
to open (vt)	oopmaak	[oəpmāk]
to close (vt)	sluit	[slœit]
to save (vt)	bewaar	[bevār]
to delete (vt)	uitvee	[œitfeə]
to copy (vt)	kopieer	[kopir]
to sort (vt)	sorteer	[sorteər]
to transfer (copy)	oorplaas	[oərplās]
program	program	[proχram]
software	sagteware	[saχtevarə]
programmer	programmeur	[proχrammøər]
to program (vt)	programmeer	[proχrammeər]
hacker	kuberkraker	[kubər·krakər]
password	wagwoord	[vaχ·woərt]

| virus | virus | [firus] |
| to find, to detect | opspoor | [opspoər] |

| byte | greep | [χreəp] |
| megabyte | megagreep | [meχaχreəp] |

| data | data | [data] |
| database | databasis | [data·basis] |

cable (USB, etc.)	kabel	[kabəl]
to disconnect (vt)	ontkoppel	[ontkoppəl]
to connect (sth to sth)	konnekteer	[konnekteər]

166. Internet. E-mail

Internet	internet	[internet]
browser	webblaaier	[veb·blājer]
search engine	soekenjin	[suk·εnʤin]
provider	verskaffer	[ferskaffər]

webmaster	webmeester	[veb·meəstər]
website	webwerf	[veb·werf]
webpage	webblad	[veb·blat]

| address (e-mail ~) | adres | [adres] |
| address book | adresboek | [adres·buk] |

mailbox	posbus	[pos·bus]
mail	pos	[pos]
full (adj)	vol	[fol]

message	boodskap	[boədskap]
incoming messages	inkomende boodskappe	[inkomendə boədskappə]
outgoing messages	uitgaande boodskappe	[œitχānde boədskappə]

sender	sender	[sendər]
to send (vt)	verstuur	[ferstɪr]
sending (of mail)	versending	[fersendiŋ]

| receiver | ontvanger | [ontfaŋər] |
| to receive (vt) | ontvang | [ontfaŋ] |

| correspondence | korrespondensie | [korrespondεŋsi] |
| to correspond (vi) | korrespondeer | [korrespondeər] |

file	lêer	[lεər]
to download (vt)	aflaai	[aflāi]
to create (vt)	skep	[skep]
to delete (vt)	uitvee	[œitfeə]
deleted (adj)	uitgevee	[œitχefeə]

connection (ADSL, etc.)	konneksie	[konneksi]
speed	spoed	[sput]
modem	modem	[modem]
access	toegang	[tuχaŋ]
port (e.g., input ~)	portaal	[portāl]

| connection (make a ~) | aansluiting | [āŋslœitiŋ] |
| to connect to ... (vi) | aansluit by ... | [āŋslœit baj ...] |

| to select (vt) | kies | [kis] |
| to search (for ...) | soek | [suk] |

167. Electricity

electricity	elektrisiteit	[εlektrisitæjt]
electric, electrical (adj)	elektries	[εlektris]
electric power plant	kragstasie	[kraχ·stasi]
energy	krag	[kraχ]
electric power	elektriese krag	[εlektrisə kraχ]

light bulb	gloeilamp	[χlui·lamp]
flashlight	flits	[flits]
street light	straatlig	[strātləχ]

light	lig	[liχ]
to turn on	aanskakel	[āŋskakəl]
to turn off	afskakel	[afskakəl]
to turn off the light	die lig afskakel	[di liχ afskakəl]

to burn out (vi)	doodbrand	[doədbrant]
short circuit	kortsluiting	[kort·slœitiŋ]
broken wire	gebreekte kabel	[χebreəktə kabəl]
contact (electrical ~)	kontak	[kontak]

light switch	ligskakelaar	[liχ·skakelār]
wall socket	muurprop	[mɪrprop]
plug	prop	[prop]
extension cord	verlengkabel	[ferleŋ·kabəl]

fuse	sekering	[sekəriŋ]
cable, wire	kabel	[kabəl]
wiring	bedrading	[bedradiŋ]

ampere	ampère	[ampɛ:r]
amperage	stroomsterkte	[stroəm·sterktə]
volt	volt	[folt]
voltage	spanning	[spanniŋ]

| electrical device | elektriese toestel | [εlektrisə tustəl] |
| indicator | aanduier | [āndœiər] |

electrician	elektrisiën	[ɛlektrisiɛn]
to solder (vt)	soldeer	[soldeər]
soldering iron	soldeerbout	[soldeər·bæʊt]
electric current	elektriese stroom	[ɛlektrisə stroəm]

168. Tools

tool, instrument	werktuig	[verktœiχ]
tools	gereedskap	[χereədskap]
equipment (factory ~)	toerusting	[turustiŋ]

hammer	hamer	[hamər]
screwdriver	skroewedraaier	[skruvə·drājer]
ax	byl	[bajl]

saw	saag	[sāχ]
to saw (vt)	saag	[sāχ]
plane (tool)	skaaf	[skāf]
to plane (vt)	skaaf	[skāf]
soldering iron	soldeerbout	[soldeər·bæʊt]
to solder (vt)	soldeer	[soldeər]

file (tool)	vyl	[fajl]
carpenter pincers	knyptang	[knajptaŋ]
lineman's pliers	tang	[taŋ]
chisel	beitel	[bæjtəl]

drill bit	boor	[boər]
electric drill	elektriese boor	[ɛlektrisə boər]
to drill (vi, vt)	boor	[boər]

knife	mes	[mes]
pocket knife	sakmes	[sakmes]
blade	lem	[lem]

sharp (blade, etc.)	skerp	[skerp]
dull, blunt (adj)	stomp	[stomp]
to get blunt (dull)	stomp raak	[stomp rāk]
to sharpen (vt)	slyp	[slajp]

bolt	bout	[bæʊt]
nut	moer	[mur]
thread (of a screw)	draad	[drāt]
wood screw	houtskroef	[hæʊt·skruf]

| nail | spyker | [spajkər] |
| nailhead | kop | [kop] |

| ruler (for measuring) | meetlat | [meətlat] |
| tape measure | meetband | [meət·bant] |

spirit level	**waterpas**	[vatərpas]
magnifying glass	**vergrootglas**	[ferχroət·χlas]
measuring instrument	**meetinstrument**	[meət·instrument]
to measure (vt)	**meet**	[meət]
scale	**skaal**	[skãl]
(of thermometer, etc.)		
readings	**lesings**	[lesiŋs]
compressor	**kompressor**	[komprɛssor]
microscope	**mikroskoop**	[mikroskoəp]
pump (e.g., water ~)	**pomp**	[pomp]
robot	**robot**	[robot]
laser	**laser**	[lasər]
wrench	**moersleutel**	[mur·sløətəl]
adhesive tape	**plakband**	[plak·bant]
glue	**gom**	[χom]
sandpaper	**skuurpapier**	[skɪr·papir]
spring	**veer**	[feər]
magnet	**magneet**	[maχneət]
gloves	**handskoene**	[handskunə]
rope	**tou**	[tæʊ]
cord	**tou**	[tæʊ]
wire (e.g., telephone ~)	**draad**	[drãt]
cable	**kabel**	[kabəl]
sledgehammer	**voorhamer**	[foər·hamər]
prybar	**breekyster**	[breəkajstər]
ladder	**leer**	[leər]
stepladder	**trapleer**	[trapleər]
to screw (tighten)	**vasskroef**	[fasskruf]
to unscrew (lid, filter, etc.)	**losskroef**	[losskruf]
to tighten	**saampars**	[sãmpars]
(e.g., with a clamp)		
to glue, to stick	**vasplak**	[fasplak]
to cut (vt)	**sny**	[snaj]
malfunction (fault)	**fout**	[fæʊt]
repair (mending)	**herstelwerk**	[herstəl·werk]
to repair, to fix (vt)	**herstel**	[herstəl]
to adjust (machine, etc.)	**stel**	[stəl]
to check (to examine)	**nagaan**	[naχãn]
checking	**kontrole**	[kontrolə]
readings	**lesings**	[lesiŋs]
reliable, solid (machine)	**betroubaar**	[betræʊbãr]
complex (adj)	**ingewikkelde**	[inχəwikkɛldə]

to rust (get rusted)	**roes**	[rus]
rusty, rusted (adj)	**verroes**	[ferrus]
rust	**roes**	[rus]

Transportation

169. Airplane

airplane	vliegtuig	[fliχtœiχ]
air ticket	lugkaartjie	[luχ·kārki]
airline	lugredery	[luχrederaj]
airport	lughawe	[luχhavə]
supersonic (adj)	supersonies	[supersonis]
captain	kaptein	[kaptæjn]
crew	bemanning	[bemanniŋ]
pilot	piloot	[piloət]
flight attendant (fem.)	lugwaardin	[luχ·wārdin]
navigator	navigator	[nafiχator]
wings	vlerke	[flerkə]
tail	stert	[stert]
cockpit	stuurkajuit	[stɪr·kajœit]
engine	enjin	[ɛnʤin]
undercarriage (landing gear)	landingstel	[landiŋ·stəl]
turbine	turbine	[turbinə]
propeller	skroef	[skruf]
black box	swart boks	[swart boks]
yoke (control column)	stuurstang	[stɪr·staŋ]
fuel	brandstof	[brantstof]
safety card	veiligheidskaart	[fæjliχæjts·kārt]
oxygen mask	suurstofmasker	[sɪrstof·maskər]
uniform	uniform	[uniform]
life vest	reddingsbaadjie	[rɛddiŋs·bāʤi]
parachute	valskerm	[fal·skerm]
takeoff	opstyging	[opstajχiŋ]
to take off (vi)	opstyg	[opstajχ]
runway	landingsbaan	[landiŋs·bān]
visibility	uitsig	[œitsəχ]
flight (act of flying)	vlug	[fluχ]
altitude	hoogte	[hoəχtə]
air pocket	lugsak	[luχsak]
seat	sitplek	[sitplek]
headphones	koptelefoon	[kop·telefoən]

folding tray (tray table)	voutafeltjie	[fæʊ·tafɛlki]
airplane window	vliegtuigvenster	[fliҳtœiҳ·fɛŋstər]
aisle	paadjie	[pādʒi]

170. Train

train	trein	[træjn]
commuter train	voorstedelike trein	[foərstedelikə træjn]
express train	sneltrein	[snɛl·træjn]
diesel locomotive	diesellokomotief	[disəl·lokomotif]
steam locomotive	stoomlokomotief	[stoəm·lokomotif]
passenger car	passasierswa	[passasirs·wa]
dining car	eetwa	[eət·wa]
rails	spoorstawe	[spoər·stavə]
railroad	spoorweg	[spoər·weҳ]
railway tie	dwarslêer	[dwarslɛer]
platform (railway ~)	perron	[perron]
track (~ 1, 2, etc.)	spoor	[spoər]
semaphore	semafoor	[semafoər]
station	stasie	[stasi]
engineer (train driver)	treindrywer	[træjn·drajvər]
porter (of luggage)	portier	[portir]
car attendant	kondukteur	[konduktøər]
passenger	passasier	[passasir]
conductor	kondukteur	[konduktøər]
(ticket inspector)		
corridor (in train)	gang	[ҳaŋ]
emergency brake	noodrem	[noədrem]
compartment	kompartiment	[kompartiment]
berth	bed	[bet]
upper berth	boonste bed	[boəŋstə bet]
lower berth	onderste bed	[ondərstə bet]
bed linen, bedding	beddegoed	[beddə·ҳut]
ticket	kaartjie	[kārki]
schedule	diensrooster	[diŋs·roəstər]
information display	informasiebord	[informasi·bort]
to leave, to depart	vertrek	[fertrek]
departure (of train)	vertrek	[fertrek]
to arrive (ab. train)	aankom	[āŋkom]
arrival	aankoms	[āŋkoms]
to arrive by train	aankom per trein	[āŋkom pər træjn]
to get on the train	in die trein klim	[in di træjn klim]

to get off the train	uit die trein klim	[œit di træjn klim]
train wreck	treinbotsing	[træjn·botsiŋ]
to derail (vi)	ontspoor	[ontspoər]

steam locomotive	stoomlokomotief	[stoəm·lokomotif]
stoker, fireman	stoker	[stokər]
firebox	stookplek	[stoəkplek]
coal	steenkool	[steən·koəl]

171. Ship

| ship | skip | [skip] |
| vessel | vaartuig | [fārtœiχ] |

steamship	stoomboot	[stoəm·boət]
riverboat	rivierboot	[rifir·boət]
cruise ship	toerskip	[tur·skip]
cruiser	kruiser	[krœisər]

yacht	jag	[jaχ]
tugboat	sleepboot	[sleəp·boət]
barge	vragskuit	[fraχ·skœit]
ferry	veerboot	[feər·boət]

| sailing ship | seilskip | [sæjl·skip] |
| brigantine | skoenerbrik | [skunər·brik] |

| ice breaker | ysbreker | [ajs·brekər] |
| submarine | duikboot | [dœik·boət] |

boat (flat-bottomed ~)	roeiboot	[ruiboət]
dinghy	bootjie	[boəki]
lifeboat	reddingsboot	[rɛddiŋs·boət]
motorboat	motorboot	[motor·boət]

captain	kaptein	[kaptæjn]
seaman	seeman	[seəman]
sailor	matroos	[matroəs]
crew	bemanning	[bemanniŋ]

boatswain	bootsman	[boətsman]
ship's boy	skeepsjonge	[skeəps·joŋə]
cook	kok	[kok]
ship's doctor	skeepsdokter	[skeəps·doktər]

deck	dek	[dek]
mast	mas	[mas]
sail	seil	[sæjl]
hold	skeepsruim	[skeəps·rœim]
bow (prow)	boeg	[buχ]

stern	agterstewe	[aχtərstevə]
oar	roeispaan	[ruis·pān]
screw propeller	skroef	[skruf]

cabin	kajuit	[kajœit]
wardroom	offisierskajuit	[offisirs·kajœit]
engine room	enjinkamer	[ɛndʒin·kamər]
bridge	brug	[bruχ]
radio room	radiokamer	[radio·kamər]

| wave (radio) | golf | [χolf] |
| logbook | logboek | [loχbuk] |

spyglass	verkyker	[ferkajkər]
bell	bel	[bəl]
flag	vlag	[flaχ]

| hawser (mooring ~) | kabel | [kabəl] |
| knot (bowline, etc.) | knoop | [knoəp] |

| deckrails | dekleuning | [dek·løənin] |
| gangway | gangplank | [χaŋ·plank] |

| anchor | anker | [ankər] |
| to weigh anchor | anker lig | [ankər ləχ] |

| to drop anchor | anker uitgooi | [ankər œitχoj] |
| anchor chain | ankerketting | [ankər·kɛttiŋ] |

| port (harbor) | hawe | [havə] |
| quay, wharf | kaai | [kāi] |

| to berth (moor) | vasmeer | [fasmeər] |
| to cast off | vertrek | [fertrek] |

| trip, voyage | reis | [ræjs] |
| cruise (sea trip) | cruise | [kru:s] |

| course (route) | koers | [kurs] |
| route (itinerary) | roete | [rutə] |

fairway (safe water channel)	vaarwater	[fār·vatər]
shallows	sandbank	[sand·bank]
to run aground	strand	[strant]

storm	storm	[storm]
signal	sienjaal	[sinjāl]
to sink (vi)	sink	[sink]
Man overboard!	Man oorboord!	[man oərboərd!]
SOS (distress signal)	SOS	[sos]
ring buoy	reddingsboei	[rɛddiŋs·bui]

172. Airport

airport	lughawe	[luχhavə]
airplane	vliegtuig	[fliχtœiχ]
airline	lugredery	[luχrederaj]
air traffic controller	lugverkeersleier	[luχ·ferkeərs·læjer]

departure	vertrek	[fertrek]
arrival	aankoms	[ānkoms]
to arrive (by plane)	aankom	[ānkom]

| departure time | vertrektyd | [fertrək·tajt] |
| arrival time | aankomstyd | [ānkoms·tajt] |

| to be delayed | vertraag wees | [fertrāχ veəs] |
| flight delay | vlugvertraging | [fluχ·fertraχiŋ] |

information board	informasiebord	[informasi·bort]
information	informasie	[informasi]
to announce (vt)	aankondig	[ānkondəχ]
flight (e.g., next ~)	vlug	[fluχ]

| customs | doeane | [duanə] |
| customs officer | doeanebeampte | [duanə·beamptə] |

customs declaration	doeaneverklaring	[duanə·ferklariŋ]
to fill out (vt)	invul	[inful]
passport control	paspoortkontrole	[paspoərt·kontrolə]

luggage	bagasie	[baχasi]
hand luggage	handbagasie	[hand·baχasi]
luggage cart	bagasiekarretjie	[baχasi·karrəki]

landing	landing	[landiŋ]
landing strip	landingsbaan	[landiŋs·bān]
to land (vi)	land	[lant]
airstairs	vliegtuigtrap	[fliχtœiχ·trap]

check-in	na die vertrektoonbank	[na di fertrək·toənbank]
check-in counter	vertrektoonbank	[fertrək·toənbank]
to check-in (vi)	na die vertrektoonbank gaan	[na di fertrək·toənbank χān]

| boarding pass | instapkaart | [instap·kārt] |
| departure gate | vertrekuitgang | [fertrek·œitχaŋ] |

transit	transito	[traŋsito]
to wait (vt)	wag	[vaχ]
departure lounge	vertreksaal	[fertrək·sāl]
to see off	afsien	[afsin]
to say goodbye	afskeid neem	[afskæjt neəm]

173. Bicycle. Motorcycle

bicycle	**fiets**	[fits]
scooter	**bromponie**	[bromponi]
motorcycle, bike	**motorfiets**	[motorfits]
to go by bicycle	**per fiets ry**	[pər fits raj]
handlebars	**stuurstang**	[stɪr·staŋ]
pedal	**pedaal**	[pedāl]
brakes	**remme**	[remmə]
bicycle seat (saddle)	**fietssaal**	[fits·sāl]
pump	**pomp**	[pomp]
luggage rack	**bagasierak**	[baχasi·rak]
front lamp	**fietslamp**	[fits·lamp]
helmet	**helmet**	[hɛlmet]
wheel	**wiel**	[vil]
fender	**modderskerm**	[moddər·skerm]
rim	**velling**	[fɛlliŋ]
spoke	**speek**	[speək]

Cars

174. Types of cars

automobile, car	**motor**	[motor]
sports car	**sportmotor**	[sport·motor]
limousine	**limousine**	[limæʊsinə]
off-road vehicle	**veldvoertuig**	[fɛlt·furtœix]
convertible (n)	**met afslaandak**	[met afslãndak]
minibus	**bussie**	[bussi]
ambulance	**ambulans**	[ambulaŋs]
snowplow	**sneeuploeg**	[sniʊ·pluχ]
truck	**vragmotor**	[fraχ·motor]
tanker truck	**tenkwa**	[tɛnk·wa]
van (small truck)	**bestelwa**	[bestəl·wa]
road tractor (trailer truck)	**padtrekker**	[pad·trɛkkər]
trailer	**aanhangwa**	[ãnhaŋ·wa]
comfortable (adj)	**gemaklik**	[χemaklik]
used (adj)	**gebruik**	[χebrœik]

175. Cars. Bodywork

hood	**enjinkap**	[ɛndʒin·kap]
fender	**modderskerm**	[moddər·skerm]
roof	**dak**	[dak]
windshield	**voorruit**	[foər·rœit]
rear-view mirror	**truspieël**	[tru·spiɛl]
windshield washer	**voorruitsproer**	[foər·rœitsprur]
windshield wipers	**ruitveërs**	[rœit·feɛrs]
side window	**syvenster**	[saj·fɛŋstər]
window lift (power window)	**vensterhyser**	[fɛŋstər·hajsər]
antenna	**lugdraad**	[luχdrãt]
sunroof	**sondak**	[sondak]
bumper	**buffer**	[buffər]
trunk	**bagasiebak**	[baχasi·bak]
roof luggage rack	**dakreling**	[dak·reliŋ]
door	**deur**	[døər]

door handle	**handvatsel**	[hand·fatsəl]
door lock	**deurslot**	[døər·slot]
license plate	**nommerplaat**	[nommər·plāt]
muffler	**knaldemper**	[knal·dempər]
gas tank	**petroltenk**	[petrol·tɛnk]
tailpipe	**uitlaatpyp**	[œitlāt·pajp]
gas, accelerator	**gaspedaal**	[χas·pedāl]
pedal	**pedaal**	[pedāl]
gas pedal	**gaspedaal**	[χas·pedāl]
brake	**rem**	[rem]
brake pedal	**rempedaal**	[rem·pedāl]
to brake (use the brake)	**remtrap**	[remtrap]
parking brake	**parkeerrem**	[parkeər·rem]
clutch	**koppelaar**	[koppelār]
clutch pedal	**koppelaarpedaal**	[koppelār·pedāl]
clutch disc	**koppelaarskyf**	[koppelār·skajf]
shock absorber	**skokbreker**	[skok·brekər]
wheel	**wiel**	[vil]
spare tire	**spaarwiel**	[spār·wil]
tire	**band**	[bant]
hubcap	**wieldop**	[wil·dop]
driving wheels	**dryfwiele**	[drajf·wilə]
front-wheel drive (as adj)	**voorwielaandrywing**	[foərwil·āndrajviŋ]
rear-wheel drive (as adj)	**agterwielaandrywing**	[aχtərwil·āndrajviŋ]
all-wheel drive (as adj)	**vierwielaandrywing**	[firwil·āndrajviŋ]
gearbox	**ratkas**	[ratkas]
automatic (adj)	**outomaties**	[æʊtomatis]
mechanical (adj)	**meganies**	[meχanis]
gear shift	**ratwisselaar**	[ratwisselār]
headlight	**koplig**	[kopləχ]
headlights	**kopligte**	[kopliχtə]
low beam	**dempstraal**	[demp·strāl]
high beam	**hoofstraal**	[hoəf·strāl]
brake light	**remlig**	[remləχ]
parking lights	**parkeerlig**	[parkeər·ləχ]
hazard lights	**gevaarligte**	[χefār·liχtə]
fog lights	**mislampe**	[mis·lampə]
turn signal	**draaiwyser**	[drāj·vajsər]
back-up light	**trulig**	[truləχ]

176. Cars. Passenger compartment

car inside (interior)	**interieur**	[interiøər]
leather (as adj)	**leer-**	[leər-]
velour (as adj)	**fluweel-**	[fluveəl-]
upholstery	**bekleding**	[beklediŋ]
instrument (gage)	**instrument**	[instrument]
dashboard	**voorpaneel**	[foər·paneəl]
speedometer	**spoedmeter**	[spud·metər]
needle (pointer)	**wyster**	[vajstər]
odometer	**afstandmeter**	[afstant·metər]
indicator (sensor)	**sensor**	[sɛŋsor]
level	**vlak**	[flak]
warning light	**waarskulig**	[vārskuləχ]
steering wheel	**stuurwiel**	[stɪr·wil]
horn	**toeter**	[tutər]
button	**knop**	[knɔp]
switch	**skakelaar**	[skakəlār]
seat	**sitplek**	[sitplek]
backrest	**rugsteun**	[ruχ·støən]
headrest	**kopstut**	[kɔpstut]
seat belt	**veiligheidsgordel**	[fæjliχæjts·χordəl]
to fasten the belt	**die gordel vasmaak**	[di χordəl fasmāk]
adjustment (of seats)	**verstelling**	[ferstɛliŋ]
airbag	**lugsak**	[luχsak]
air-conditioner	**lugversorger**	[luχfersorχər]
radio	**radio**	[radio]
CD player	**CD-speler**	[se·de spelər]
to turn on	**aanskakel**	[āŋskakəl]
antenna	**lugdraad**	[luχdrāt]
glove box	**paneelkassie**	[paneəl·kassi]
ashtray	**asbak**	[asbak]

177. Cars. Engine

engine	**enjin**	[ɛndʒin]
motor	**motor**	[motor]
diesel (as adj)	**diesel**	[disəl]
gasoline (as adj)	**petrol**	[petrol]
engine volume	**enjininhoud**	[ɛndʒin·inhæʊt]
power	**krag**	[kraχ]
horsepower	**perdekrag**	[perdə·kraχ]

piston	suier	[sœier]
cylinder	silinder	[silindər]
valve	klep	[klep]

injector	inspuiting	[inspœitiŋ]
generator (alternator)	generator	[χenerator]
carburetor	vergasser	[ferχassər]
motor oil	motorolie	[motor·oli]

radiator	verkoeler	[ferkulər]
coolant	koelmiddel	[kul·middəl]
cooling fan	waaier	[vãjer]

battery (accumulator)	battery	[battəraj]
starter	aansitter	[ãŋsittər]
ignition	ontsteking	[ontstekiŋ]
spark plug	vonkprop	[fonk·prop]

terminal (of battery)	pool	[poəl]
positive terminal	positiewe pool	[positivə poəl]
negative terminal	negatiewe pool	[neχativə poəl]
fuse	sekering	[sekəriŋ]

air filter	lugfilter	[luχ·filtər]
oil filter	oliefilter	[oli·filtər]
fuel filter	brandstoffilter	[brantstof·filtər]

178. Cars. Crash. Repair

car crash	motorbotsing	[motor·botsiŋ]
traffic accident	verkeersongeluk	[ferkeərs·onχəluk]
to crash (into the wall, etc.)	bots	[bots]

to get smashed up	verongeluk	[feronχəluk]
damage	skade	[skadə]
intact (unscathed)	onbeskadig	[onbeskadəχ]

breakdown	onklaar raak	[onklãr rãk]
to break down (vi)	onklaar raak	[onklãr rãk]
towrope	sleeptou	[sleəp·tæʊ]

puncture	papwiel	[pap·wil]
to be flat	pap wees	[pap veəs]
to pump up	oppomp	[oppomp]
pressure	druk	[druk]
to check (to examine)	nagaan	[naχãn]

repair	herstel	[herstəl]
auto repair shop	garage	[χaraʒə]
spare part	onderdeel	[ondərdeəl]

part	onderdeel	[onderdeel]
bolt (with nut)	bout	[bæʋt]
screw (fastener)	skroef	[skruf]
nut	moer	[mur]
washer	waster	[vaster]
bearing	koeëllaer	[kuɛllaer]

tube	pyp	[pajp]
gasket (head ~)	pakstuk	[pakstuk]
cable, wire	kabel	[kabel]

jack	domkrag	[domkraχ]
wrench	moersleutel	[mur·sløetel]
hammer	hamer	[hamer]
pump	pomp	[pomp]
screwdriver	skroewedraaier	[skruve·drājer]

fire extinguisher	brandblusser	[brant·blusser]
warning triangle	gevaardriehoek	[χefār·drihuk]

to stall (vi)	stol	[stol]
stall (n)	stol	[stol]
to be broken	stukkend wees	[stukkent vees]

to overheat (vi)	oorverhit	[oerferhit]
to be clogged up	verstop raak	[ferstop rāk]
to freeze up (pipes, etc.)	vries	[fris]
to burst (vi, ab. tube)	bars	[bars]

pressure	druk	[druk]
level	vlak	[flak]
slack (~ belt)	slap	[slap]

dent	duik	[dœik]
knocking noise (engine)	klopgeluid	[klop·χelœit]
crack	kraak	[krāk]
scratch	skraap	[skrāp]

179. Cars. Road

road	pad	[pat]
highway	deurpad	[døerpat]
freeway	deurpad	[døerpat]
direction (way)	rigting	[riχtiŋ]
distance	afstand	[afstant]

bridge	brug	[bruχ]
parking lot	parkeerterrein	[parkeer·terræjn]
square	plein	[plæjn]
interchange	padknoop	[pad·knoəp]

tunnel	tonnel	[tonnəl]
gas station	petrolstasie	[petrol·stasi]
parking lot	parkeerterrein	[parkeər·terræjn]
gas pump (fuel dispenser)	petrolpomp	[petrol·pomp]
auto repair shop	garage	[χaraʒə]
to get gas (to fill up)	volmaak	[folmāk]
fuel	brandstof	[brantstof]
jerrycan	petrolblik	[petrol·blik]

asphalt	teer	[teər]
road markings	padmerktekens	[pad·merktekɛns]
curb	randsteen	[rand·steen]
guardrail	skutreling	[skut·reliŋ]
ditch	donga	[donχa]
roadside (shoulder)	skouer	[skæʊər]
lamppost	lamppaal	[lamp·pāl]

to drive (a car)	bestuur	[bestɪr]
to turn (e.g., ~ left)	draai	[drāi]
to make a U-turn	U-draai maak	[u-drāj māk]
reverse (~ gear)	tru-	[tru-]

to honk (vi)	toeter	[tutər]
honk (sound)	toeter	[tutər]
to get stuck (in the mud, etc.)	vassteek	[fassteək]
to spin the wheels	die wiele laat tol	[di vilə lāt tol]
to cut, to turn off (vt)	afskakel	[afskakəl]

speed	spoed	[sput]
to exceed the speed limit	die spoedgrens oortree	[di sputχrɛns oərtreə]
traffic lights	robot	[robot]
driver's license	bestuurslisensie	[bestɪrs·lisɛŋsi]

grade crossing	treinoorgang	[træjn·oərχaŋ]
intersection	kruispunt	[krœis·punt]
crosswalk	sebraoorgang	[sebra·oərχaŋ]
bend, curve	draai	[drāi]
pedestrian zone	voetgangerstraat	[futχaŋər·strāt]

180. Traffic signs

rules of the road	padreëls	[pad·reɛls]
road sign (traffic sign)	padteken	[pad·tekən]
passing (overtaking)	verbysteek	[ferbajsteək]
curve	draai	[drāi]
U-turn	U-draai	[u-drāi]
traffic circle	verkeerssirkel	[ferkeərs·sirkəl]
No vehicles allowed	Geen voertuie toegelaat nie	[χeən furtœiə tuχelāt ni]

No entry	Geen toegang	[χeən tuχaŋ]
No passing	Verbysteek verbode	[ferbajsteək ferbodə]
No parking	Parkeerverbod	[parkeər·ferbot]
No stopping	Nie stilhou nie	[ni stilhæʊ ni]

dangerous bend	gevaarlike draai	[χefārlikə drāi]
steep descent	steil afdraande	[stæjl afdrāndə]
one-way traffic	eenrigtingverkeer	[eənriχtiŋ·ferkeər]
crosswalk	Voetoorgang voor	[futoərχaŋ foər]
slippery road	Glibberige pad voor	[χlibbəriχə pat foər]
YIELD	TOEGEE	[tuχeə]

PEOPLE. LIFE EVENTS

Life events

181. Holidays. Event

celebration, holiday	partytjie	[partajki]
national day	nasionale dag	[naʃionalə daχ]
public holiday	openbare vakansiedag	[openbarə fakaŋsi·daχ]
to commemorate (vt)	herdenk	[herdenk]
event (happening)	gebeurtenis	[χebøørtenis]
event (organized activity)	gebeurtenis	[χebøørtenis]
banquet (party)	banket	[banket]
reception (formal party)	onthaal	[onthāl]
feast	feesmaal	[fees·māl]
anniversary	verjaardag	[ferjār·daχ]
jubilee	jubileum	[jubiløøm]
to celebrate (vt)	vier	[fir]
New Year	Nuwejaar	[nuvejār]
Happy New Year!	Voorspoedige Nuwejaar	[foərspudiχə nuvejār]
Santa Claus	Kersvader	[kers·fadər]
Christmas	Kersfees	[kersfees]
Merry Christmas!	Geseënde Kersfees	[χeseɛndə kersfeɛs]
Christmas tree	Kersboom	[kers·boəm]
fireworks (fireworks show)	vuurwerk	[fɪrwerk]
wedding	bruilof	[brœilof]
groom	bruidegom	[brœideχom]
bride	bruid	[brœit]
to invite (vt)	uitnooi	[œitnoj]
invitation card	uitnodiging	[œitnodəχiŋ]
guest	gas	[χas]
to visit	besoek	[besuk]
(~ your parents, etc.)		
to meet the guests	die gaste ontmoet	[di χastə ontmut]
gift, present	present	[present]
to give (sth as present)	gee	[χeə]
to receive gifts	presente ontvang	[presentə ontfaŋ]

181

bouquet (of flowers)	boeket	[buket]
congratulations	gelukwense	[χelukwɛŋsə]
to congratulate (vt)	gelukwens	[χelukwɛŋs]
greeting card	geleentheidskaartjie	[χeleenthæjts·kãrki]

toast	heildronk	[hæjldronk]
to offer (a drink, etc.)	aanbied	[ãnbit]
champagne	sjampanje	[ʃampanje]

to enjoy oneself	jouself geniet	[jæʊsɛlf χenit]
merriment (gaiety)	pret	[pret]
joy (emotion)	vreugde	[frøəχdə]

| dance | dans | [daŋs] |
| to dance (vi, vt) | dans | [daŋs] |

| waltz | wals | [vals] |
| tango | tango | [tanχo] |

182. Funerals. Burial

cemetery	begraafplaas	[beχrãf·plãs]
grave, tomb	graf	[χraf]
cross	kruis	[krœis]
gravestone	grafsteen	[χrafsteən]
fence	heining	[hæjniŋ]
chapel	kapel	[kapəl]

death	dood	[doət]
to die (vi)	doodgaan	[doədχãn]
the deceased	oorledene	[oərledenə]
mourning	rou	[ræʊ]

to bury (vt)	begrawe	[beχravə]
funeral home	begrafnisonderneming	[beχrafnis·ondərnemiŋ]
funeral	begrafnis	[beχrafnis]

| wreath | krans | [kraŋs] |
| casket, coffin | doodskis | [doədskis] |

| hearse | lykswa | [lajks·wa] |
| shroud | lykkleed | [lajk·kleət] |

funeral procession	begrafnisstoet	[beχrafnis·stut]
funerary urn	urn	[urn]
crematory	krematorium	[krematorium]

obituary	doodsberig	[doəds·berəχ]
to cry (weep)	huil	[hœil]
to sob (vi)	snik	[snik]

183. War. Soldiers

platoon	peleton	[peleton]
company	kompanie	[kompani]
regiment	regiment	[reχiment]
army	leër	[leɛr]
division	divisie	[difisi]
section, squad	afdeling	[afdeliŋ]
host (army)	leërskare	[leɛrskarə]
soldier	soldaat	[soldãt]
officer	offisier	[offisir]
private	soldaat	[soldãt]
sergeant	sersant	[sersant]
lieutenant	luitenant	[lœitənant]
captain	kaptein	[kaptæjn]
major	majoor	[majoər]
colonel	kolonel	[kolonəl]
general	generaal	[χenerãl]
sailor	matroos	[matroəs]
captain	kaptein	[kaptæjn]
boatswain	bootsman	[boətsman]
artilleryman	artilleris	[artilleris]
paratrooper	valskermsoldaat	[falskerm·soldãt]
pilot	piloot	[piloət]
navigator	navigator	[nafiχator]
mechanic	werktuigkundige	[verktœiχ·kundiχə]
pioneer (sapper)	sappeur	[sappøər]
parachutist	valskermspringer	[falskerm·spriŋər]
reconnaissance scout	verkenner	[ferkɛnnər]
sniper	skerpskut	[skerp·skut]
patrol (group)	patrollie	[patrolli]
to patrol (vt)	patrolleer	[patrolleər]
sentry, guard	wag	[vaχ]
warrior	vegter	[feχtər]
patriot	patriot	[patriot]
hero	held	[hɛlt]
heroine	heldin	[hɛldin]
traitor	verraaier	[ferrãjer]
to betray (vt)	verraai	[ferrãi]
deserter	droster	[drostər]
to desert (vi)	dros	[dros]

mercenary	huursoldaat	[hɪr·soldāt]
recruit	rekruteer	[rekruteər]
volunteer	vrywilliger	[frajvillixər]

dead (n)	dooie	[doje]
wounded (n)	gewonde	[xevondə]
prisoner of war	krygsgevangene	[krajxs·xefaŋənə]

184. War. Military actions. Part 1

war	oorlog	[oərloχ]
to be at war	oorlog voer	[oərloχ fur]
civil war	burgeroorlog	[burgər·oərloχ]

treacherously (adv)	valslik	[falslik]
declaration of war	oorlogsverklaring	[oərloχs·ferklariŋ]
to declare (~ war)	oorlog verklaar	[oərloχ ferklār]
aggression	aggressie	[aχrɛssi]
to attack (invade)	aanval	[ānfal]

to invade (vt)	binneval	[binnəfal]
invader	binnevaller	[binnəfallər]
conqueror	veroweraar	[feroverār]

defense	verdediging	[ferdedəxiŋ]
to defend (a country, etc.)	verdedig	[ferdedəx]
to defend (against ...)	jouself verdedig	[jæʊsɛlf ferdedəχ]

enemy	vyand	[fajant]
foe, adversary	teëstander	[tɛɛstandər]
enemy (as adj)	vyandig	[fajandəx]

| strategy | strategie | [strateχi] |
| tactics | taktiek | [taktik] |

order	bevel	[befəl]
command (order)	bevel	[befəl]
to order (vt)	beveel	[befeəl]
mission	opdrag	[opdraχ]
secret (adj)	geheim	[χəhæjm]

| battle | veldslag | [fɛltslaχ] |
| combat | geveg | [χefeχ] |

attack	aanval	[ānfal]
charge (assault)	bestorming	[bestormiŋ]
to storm (vt)	bestorm	[bestorm]
siege (to be under ~)	beleg	[beleχ]
offensive (n)	aanval	[ānfal]
to go on the offensive	tot die offensief oorgaan	[tot di offɛŋsif oərχān]

retreat	terugtrekking	[teruχ·trɛkkiŋ]
to retreat (vi)	terugtrek	[teruχtrek]
encirclement	omsingeling	[omsinχəliŋ]
to encircle (vt)	omsingel	[omsiŋəl]
bombing (by aircraft)	bombardement	[bombardement]
to bomb (vt)	bombardeer	[bombardeər]
explosion	ontploffing	[ontploffiŋ]
shot	skoot	[skoət]
firing (burst of ~)	skiet	[skit]
to aim (to point a weapon)	mik op	[mik op]
to point (a gun)	rig	[riχ]
to hit (the target)	tref	[tref]
to sink (~ a ship)	sink	[sink]
hole (in a ship)	gat	[χat]
to founder, to sink (vi)	sink	[sink]
front (war ~)	front	[front]
evacuation	evakuasie	[ɛfakuasi]
to evacuate (vt)	evakueer	[ɛfakueər]
trench	loopgraaf	[loəpχrāf]
barbwire	doringdraad	[doriŋ·drāt]
barrier (anti tank ~)	versperring	[fersperriŋ]
watchtower	wagtoring	[vaχ·toriŋ]
military hospital	militêre hospitaal	[militæərə hospitāl]
to wound (vt)	wond	[vont]
wound	wond	[vont]
wounded (n)	gewonde	[χevondə]
to be wounded	gewond	[χevont]
serious (wound)	ernstig	[ɛrnstəχ]

185. War. Military actions. Part 2

captivity	gevangenskap	[χefaŋənskap]
to take captive	gevange neem	[χefaŋə neəm]
to be held captive	in gevangenskap wees	[in χefaŋənskap veəs]
to be taken captive	in gevangenskap geneem word	[in χefaŋənskap χeneəm vort]
concentration camp	konsentrasiekamp	[kɔŋsentrasi·kamp]
prisoner of war	krygsgevangene	[krajχs·χefaŋənə]
to escape (vi)	ontsnap	[ontsnap]
to betray (vt)	verraai	[ferrāi]
betrayer	verraaier	[ferrājer]

betrayal	verraad	[ferrãt]
to execute (by firing squad)	eksekuteer	[ɛksekuteǝr]
execution (by firing squad)	eksekusie	[ɛksekusi]

equipment (military gear)	toerusting	[turustiŋ]
shoulder board	skouerstrook	[skæʊǝr·stroǝk]
gas mask	gasmasker	[χas·maskǝr]

field radio	veldradio	[fɛlt·radio]
cipher, code	geheime kode	[χǝhæjmǝ kodǝ]
secrecy	geheimhouding	[χǝhæjm·hæʊdiŋ]
password	wagwoord	[vaχ·woǝrt]

land mine	landmyn	[land·majn]
to mine (road, etc.)	bemyn	[bemajn]
minefield	mynveld	[majn·fɛlt]

air-raid warning	lugalarm	[luχ·alarm]
alarm (alert signal)	alarm	[alarm]
signal	sienjaal	[sinjãl]
signal flare	fakkel	[fakkel]

headquarters	hoofkwartier	[hoǝf·kwartir]
reconnaissance	verkenningstog	[ferkɛnniŋs·toχ]
situation	toestand	[tustant]
report	verslag	[ferslaχ]
ambush	hinderlaag	[hindǝr·lãχ]
reinforcement (of army)	versterking	[ferstǝrkiŋ]

target	doel	[dul]
proving ground	proefterrein	[pruf·terræjn]
military exercise	militêre oefening	[militærǝ ufeniŋ]

panic	paniek	[panik]
devastation	verwoesting	[ferwustiŋ]
destruction, ruins	verwoesting	[ferwustiŋ]
to destroy (vt)	verwoes	[ferwus]

to survive (vi, vt)	oorleef	[oǝrleǝf]
to disarm (vt)	ontwapen	[ontvapen]
to handle (~ a gun)	hanteer	[hanteǝr]

| Attention! | Aandag! | [ãndaχ!] |
| At ease! | Op die plek rus! | [op di plek rus!] |

act of courage	heldedaad	[hɛldǝ·dãt]
oath (vow)	eed	[eǝt]
to swear (an oath)	sweer	[sweǝr]

| decoration (medal, etc.) | dekorasie | [dekorasiǝ] |
| to award (give medal to) | toeken | [tuken] |

| medal | medalje | [medalje] |
| order (e.g., ~ of Merit) | orde | [ordə] |

victory	oorwinning	[oərwinniŋ]
defeat	nederlaag	[nedərlāχ]
armistice	wapenstilstand	[vapɛn·stilstant]

standard (battle flag)	vaandel	[fāndəl]
glory (honor, fame)	roem	[rum]
parade	parade	[paradə]
to march (on parade)	marseer	[marseər]

186. Weapons

weapons	wapens	[vapɛns]
firearms	vuurwapens	[fɪr·vapɛns]
cold weapons (knives, etc.)	messe	[mɛssə]

chemical weapons	chemiese wapens	[χemisə vapɛns]
nuclear (adj)	kern-	[kern-]
nuclear weapons	kernwapens	[kern·vapɛns]

| bomb | bom | [bom] |
| atomic bomb | atoombom | [atoəm·bom] |

pistol (gun)	pistool	[pistoəl]
rifle	geweer	[χeveər]
submachine gun	aanvalsgeweer	[ānvals·χeveər]
machine gun	masjiengeweer	[maʃin·χeveər]

muzzle	loop	[loəp]
barrel	loop	[loəp]
caliber	kaliber	[kalibər]

trigger	sneller	[snɛllər]
sight (aiming device)	visier	[fisir]
magazine	magasyn	[maχasajn]
butt (shoulder stock)	kolf	[kolf]

| hand grenade | handgranaat | [hand·χranāt] |
| explosive | springstof | [spriŋstof] |

bullet	koeël	[kuɛl]
cartridge	patroon	[patroən]
charge	lading	[ladiŋ]
ammunition	ammunisie	[ammunisi]

| bomber (aircraft) | bomwerper | [bom·werpər] |
| fighter | straalvegter | [strāl·feχtər] |

helicopter	helikopter	[helikoptər]
anti-aircraft gun	lugafweer	[luχafweər]
tank	tenk	[tɛnk]
tank gun	tenkkanon	[tɛnk·kanon]

artillery	artillerie	[artilleri]
gun (cannon, howitzer)	kanon	[kanon]
to lay (a gun)	aanlê	[ānlɛ:]

shell (projectile)	projektiel	[projektil]
mortar bomb	mortierbom	[mortir·bom]
mortar	mortier	[mortir]
splinter (shell fragment)	skrapnel	[skrapnəl]

submarine	duikboot	[dœik·boət]
torpedo	torpedo	[torpedo]
missile	vuurpyl	[fɪr·pajl]

to load (gun)	laai	[lāi]
to shoot (vi)	skiet	[skit]
to point at (the cannon)	rig op	[riχ op]
bayonet	bajonet	[bajonet]

rapier	rapier	[rapir]
saber (e.g., cavalry ~)	sabel	[sabəl]
spear (weapon)	spies	[spis]
bow	boog	[boəχ]
arrow	pyl	[pajl]
musket	musket	[musket]
crossbow	kruisboog	[krœis·boəχ]

187. Ancient people

primitive (prehistoric)	primitief	[primitif]
prehistoric (adj)	prehistories	[prehistoris]
ancient (~ civilization)	antiek	[antik]

Stone Age	Steentydperk	[steən·tajtperk]
Bronze Age	Bronstydperk	[brɔŋs·tajtperk]
Ice Age	Ystydperk	[ajs·tajtperk]

tribe	stam	[stam]
cannibal	mensvreter	[mɛŋs·fretər]
hunter	jagter	[jaχtər]
to hunt (vi, vt)	jag	[jaχ]
mammoth	mammoet	[mammut]

cave	grot	[χrot]
fire	vuur	[fɪr]
campfire	kampvuur	[kampfɪr]

cave painting	rotstekening	[rots·tekəniŋ]
tool (e.g., stone ax)	werktuig	[verktœiχ]
spear	spies	[spis]
stone ax	klipbyl	[klip·bajl]
to be at war	oorlog voer	[oərloχ fur]
to domesticate (vt)	tem	[tem]

idol	afgod	[afχot]
to worship (vt)	aanbid	[ānbit]
superstition	bygeloof	[bajχəloəf]
rite	ritueel	[ritueəl]

evolution	evolusie	[ɛfolusi]
development	ontwikkeling	[ontwikkeliŋ]
disappearance (extinction)	verdwyning	[ferdwajniŋ]
to adapt oneself	jou aanpas	[jæʊ ānpas]

archeology	argeologie	[arχeoloχi]
archeologist	argeoloog	[arχeoloəχ]
archeological (adj)	argeologies	[arχeoloχis]

excavation site	opgrawingsplek	[opχraviŋs·plek]
excavations	opgrawingsplekke	[opχraviŋs·plɛkkə]
find (object)	vonds	[fonds]
fragment	fragment	[fraχment]

188. Middle Ages

people (ethnic group)	volk	[folk]
peoples	bevolking	[befolkiŋ]
tribe	stam	[stam]
tribes	stamme	[stammə]

barbarians	barbare	[barbarə]
Gauls	Galliërs	[χalliɛrs]
Goths	Gote	[χote]
Slavs	Slawe	[slavə]
Vikings	Vikings	[vikiŋs]

| Romans | Romeine | [romæjnə] |
| Roman (adj) | Romeins | [romæjns] |

Byzantines	Bisantyne	[bisantajnə]
Byzantium	Bisantium	[bisantium]
Byzantine (adj)	Bisantyns	[bisantajns]

emperor	keiser	[kæjsər]
leader, chief (tribal ~)	leier	[læjer]
powerful (~ king)	magtig	[maχtəχ]
king	koning	[koniŋ]

ruler (sovereign)	heerser	[heərsər]
knight	ridder	[riddər]
feudal lord	feodale heerser	[feodale heərsər]
feudal (adj)	feodaal	[feodāl]
vassal	vasal	[fasal]
duke	hertog	[hertoχ]
earl	graaf	[χrāf]
baron	baron	[baron]
bishop	biskop	[biskop]
armor	harnas	[harnas]
shield	skild	[skilt]
sword	swaard	[swārt]
visor	visier	[fisir]
chainmail	maliehemp	[mali·hemp]
Crusade	Kruistog	[krœis·toχ]
crusader	kruisvaarder	[krœis·fārdər]
territory	gebied	[χebit]
to attack (invade)	aanval	[ānfal]
to conquer (vt)	verower	[ferovər]
to occupy (invade)	beset	[beset]
siege (to be under ~)	beleg	[beleχ]
besieged (adj)	beleërde	[beleɛrdə]
to besiege (vt)	beleër	[beleɛr]
inquisition	inkwisisie	[inkvisisi]
inquisitor	inkwisiteur	[inkvisitøər]
torture	marteling	[martəliŋ]
cruel (adj)	wreed	[vreet]
heretic	ketter	[kɛttər]
heresy	kettery	[kɛtteraj]
seafaring	seevaart	[see·fārt]
pirate	piraat, seerower	[pirāt], [see·rovər]
piracy	pirateraj, seerowery	[pirateraj], [see·roveraj]
boarding (attack)	enter	[ɛntər]
loot, booty	buit	[bœit]
treasures	skatte	[skattə]
discovery	ontdekking	[ontdɛkkiŋ]
to discover (new land, etc.)	ontdek	[ontdek]
expedition	ekspedisie	[ɛkspedisi]
musketeer	musketier	[musketir]
cardinal	kardinaal	[kardināl]
heraldry	heraldiek	[heraldik]
heraldic (adj)	heraldies	[heraldis]

189. Leader. Chief. Authorities

king	**koning**	[koniŋ]
queen	**koningin**	[koniŋin]
royal (adj)	**koninklik**	[koninklik]
kingdom	**koninkryk**	[koninkrajk]
prince	**prins**	[prins]
princess	**prinses**	[prinsəs]
president	**president**	[president]
vice-president	**vise-president**	[fise-president]
senator	**senator**	[senator]
monarch	**monarg**	[monarχ]
ruler (sovereign)	**heerser**	[heərsər]
dictator	**diktator**	[diktator]
tyrant	**tiran**	[tiran]
magnate	**magnaat**	[maχnãt]
director	**direkteur**	[direktøər]
chief	**baas**	[bãs]
manager (director)	**bestuurder**	[bestɪrdər]
boss	**baas**	[bãs]
owner	**eienaar**	[æjenãr]
leader	**leier**	[læjer]
head (~ of delegation)	**hoof**	[hoəf]
authorities	**outoriteite**	[æʊtoritæjtə]
superiors	**hoofde**	[hoəfdə]
governor	**goewerneur**	[χuvernøər]
consul	**konsul**	[kɔŋsul]
diplomat	**diplomaat**	[diplomãt]
mayor	**burgermeester**	[burgər·meəstər]
sheriff	**sheriff**	[sheriff]
emperor	**keiser**	[kæjsər]
tsar, czar	**tsaar**	[tsãr]
pharaoh	**farao**	[farao]
khan	**kan**	[kan]

190. Road. Way. Directions

road	**pad**	[pat]
way (direction)	**pad**	[pat]
freeway	**deurpad**	[døərpat]
highway	**deurpad**	[døərpat]

interstate	nasionale pad	[naʃionalə pat]
main road	hoofweg	[hoəf·weχ]
dirt road	grondpad	[χront·pat]

| pathway | paadjie | [pādʒi] |
| footpath (troddenpath) | paadjie | [pādʒi] |

Where?	Waar?	[vār?]
Where (to)?	Waarheen?	[vārheən?]
From where?	Waarvandaan?	[vārfandān?]

| direction (way) | rigting | [riχtiŋ] |
| to point (~ the way) | wys | [vajs] |

to the left	na links	[na links]
to the right	na regs	[na reχs]
straight ahead (adv)	reguit	[reχœit]
back (e.g., to turn ~)	terug	[teruχ]
bend, curve	draai	[drāi]
to turn (e.g., ~ left)	draai	[drāi]
to make a U-turn	U-draai maak	[u-drāj māk]

to be visible	sigbaar wees	[siχbār veəs]
(mountains, castle, etc.)		
to appear (come into view)	verskyn	[ferskajn]

stop, halt	stop	[stop]
(e.g., during a trip)		
to rest, to pause (vi)	pouseer	[pæʊseər]
rest (pause)	ruspouse	[ruspæʊsə]

to lose one's way	verdwaal	[ferdwāl]
to lead to … (ab. road)	lei na …	[læj na …]
to come out	uitkom by	[œitkom baj]
(e.g., on the highway)		
stretch (of road)	stuk pad	[stuk pat]

asphalt	teer	[teər]
curb	randsteen	[rand·steən]
ditch	donga	[donχa]
manhole	mangat	[manχat]
roadside (shoulder)	skouer	[skæʊər]
pit, pothole	slaggat	[slaχχat]

| to go (on foot) | gaan | [χān] |
| to pass (overtake) | verbysteek | [ferbajsteək] |

step (footstep)	tree	[treə]
on foot (adv)	te voet	[tə fut]
to block (road)	blokkeer	[blokkeər]
boom gate	hefboom	[hefboəm]
dead end	doodloopstraat	[doədloəp·strāt]

191. Breaking the law. Criminals. Part 1

bandit	**bandiet**	[bandit]
crime	**misdaad**	[misdāt]
criminal (person)	**misdadiger**	[misdadiχər]
thief	**dief**	[dif]
to steal (vi, vt)	**steel**	[steəl]
stealing (larceny)	**steel**	[steəl]
theft	**diefstal**	[difstal]
to kidnap (vt)	**ontvoer**	[ontfur]
kidnapping	**ontvoering**	[ontfuriŋ]
kidnapper	**ontvoerder**	[ontfurdər]
ransom	**losgeld**	[losχɛlt]
to demand ransom	**losgeld eis**	[losχɛlt æjs]
to rob (vt)	**besteel**	[besteəl]
robbery	**oorval**	[oərfal]
robber	**boef**	[buf]
to extort (vt)	**afpers**	[afpers]
extortionist	**afperser**	[afpersər]
extortion	**afpersing**	[afpersiŋ]
to murder, to kill	**vermoor**	[fermoər]
murder	**moord**	[moərt]
murderer	**moordenaar**	[moərdenār]
gunshot	**skoot**	[skoət]
to shoot to death	**doodskiet**	[doədskit]
to shoot (vi)	**skiet**	[skit]
shooting	**skietery**	[skiteraj]
incident (fight, etc.)	**insident**	[insident]
fight, brawl	**geveg**	[χefeχ]
Help!	**Help!**	[hɛlp!]
victim	**slagoffer**	[slaχoffər]
to damage (vt)	**beskadig**	[beskadəχ]
damage	**skade**	[skadə]
dead body, corpse	**lyk**	[lajk]
grave (~ crime)	**ernstig**	[ɛrnstəχ]
to attack (vt)	**aanval**	[ānfal]
to beat (to hit)	**slaan**	[slān]
to beat up	**platslaan**	[platslān]
to take (rob of sth)	**vat**	[fat]
to stab to death	**doodsteek**	[doədsteək]
to maim (vt)	**vermink**	[fermink]

to wound (vt)	wond	[vont]
blackmail	afpersing	[afpersiŋ]
to blackmail (vt)	afpers	[afpers]
blackmailer	afperser	[afpersər]

protection racket	beskermingswendelary	[beskermiŋ·swendəlaraj]
racketeer	afperser	[afpersər]
gangster	boef	[buf]
mafia, Mob	mafia	[mafia]

pickpocket	sakkeroller	[sakkerollər]
burglar	inbreker	[inbrekər]
smuggling	smokkel	[smokkəl]
smuggler	smokkelaar	[smokkəlār]

forgery	vervalsing	[ferfalsiŋ]
to forge (counterfeit)	verval	[ferfal]
fake (forged)	vals	[fals]

192. Breaking the law. Criminals. Part 2

rape	verkragting	[ferkraχtiŋ]
to rape (vt)	verkrag	[ferkraχ]
rapist	verkragter	[ferkraχtər]
maniac	maniak	[maniak]

prostitute (fem.)	prostituut	[prostitɪt]
prostitution	prostitusie	[prostitusi]
pimp	pooier	[pojer]

| drug addict | dwelmslaaf | [dwɛlm·slāf] |
| drug dealer | dwelmhandelaar | [dwɛlm·handəlār] |

to blow up (bomb)	opblaas	[opblās]
explosion	ontploffing	[ontploffiŋ]
to set fire	aan die brand steek	[ān di brant steək]
arsonist	brandstigter	[brant·stiχtər]

terrorism	terrorisme	[terrorismə]
terrorist	terroris	[terroris]
hostage	gyselaar	[χajsəlār]

to swindle (deceive)	bedrieg	[bedrəχ]
swindle, deception	bedrog	[bedroχ]
swindler	bedrieër	[bedriɛr]

to bribe (vt)	omkoop	[omkoəp]
bribery	omkopery	[omkoperaj]
bribe	omkoopgeld	[omkoəp·χɛlt]
poison	gif	[χif]

| to poison (vt) | vergiftig | [ferχiftəχ] |
| to poison oneself | jouself vergiftig | [jæusɛlf ferχiftəχ] |

| suicide (act) | selfmoord | [sɛlfmoərt] |
| suicide (person) | selfmoordenaar | [sɛlfmoərdenãr] |

to threaten (vt)	dreig	[dræjχ]
threat	dreigement	[dræjχement]
attempt (attack)	aanslag	[ãŋslaχ]

| to steal (a car) | steel | [steəl] |
| to hijack (a plane) | kaap | [kãp] |

| revenge | wraak | [vrãk] |
| to avenge (get revenge) | wreek | [vreək] |

to torture (vt)	martel	[martəl]
torture	marteling	[martəliŋ]
to torment (vt)	folter	[foltər]

pirate	piraat, seerower	[pirãt], [seə·rovər]
hooligan	skollie	[skolli]
armed (adj)	gewapen	[χevapen]
violence	geweld	[χevɛlt]
illegal (unlawful)	onwettig	[onwɛttəχ]

| spying (espionage) | spioenasie | [spiunasi] |
| to spy (vi) | spioeneer | [spiuneər] |

193. Police. Law. Part 1

| justice | justisie | [jəstisi] |
| court (see you in ~) | geregshof | [χereχshof] |

judge	regter	[reχtər]
jurors	jurielede	[jurilede]
jury trial	jurieregspraak	[juri·reχsprãk]
to judge (vt)	bereg	[bereχ]

lawyer, attorney	advokaat	[adfokãt]
defendant	beklaagde	[beklãχdə]
dock	beklaagdebank	[beklãχdə·bank]

| charge | aanklag | [ãnklaχ] |
| accused | beskuldigde | [beskuldiχdə] |

sentence	vonnis	[fonnis]
to sentence (vt)	veroordeel	[feroərdeəl]
guilty (culprit)	skuldig	[skuldəχ]
to punish (vt)	straf	[straf]

punishment	straf	[straf]
fine (penalty)	boete	[butə]
life imprisonment	lewenslange gevangenisstraf	[levɛŋslaŋə χefaŋenis·straf]
death penalty	doodstraf	[doədstraf]
electric chair	elektriese stoel	[ɛlektrisə stul]
gallows	galg	[χalχ]

| to execute (vt) | eksekuteer | [ɛksekuteər] |
| execution | eksekusie | [ɛksekusi] |

| prison, jail | tronk | [tronk] |
| cell | sel | [səl] |

escort	eskort	[ɛskort]
prison guard	tronkbewaarder	[tronk·bevārdər]
prisoner	gevangene	[χefaŋənə]

| handcuffs | handboeie | [hant·buje] |
| to handcuff (vt) | in die boeie slaan | [in di buje slān] |

prison break	ontsnapping	[ontsnappiŋ]
to break out (vi)	ontsnap	[ontsnap]
to disappear (vi)	verdwyn	[ferdwajn]
to release (from prison)	vrylaat	[frajlāt]
amnesty	amnestie	[amnesti]

police	polisie	[polisi]
police officer	polisieman	[polisi·man]
police station	polisiestasie	[polisi·stasi]
billy club	knuppel	[knuppəl]
bullhorn	megafoon	[meχafoən]

patrol car	patrolliemotor	[patrolli·motor]
siren	sirene	[sirenə]
to turn on the siren	die sirene aanskakel	[di sirenə āŋskakəl]
siren call	sirenegeloei	[sirenə·χelui]

crime scene	misdaadtoneel	[misdād·toneəl]
witness	getuie	[χetœie]
freedom	vryheid	[frajhæjt]
accomplice	medepligtige	[medə·pliχtiχə]
to flee (vi)	ontvlug	[ontfluχ]
trace (to leave a ~)	spoor	[spoər]

194. Police. Law. Part 2

search (investigation)	soektog	[suktoχ]
to look for ...	soek ...	[suk ...]
suspicion	verdenking	[ferdɛnkiŋ]

suspicious (e.g., ~ vehicle)	**verdag**	[ferdaχ]
to stop (cause to halt)	**teëhou**	[teɛhæʊ]
to detain (keep in custody)	**aanhou**	[ānhæʊ]
case (lawsuit)	**hofsaak**	[hofsāk]
investigation	**ondersoek**	[ondərsuk]
detective	**speurder**	[spøørdər]
investigator	**speurder**	[spøørdər]
hypothesis	**hipotese**	[hipotesə]
motive	**motief**	[motif]
interrogation	**ondervraging**	[ondərfraχiŋ]
to interrogate (vt)	**ondervra**	[ondərfra]
to question	**verhoor**	[ferhoər]
(~ neighbors, etc.)		
check (identity ~)	**kontroleer**	[kontroleər]
round-up	**klopjag**	[klopjaχ]
search (~ warrant)	**huissoeking**	[hœis·sukiŋ]
chase (pursuit)	**agtervolging**	[aχtərfolχiŋ]
to pursue, to chase	**agtervolg**	[aχtərfolχ]
to track (a criminal)	**opspoor**	[opspoər]
arrest	**inhegtenisneming**	[inheχtenis·nemiŋ]
to arrest (sb)	**arresteer**	[arresteər]
to catch (thief, etc.)	**vang**	[faŋ]
capture	**opsporing**	[opsporiŋ]
document	**dokument**	[dokument]
proof (evidence)	**bewys**	[bevajs]
to prove (vt)	**bewys**	[bevajs]
footprint	**voetspoor**	[futspoər]
fingerprints	**vingerafdrukke**	[fiŋər·afdrukkə]
piece of evidence	**bewysstuk**	[bevajs·stuk]
alibi	**alibi**	[alibi]
innocent (not guilty)	**onskuldig**	[ɔŋskuldəχ]
injustice	**onreg**	[onreχ]
unjust, unfair (adj)	**onregverdig**	[onreχferdəχ]
criminal (adj)	**krimineel**	[krimineəl]
to confiscate (vt)	**in beslag neem**	[in beslaχ neəm]
drug (illegal substance)	**dwelm**	[dwɛlm]
weapon, gun	**wapen**	[vapen]
to disarm (vt)	**ontwapen**	[ontvapen]
to order (command)	**beveel**	[befeəl]
to disappear (vi)	**verdwyn**	[ferdwajn]
law	**wet**	[vet]
legal, lawful (adj)	**wettig**	[vɛttəχ]
illegal, illicit (adj)	**onwettig**	[onwɛttəχ]
responsibility (blame)	**verantwoordelikheid**	[ferant·voərdelikhæjt]
responsible (adj)	**verantwoordelik**	[ferant·voərdelik]

NATURE

The Earth. Part 1

195. Outer space

space	kosmos	[kosmos]
space (as adj)	kosmies	[kosmis]
outer space	buitenste ruimte	[bœitɛŋstə rajmtə]
world	wêreld	[værɛlt]
universe	heelal	[heəlal]
galaxy	sterrestelsel	[sterrə·stɛlsəl]
star	ster	[ster]
constellation	sterrebeeld	[sterrə·beəlt]
planet	planeet	[planeət]
satellite	satelliet	[satɛllit]
meteorite	meteoriet	[meteorit]
comet	komeet	[komeət]
asteroid	asteroïed	[asteroïət]
orbit	baan	[bān]
to revolve	draai	[drāi]
(~ around the Earth)		
atmosphere	atmosfeer	[atmosfeər]
the Sun	die Son	[di son]
solar system	sonnestelsel	[sonnə·stɛlsəl]
solar eclipse	sonsverduistering	[sɔŋs·ferdœisteriŋ]
the Earth	die Aarde	[di ārdə]
the Moon	die Maan	[di mān]
Mars	Mars	[mars]
Venus	Venus	[fenus]
Jupiter	Jupiter	[jupitər]
Saturn	Saturnus	[saturnus]
Mercury	Mercurius	[merkurius]
Uranus	Uranus	[uranus]
Neptune	Neptunus	[neptunus]
Pluto	Pluto	[pluto]
Milky Way	Melkweg	[melk·weχ]

| Great Bear (Ursa Major) | Groot Beer | [χroət beər] |
| North Star | Poolster | [poəl·stər] |

Martian	marsbewoner	[mars·bevonər]
extraterrestrial (n)	buiteaardse wese	[bœite·ārdsə vesə]
alien	ruimtewese	[rœimtə·vesə]
flying saucer	vlieënde skottel	[flіɛndə skottəl]

spaceship	ruimteskip	[rœimtə·skip]
space station	ruimtestasie	[rœimtə·stasi]
blast-off	vertrek	[fertrek]

engine	enjin	[ɛndʒin]
nozzle	uitlaatpyp	[œitlāt·pajp]
fuel	brandstof	[brantstof]

cockpit, flight deck	stuurkajuit	[stır·kajœit]
antenna	lugdraad	[luχdrāt]
porthole	patryspoort	[patrajs·poərt]
solar panel	sonpaneel	[son·paneəl]
spacesuit	ruimtepak	[rœimtə·pak]

| weightlessness | gewigloosheid | [χeviχloəshæjt] |
| oxygen | suurstof | [sırstof] |

| docking (in space) | koppeling | [koppeliŋ] |
| to dock (vi, vt) | koppel | [koppəl] |

observatory	observatorium	[observatorium]
telescope	teleskoop	[teleskoəp]
to observe (vt)	waarneem	[vārneəm]
to explore (vt)	eksploreer	[ɛksploreər]

196. The Earth

the Earth	die Aarde	[di ārdə]
the globe (the Earth)	die aardbol	[di ārdbol]
planet	planeet	[planeət]

atmosphere	atmosfeer	[atmosfeər]
geography	geografie	[χeoχrafi]
nature	natuur	[natır]

globe (table ~)	aardbol	[ārd·bol]
map	kaart	[kārt]
atlas	atlas	[atlas]

Europe	Europa	[øəropa]
Asia	Asië	[asiɛ]
Africa	Afrika	[afrika]

Australia	**Australië**	[ɔustraliɛ]
America	**Amerika**	[amerika]
North America	**Noord-Amerika**	[noərd-amerika]
South America	**Suid-Amerika**	[sœid-amerika]

| Antarctica | **Suidpool** | [sœid·poəl] |
| the Arctic | **Noordpool** | [noərd·poəl] |

197. Cardinal directions

north	**noorde**	[noərdə]
to the north	**na die noorde**	[na di noərdə]
in the north	**in die noorde**	[in di noərdə]
northern (adj)	**noordelik**	[noərdəlik]

south	**suide**	[sœidə]
to the south	**na die suide**	[na di sœidə]
in the south	**in die suide**	[in di sœidə]
southern (adj)	**suidelik**	[sœidəlik]

west	**weste**	[vestə]
to the west	**na die weste**	[na di vestə]
in the west	**in die weste**	[in di vestə]
western (adj)	**westelik**	[vestelik]

east	**ooste**	[oəstə]
to the east	**na die ooste**	[na di oəstə]
in the east	**in die ooste**	[in di oəstə]
eastern (adj)	**oostelik**	[oəstəlik]

198. Sea. Ocean

sea	**see**	[seə]
ocean	**oseaan**	[oseãn]
gulf (bay)	**golf**	[χolf]
straits	**straat**	[strãt]

| land (solid ground) | **land** | [lant] |
| continent (mainland) | **kontinent** | [kontinent] |

island	**eiland**	[æjlant]
peninsula	**skiereiland**	[skir·æjlant]
archipelago	**argipel**	[arχipəl]

bay, cove	**baai**	[bãi]
harbor	**hawe**	[havə]
lagoon	**strandmeer**	[strand·meər]
cape	**kaap**	[kãp]

atoll	**atol**	[atol]
reef	**rif**	[rif]
coral	**koraal**	[korāl]
coral reef	**koraalrif**	[korāl·rif]

deep (adj)	**diep**	[dip]
depth (deep water)	**diepte**	[diptə]
abyss	**afgrond**	[afχront]
trench (e.g., Mariana ~)	**trog**	[troχ]
current (Ocean ~)	**stroming**	[stromiŋ]
to surround (bathe)	**omring**	[omriŋ]

| shore | **oewer** | [uvər] |
| coast | **kus** | [kus] |

flow (flood tide)	**hoogwater**	[hoəχ·vatər]
ebb (ebb tide)	**laagwater**	[lāχ·vatər]
shoal	**sandbank**	[sand·bank]
bottom (~ of the sea)	**bodem**	[bodem]

wave	**golf**	[χolf]
crest (~ of a wave)	**kruin**	[krœin]
spume (sea foam)	**skuim**	[skœim]
storm (sea storm)	**storm**	[storm]
hurricane	**orkaan**	[orkān]
tsunami	**tsunami**	[tsunami]
calm (dead ~)	**windstilte**	[vindstiltə]
quiet, calm (adj)	**kalm**	[kalm]

| pole | **pool** | [poəl] |
| polar (adj) | **polêr** | [polær] |

latitude	**breedtegraad**	[breədtə·χrāt]
longitude	**lengtegraad**	[leŋtə·χrāt]
parallel	**parallel**	[parallel]
equator	**ewenaar**	[ɛvenār]

sky	**hemel**	[hemel]
horizon	**horison**	[horison]
air	**lug**	[luχ]

lighthouse	**vuurtoring**	[fɪrtoriŋ]
to dive (vi)	**duik**	[dœik]
to sink (ab. boat)	**sink**	[sink]
treasures	**skatte**	[skattə]

199. Seas' and Oceans' names

| Atlantic Ocean | **Atlantiese oseaan** | [atlantisə oseān] |
| Indian Ocean | **Indiese Oseaan** | [indisə oseān] |

| Pacific Ocean | Stille Oseaan | [stillə oseān] |
| Arctic Ocean | Noordelike Yssee | [noərdelikə ajs·see] |

Black Sea	Swart See	[swart see]
Red Sea	Rooi See	[roj see]
Yellow Sea	Geel See	[χeəl see]
White Sea	Witsee	[vit·see]

Caspian Sea	Kaspiese See	[kaspisə see]
Dead Sea	Dooie See	[doje see]
Mediterranean Sea	Middellandse See	[middəllandsə see]

| Aegean Sea | Egeïese See | [εχejesə see] |
| Adriatic Sea | Adriatiese See | [adriatisə see] |

Arabian Sea	Arabiese See	[arabisə see]
Sea of Japan	Japanse See	[japaŋsə see]
Bering Sea	Beringsee	[beriŋ·see]
South China Sea	Suid-Sjinese See	[sœid-ʃinesə see]

Coral Sea	Koraalsee	[korāl·see]
Tasman Sea	Tasmansee	[tasmaŋ·see]
Caribbean Sea	Karibiese See	[karibisə see]

| Barents Sea | Barentssee | [barents·see] |
| Kara Sea | Karasee | [kara·see] |

North Sea	Noordsee	[noərd·see]
Baltic Sea	Baltiese See	[baltisə see]
Norwegian Sea	Noorse See	[noərsə see]

200. Mountains

mountain	berg	[berχ]
mountain range	bergreeks	[berχ·reəks]
mountain ridge	bergrug	[berχ·ruχ]

summit, top	top	[top]
peak	piek	[pik]
foot (~ of the mountain)	voet	[fut]
slope (mountainside)	helling	[hεlliŋ]

volcano	vulkaan	[fulkān]
active volcano	aktiewe vulkaan	[aktivə fulkān]
dormant volcano	rustende vulkaan	[rustendə fulkān]

eruption	uitbarsting	[œitbarstiŋ]
crater	krater	[kratər]
magma	magma	[maχma]
lava	lawa	[lava]

molten (~ lava)	gloeiende	[χlujendə]
canyon	diepkloof	[dip·kloəf]
gorge	kloof	[kloəf]
crevice	skeur	[skøər]
abyss (chasm)	afgrond	[afχront]

pass, col	bergpas	[berχ·pas]
plateau	plato	[plato]
cliff	krans	[kraŋs]
hill	kop	[kop]

glacier	gletser	[χletsər]
waterfall	waterval	[vatər·fal]
geyser	geiser	[χæjsər]
lake	meer	[meər]

plain	vlakte	[flaktə]
landscape	landskap	[landskap]
echo	eggo	[εχχo]

alpinist	alpinis	[alpinis]
rock climber	bergklimmer	[berχ·klimmər]
to conquer (in climbing)	baasraak	[bāsrāk]
climb (an easy ~)	beklimming	[beklimmiŋ]

201. Mountains names

The Alps	die Alpe	[di alpə]
Mont Blanc	Mont Blanc	[mon blan]
The Pyrenees	die Pireneë	[di pireneε]

The Carpathians	die Karpate	[di karpatə]
The Ural Mountains	die Oeralgebergte	[di ural·χəberχtə]
The Caucasus Mountains	die Koukasus Gebergte	[di kæʊkasus χəberχtə]
Mount Elbrus	Elbroes	[εlbrus]

The Altai Mountains	die Altai-gebergte	[di altaj-χəberχtə]
The Tian Shan	die Tian Shan	[di tian ʃan]
The Pamir Mountains	die Pamir	[di pamir]
The Himalayas	die Himalajas	[di himalajas]
Mount Everest	Everest	[εverest]
The Andes	die Andes	[di andes]
Mount Kilimanjaro	Kilimanjaro	[kilimandʒaro]

202. Rivers

| river | rivier | [rifir] |
| spring (natural source) | bron | [bron] |

riverbed (river channel)	rivierbed	[rifir·bet]
basin (river valley)	stroomgebied	[stroəm·χebit]
to flow into ...	uitmond in ...	[œitmont in ...]

| tributary | syrivier | [saj·rifir] |
| bank (of river) | oewer | [uvər] |

current (stream)	stroming	[stromiŋ]
downstream (adv)	stroomafwaarts	[stroəm·afvãrts]
upstream (adv)	stroomopwaarts	[stroəm·opvãrts]

inundation	oorstroming	[oərstromiŋ]
flooding	oorstroming	[oərstromiŋ]
to overflow (vi)	oor sy walle loop	[oər saj vallə loəp]
to flood (vt)	oorstroom	[oərstroəm]

| shallow (shoal) | sandbank | [sand·bank] |
| rapids | stroomversnellings | [stroəm·fersnɛlliŋs] |

dam	damwal	[dam·wal]
canal	kanaal	[kanãl]
reservoir (artificial lake)	opgaardam	[opχãr·dam]
sluice, lock	sluis	[slœis]

water body (pond, etc.)	dam	[dam]
swamp (marshland)	moeras	[muras]
bog, marsh	vlei	[flæj]
whirlpool	draaikolk	[drãj·kolk]

stream (brook)	spruit	[sprœit]
drinking (ab. water)	drink-	[drink-]
fresh (~ water)	vars	[fars]

| ice | ys | [ajs] |
| to freeze over (ab. river, etc.) | bevries | [befris] |

203. Rivers' names

| Seine | Seine | [sæjn] |
| Loire | Loire | [lua:r] |

Thames	Teems	[tems]
Rhine	Ryn	[rajn]
Danube	Donau	[donɔu]

Volga	Wolga	[volga]
Don	Don	[don]
Lena	Lena	[lena]
Yellow River	Geel Rivier	[χeəl rifir]

Yangtze	Blou Rivier	[blæʊ rifir]
Mekong	Mekong	[mekoŋ]
Ganges	Ganges	[xaŋəs]

Nile River	Nyl	[najl]
Congo River	Kongorivier	[kongo·rifir]
Okavango River	Okavango	[okavango]
Zambezi River	Zambezi	[sambesi]
Limpopo River	Limpopo	[limpopo]
Mississippi River	Mississippi	[mississippi]

204. Forest

| forest, wood | bos | [bos] |
| forest (as adj) | bos- | [bos-] |

thick forest	woud	[væʊt]
grove	boord	[boərt]
forest clearing	oopte	[oəptə]

| thicket | struikgewas | [strœik·xevas] |
| scrubland | struikveld | [strœik·fɛlt] |

| footpath (troddenpath) | paadjie | [pādʒi] |
| gully | donga | [donχa] |

tree	boom	[boəm]
leaf	blaar	[blār]
leaves (foliage)	blare	[blarə]

fall of leaves	val van die blare	[fal fan di blarə]
to fall (ab. leaves)	val	[fal]
top (of the tree)	boomtop	[boəm·top]

branch	tak	[tak]
bough	tak	[tak]
bud (on shrub, tree)	knop	[knop]
needle (of pine tree)	naald	[nālt]
pine cone	dennebol	[dɛnnə·bol]

hollow (in a tree)	holte	[holtə]
nest	nes	[nes]
burrow (animal hole)	gat	[χat]

trunk	stam	[stam]
root	wortel	[vortəl]
bark	bas	[bas]
moss	mos	[mos]
to uproot (remove trees or tree stumps)	ontwortel	[ontwortəl]

to chop down	omkap	[omkap]
to deforest (vt)	ontbos	[ontbos]
tree stump	boomstomp	[boəm·stomp]

campfire	kampvuur	[kampfɪr]
forest fire	bosbrand	[bos·brant]
to extinguish (vt)	blus	[blus]

forest ranger	boswagter	[bos·waχtər]
protection	beskerming	[beskermiŋ]
to protect (~ nature)	beskerm	[beskerm]
poacher	wildstroper	[vilt·stropər]
steel trap	slagyster	[slaχ·ajstər]

to gather, to pick (vt)	pluk	[pluk]
to lose one's way	verdwaal	[ferdwāl]

205. Natural resources

natural resources	natuurlike bronne	[natɪrlikə bronnə]
minerals	minerale	[mineralə]
deposits	lae	[laə]
field (e.g., oilfield)	veld	[fɛlt]

to mine (extract)	myn	[majn]
mining (extraction)	myn	[majn]
ore	erts	[ɛrts]
mine (e.g., for coal)	myn	[majn]
shaft (mine ~)	mynskag	[majn·skaχ]
miner	mynwerker	[majn·werkər]

gas (natural ~)	gas	[χas]
gas pipeline	gaspyp	[χas·pajp]

oil (petroleum)	olie	[oli]
oil pipeline	olipypleiding	[oli·pajp·læjdiŋ]
oil well	oliebron	[oli·bron]
derrick (tower)	boortoring	[boər·toriŋ]
tanker	tenkskip	[tɛnk·skip]

sand	sand	[sant]
limestone	kalksteen	[kalksteən]
gravel	gruis	[χrœis]
peat	veengrond	[feənχront]
clay	klei	[klæj]
coal	steenkool	[steən·koəl]

iron (ore)	yster	[ajstər]
gold	goud	[χæʊt]
silver	silwer	[silwər]

| nickel | nikkel | [nikkəl] |
| copper | koper | [kopər] |

zinc	sink	[sink]
manganese	mangaan	[manχān]
mercury	kwik	[kwik]
lead	lood	[loət]

mineral	mineraal	[minerāl]
crystal	kristal	[kristal]
marble	marmer	[marmər]
uranium	uraan	[urān]

The Earth. Part 2

206. Weather

weather	weer	[veər]
weather forecast	weersvoorspelling	[veərs·foərspɛliŋ]
temperature	temperatuur	[temperatɪr]
thermometer	termometer	[termometər]
barometer	barometer	[barometər]
humid (adj)	klam	[klam]
humidity	vogtigheid	[foχtiχæejt]
heat (extreme ~)	hitte	[hittə]
hot (torrid)	heet	[heət]
it's hot	dis vrekwarm	[dis frekvarm]
it's warm	dit is warm	[dit is varm]
warm (moderately hot)	louwarm	[læʊvarm]
it's cold	dis koud	[dis kæʊt]
cold (adj)	koud	[kæʊt]
sun	son	[son]
to shine (vi)	skyn	[skajn]
sunny (day)	sonnig	[sonnəχ]
to come up (vi)	opkom	[opkom]
to set (vi)	ondergaan	[ondərχān]
cloud	wolk	[volk]
cloudy (adj)	bewolk	[bevolk]
rain cloud	reënwolk	[reɛn·wolk]
somber (gloomy)	somber	[sombər]
rain	reën	[reɛn]
it's raining	dit reën	[dit reɛn]
rainy (~ day, weather)	reënerig	[reɛnerəχ]
to drizzle (vi)	motreën	[motreɛn]
pouring rain	stortbui	[stortbœi]
downpour	reënvlaag	[reɛn·flāχ]
heavy (e.g., ~ rain)	swaar	[swār]
puddle	poeletjie	[puləki]
to get wet (in rain)	nat word	[nat vort]
fog (mist)	mis	[mis]
foggy	mistig	[mistəχ]

| snow | sneeu | [sniʊ] |
| it's snowing | dit sneeu | [dit sniʊ] |

207. Severe weather. Natural disasters

thunderstorm	donderstorm	[dondər·storm]
lightning (~ strike)	weerlig	[veərləχ]
to flash (vi)	flits	[flits]

thunder	donder	[dondər]
to thunder (vi)	donder	[dondər]
it's thundering	dit donder	[dit dondər]

| hail | hael | [haəl] |
| it's hailing | dit hael | [dit haəl] |

| to flood (vt) | oorstroom | [oərstroəm] |
| flood, inundation | oorstroming | [oərstromiŋ] |

earthquake	aardbewing	[ārd·beviŋ]
tremor, quake	aardskok	[ārd·skok]
epicenter	episentrum	[ɛpisentrum]

| eruption | uitbarsting | [œitbarstiŋ] |
| lava | lawa | [lava] |

| twister, tornado | tornado | [tornado] |
| typhoon | tifoon | [tifoən] |

hurricane	orkaan	[orkān]
storm	storm	[storm]
tsunami	tsunami	[tsunami]

cyclone	sikloon	[sikloən]
bad weather	slegte weer	[sleχtə veər]
fire (accident)	brand	[brant]
disaster	ramp	[ramp]
meteorite	meteoriet	[meteorit]

avalanche	lawine	[lavinə]
snowslide	sneeulawine	[sniʊ·lavinə]
blizzard	sneeustorm	[sniʊ·storm]
snowstorm	sneeustorm	[sniʊ·storm]

208. Noises. Sounds

| silence (quiet) | stilte | [stiltə] |
| sound | geluid | [χelœit] |

noise	**geraas**	[xerãs]
to make noise	**geraas maak**	[xerãs mãk]
noisy (adj)	**lawaaierig**	[lavajerəx]

loudly (to speak, etc.)	**hard**	[hart]
loud (voice, etc.)	**hard**	[hart]
constant (e.g., ~ noise)	**aanhoudend**	[ãnhæʊdent]

cry, shout (n)	**skreeu**	[skriʊ]
to cry, to shout (vi)	**skreeu**	[skriʊ]
whisper	**gefluister**	[xeflœeistər]
to whisper (vi, vt)	**fluister**	[flœeistər]

barking (dog's ~)	**geblaf**	[xeblaf]
to bark (vi)	**blaf**	[blaf]

groan (of pain, etc.)	**gekreun**	[xekrøən]
to groan (vi)	**kreun**	[krøən]
cough	**hoes**	[hus]
to cough (vi)	**hoes**	[hus]

whistle	**gefluit**	[xeflœeit]
to whistle (vi)	**fluit**	[flœeit]
knock (at the door)	**klop**	[klop]
to knock (at the door)	**klop**	[klop]

to crack (vi)	**kraak**	[krãk]
crack (cracking sound)	**gekraak**	[xekrãk]

siren	**sirene**	[sirenə]
whistle (factory ~, etc.)	**fluit**	[flœeit]
to whistle (ab. train)	**fluit**	[flœeit]
honk (car horn sound)	**toeter**	[tutər]
to honk (vi)	**toeter**	[tutər]

209. Winter

winter (n)	**winter**	[vintər]
winter (as adj)	**winter-**	[vintər-]
in winter	**in die winter**	[in di vintər]

snow	**sneeu**	[sniʊ]
it's snowing	**dit sneeu**	[dit sniʊ]
snowfall	**sneeuval**	[sniʊ·fal]
snowdrift	**sneeuhoop**	[sniʊ·hoəp]

snowflake	**sneeuvlokkie**	[sniʊ·flokki]
snowball	**sneeubal**	[sniʊ·bal]
snowman	**sneeuman**	[sniʊ·man]
icicle	**yskeël**	[ajskeɛl]

December	Desember	[desembər]
January	Januarie	[januari]
February	Februarie	[februari]

| frost (severe ~, freezing cold) | ryp | [rajp] |
| frosty (weather, air) | vries- | [fris-] |

below zero (adv)	onder nul	[ondər nul]
first frost	eerste ryp	[eərstə rajp]
hoarfrost	ruigryp	[rœiχ·rajp]

| cold (cold weather) | koue | [kæʋə] |
| it's cold | dis koud | [dis kæʋt] |

| fur coat | pelsjas | [pelʃas] |
| mittens | duimhandskoene | [dœim·handskunə] |

| to get sick | siek word | [sik vort] |
| cold (illness) | verkoue | [ferkæʋə] |

ice	ys	[ajs]
black ice	gevriesde reën	[χefrisdə reɛn]
to freeze over (ab. river, etc.)	bevries	[befris]
ice floe	ysskotse	[ajs·skotsə]

skier	skiër	[skiɛr]
to ski (vi)	ski	[ski]
to skate (vi)	ysskaats	[ajs·skāts]

Fauna

210. Mammals. Predators

predator	roofdier	[roəf·dir]
tiger	tier	[tir]
lion	leeu	[liʊ]
wolf	wolf	[volf]
fox	vos	[fos]
jaguar	jaguar	[jaχuar]
leopard	luiperd	[lœipert]
cheetah	jagluiperd	[jaχ·lœipert]
black panther	swart luiperd	[swart lœipert]
puma	poema	[puma]
snow leopard	sneeuluiperd	[sniʊ·lœipert]
lynx	los	[los]
coyote	prêriewolf	[præri·volf]
jackal	jakkals	[jakkals]
hyena	hiëna	[hiɛna]

211. Wild animals

animal	dier	[dir]
beast (animal)	beest	[beəst]
squirrel	eekhoring	[eəkhoriŋ]
hedgehog	krimpvarkie	[krimpfarki]
hare	hasie	[hasi]
rabbit	konyn	[konajn]
badger	das	[das]
raccoon	wasbeer	[vasbeər]
hamster	hamster	[hamstər]
marmot	marmot	[marmot]
mole	mol	[mol]
mouse	muis	[mœis]
rat	rot	[rot]
bat	vlermuis	[fler·mœis]
ermine	hermelyn	[herməlajn]
sable	sabel, sabeldier	[sabəl], [sabəl·dir]

marten	marter	[martər]
weasel	wesel	[vesəl]
mink	nerts	[nerts]

| beaver | bewer | [bevər] |
| otter | otter | [ottər] |

horse	perd	[pert]
moose	eland	[ɛlant]
deer	hert	[hert]
camel	kameel	[kameəl]

bison	bison	[bison]
aurochs	wisent	[visent]
buffalo	buffel	[buffəl]

zebra	sebra, kwagga	[sebra], [kwaχχa]
antelope	wildsbok	[vilds·bok]
roe deer	reebok	[reəbok]
fallow deer	damhert	[damhert]
chamois	gems	[χems]
wild boar	wildevark	[vildə·fark]

whale	walvis	[valfis]
seal	seehond	[seə·hont]
walrus	walrus	[valrus]
fur seal	seebeer	[seə·beər]
dolphin	dolfyn	[dolfajn]

bear	beer	[beər]
polar bear	ysbeer	[ajs·beər]
panda	panda	[panda]

monkey	aap	[āp]
chimpanzee	sjimpansee	[ʃimpaŋseə]
orangutan	orangoetang	[oraŋχutaŋ]
gorilla	gorilla	[χorilla]
macaque	makaak	[makāk]
gibbon	gibbon	[χibbon]

elephant	olifant	[olifant]
rhinoceros	renoster	[renostər]
giraffe	kameelperd	[kameəl·pert]
hippopotamus	seekoei	[seə·kui]

| kangaroo | kangaroe | [kanχaru] |
| koala (bear) | koala | [koala] |

mongoose	muishond	[mœis·hont]
chinchilla	chinchilla, tjintjilla	[tʃin·tʃila]
skunk	stinkmuishond	[stinkmœis·hont]
porcupine	ystervark	[ajstər·fark]

212. Domestic animals

cat	kat	[kat]
tomcat	kater	[katər]
dog	hond	[hont]
horse	perd	[pert]
stallion (male horse)	hings	[hiŋs]
mare	merrie	[merri]
cow	koei	[kui]
bull	bul	[bul]
ox	os	[os]
sheep (ewe)	skaap	[skāp]
ram	ram	[ram]
goat	bok	[bok]
billy goat, he-goat	bokram	[bok·ram]
donkey	donkie, esel	[donki], [eisəl]
mule	muil	[mœil]
pig, hog	vark	[fark]
piglet	varkie	[farki]
rabbit	konyn	[konajn]
hen (chicken)	hoender, hen	[hundər], [hen]
rooster	haan	[hān]
duck	eend	[eent]
drake	mannetjieseend	[mannekis·eent]
goose	gans	[χaŋs]
tom turkey, gobbler	kalkoenmannetjie	[kalkun·manneki]
turkey (hen)	kalkoen	[kalkun]
domestic animals	huisdiere	[hœis·dirə]
tame (e.g., ~ hamster)	mak	[mak]
to tame (vt)	mak maak	[mak māk]
to breed (vt)	teel	[teəl]
farm	plaas	[plās]
poultry	pluimvee	[plœimfeə]
cattle	beeste	[beəstə]
herd (cattle)	kudde	[kuddə]
stable	stal	[stal]
pigpen	varkstal	[fark·stal]
cowshed	koeistal	[kui·stal]
rabbit hutch	konynehok	[konajnə·hok]
hen house	hoenderhok	[hundər·hok]

213. Dogs. Dog breeds

dog	hond	[hont]
sheepdog	herdershond	[herdərs·hont]
German shepherd	Duitse herdershond	[dœitsə herdərs·hont]
poodle	poedel	[pudəl]
dachshund	worshond	[vors·hont]

bulldog	bulhond	[bul·hont]
boxer	bokser	[boksər]
mastiff	mastiff	[mastif]
Rottweiler	Rottweiler	[rottwæjlər]
Doberman	Dobermann	[dobermann]

basset	basset	[basset]
bobtail	bobtail	[bobtajl]
Dalmatian	Dalmatiese hond	[dalmatisə hont]
cocker spaniel	sniphond	[snip·hont]

| Newfoundland | Newfoundlander | [njufæʊntlandər] |
| Saint Bernard | Sint Bernard | [sint bernart] |

husky	poolhond, husky	[pulhont], [huski]
Chow Chow	chowchow	[tʃau·tʃau]
spitz	spitshond	[spits·hont]
pug	mopshond	[mops·hont]

214. Sounds made by animals

barking (n)	geblaf	[χeblaf]
to bark (vi)	blaf	[blaf]
to meow (vi)	miaau	[miāu]
to purr (vi)	spin	[spin]

to moo (vi)	loei	[lui]
to bellow (bull)	bulk	[bulk]
to growl (vi)	grom	[χrom]

howl (n)	gehuil	[χehœil]
to howl (vi)	huil	[hœil]
to whine (vi)	tjank	[tʃank]

to bleat (sheep)	blêr	[blær]
to oink, to grunt (pig)	snork	[snork]
to squeal (vi)	gil	[χil]
to croak (vi)	kwaak	[kwāk]
to buzz (insect)	zoem	[zum]
to chirp (crickets, grasshopper)	kriek	[krik]

215. Young animals

cub	kleintjie	[klæjnki]
kitten	katjie	[kaki]
baby mouse	muisie	[mœisi]
puppy	hondjie	[hondʒi]
leveret	hasie	[hasi]
baby rabbit	konyntjie	[konajnki]
wolf cub	wolfie	[volfi]
fox cub	vossie	[fossi]
bear cub	beertjie	[beərki]
lion cub	leeutjie	[liʋki]
tiger cub	tiertjie	[tirki]
elephant calf	olifantjie	[olifanki]
piglet	varkie	[farki]
calf (young cow, bull)	kalfie	[kalfi]
kid (young goat)	bokkie	[bokki]
lamb	lam	[lam]
fawn (young deer)	bokkie	[bokki]
young camel	kameeltjie	[kameəlki]
snakelet (baby snake)	slangetjie	[slaŋəki]
froglet (baby frog)	paddatjie	[pad·daki]
baby bird	voëltjie	[foɛlki]
chick (of chicken)	kuiken	[kœiken]
duckling	eendjie	[eəndʒi]

216. Birds

bird	voël	[foɛl]
pigeon	duif	[dœif]
sparrow	mossie	[mossi]
tit (great tit)	mees	[meəs]
magpie	ekster	[ɛkstər]
raven	raaf	[rãf]
crow	kraai	[krãi]
jackdaw	kerkkraai	[kerk·krãi]
rook	roek	[ruk]
duck	eend	[eent]
goose	gans	[ɣaŋs]
pheasant	fisant	[fisant]
eagle	arend	[arɛnt]
hawk	sperwer	[sperwər]

falcon	valk	[falk]
vulture	aasvoël	[āsfoɛl]
condor (Andean ~)	kondor	[kondor]

swan	swaan	[swān]
crane	kraanvoël	[krān·foɛl]
stork	ooievaar	[ojefār]

parrot	papegaai	[papəχāi]
hummingbird	kolibrie	[kolibri]
peacock	pou	[pæʊ]

ostrich	volstruis	[folstrœis]
heron	reier	[ræjer]
flamingo	flamink	[flamink]
pelican	pelikaan	[pelikān]

| nightingale | nagtegaal | [naχteχāl] |
| swallow | swael | [swaəl] |

thrush	lyster	[lajstər]
song thrush	sanglyster	[saŋlajstər]
blackbird	merel	[merəl]

swift	windswael	[vindswaəl]
lark	lewerik	[leverik]
quail	kwartel	[kwartəl]

woodpecker	speg	[speχ]
cuckoo	koekoek	[kukuk]
owl	uil	[œil]
eagle owl	ooruil	[oərœil]
wood grouse	auerhoen	[ɔuer·hun]
black grouse	korhoen	[korhun]
partridge	patrys	[patrajs]

starling	spreeu	[spriʊ]
canary	kanarie	[kanari]
hazel grouse	bonasa hoen	[bonasa hun]
chaffinch	gryskoppie	[χrajskoppi]
bullfinch	bloedvink	[bludfink]

seagull	seemeeu	[seəmiʊ]
albatross	albatros	[albatros]
penguin	pikkewyn	[pikkəvajn]

217. Birds. Singing and sounds

| to sing (vi) | fluit | [flœit] |
| to call (animal, bird) | roep | [rup] |

| to crow (rooster) | kraai | [krāi] |
| cock-a-doodle-doo | koekelekoe | [kukeleku] |

to cluck (hen)	kekkel	[kɛkkəl]
to caw (vi)	kras	[kras]
to quack (duck)	kwaak	[kwāk]
to cheep (vi)	piep	[pip]
to chirp, to twitter	tjilp	[tʃilp]

218. Fish. Marine animals

bream	brasem	[brasem]
carp	karp	[karp]
perch	baars	[bārs]
catfish	katvis, seebaber	[katfis], [seə·babər]
pike	snoek	[snuk]

| salmon | salm | [salm] |
| sturgeon | steur | [støər] |

herring	haring	[hariŋ]
Atlantic salmon	atlantiese salm	[atlantisə salm]
mackerel	makriel	[makril]
flatfish	platvis	[platfis]

zander, pike perch	varswatersnoek	[farswatər·snuk]
cod	kabeljou	[kabeljæʊ]
tuna	tuna	[tuna]
trout	forel	[forəl]
eel	paling	[paliŋ]
electric ray	drilvis	[drilfis]
moray eel	bontpaling	[bontpaliŋ]
piranha	piranha	[piranha]

shark	haai	[hāi]
dolphin	dolfyn	[dolfajn]
whale	walvis	[valfis]

crab	krap	[krap]
jellyfish	jellievis	[jelli·fis]
octopus	seekat	[seə·kat]

starfish	seester	[seə·stər]
sea urchin	see-egel, seekastaiing	[seə-eχel], [seə·kastajiŋ]
seahorse	seeperdjie	[seə·perdʒi]

oyster	oester	[ustər]
shrimp	garnaal	[χarnāl]
lobster	kreef	[kreəf]
spiny lobster	seekreef	[seə·kreəf]

219. Amphibians. Reptiles

snake	**slang**	[slaŋ]
venomous (snake)	**giftig**	[χiftəχ]
viper	**adder**	[addər]
cobra	**kobra**	[kobra]
python	**luislang**	[lœislaŋ]
boa	**boa, konstriktorslang**	[boa], [kɔŋstriktor·slaŋ]
grass snake	**ringslang**	[riŋ·slaŋ]
rattle snake	**ratelslang**	[ratəl·slaŋ]
anaconda	**anakonda**	[anakonda]
lizard	**akkedis**	[akkedis]
iguana	**leguaan**	[leχuãn]
monitor lizard	**likkewaan**	[likkevãn]
salamander	**salamander**	[salamandər]
chameleon	**verkleurmannetjie**	[ferkløər·manneki]
scorpion	**skerpioen**	[skerpiun]
turtle	**skilpad**	[skilpat]
frog	**padda**	[padda]
toad	**brulpadda**	[brul·padda]
crocodile	**krokodil**	[krokodil]

220. Insects

insect, bug	**insek**	[insek]
butterfly	**skoenlapper**	[skunlappər]
ant	**mier**	[mir]
fly	**vlieg**	[fliχ]
mosquito	**muskiet**	[muskit]
beetle	**kewer**	[kevər]
wasp	**perdeby**	[perdə·baj]
bee	**by**	[baj]
bumblebee	**hommelby**	[homməl·baj]
gadfly (botfly)	**perdevlieg**	[perdə·fliχ]
spider	**spinnekop**	[spinnə·kop]
spiderweb	**spinnerak**	[spinnə·rak]
dragonfly	**naaldekoker**	[nãldə·kokər]
grasshopper	**sprinkaan**	[sprinkãn]
moth (night butterfly)	**mot**	[mot]
cockroach	**kakkerlak**	[kakkerlak]
tick	**bosluis**	[boslœis]

| flea | vlooi | [floj] |
| midge | muggie | [muχχi] |

locust	treksprinkhaan	[trek·sprinkhān]
snail	slak	[slak]
cricket	kriek	[krik]

lightning bug	vuurvliegie	[fɪrfliχi]
ladybug	lieweheersbesie	[liveheers·besi]
cockchafer	lentekewer	[lentekevər]

leech	bloedsuier	[blud·sœiər]
caterpillar	ruspe	[ruspə]
earthworm	erdwurm	[ɛrd·vurm]
larva	larwe	[larvə]

221. Animals. Body parts

beak	snawel	[snavəl]
wings	vlerke	[flerkə]
foot (of bird)	poot	[poət]
feathers (plumage)	vere	[ferə]

| feather | veer | [feər] |
| crest | kuif | [kœif] |

gills	kiewe	[kivə]
spawn	viseiers	[fisæejers]
larva	larwe	[larvə]

| fin | vin | [fin] |
| scales (of fish, reptile) | skubbe | [skubbə] |

fang (canine)	slagtand	[slaχtant]
paw (e.g., cat's ~)	poot	[poət]
muzzle (snout)	muil	[mœil]
mouth (of cat, dog)	bek	[bek]

| tail | stert | [stert] |
| whiskers | snor | [snor] |

| hoof | hoef | [huf] |
| horn | horing | [horiŋ] |

carapace	rugdop	[ruχdop]
shell (of mollusk)	skulp	[skulp]
eggshell	eierdop	[æejer·dop]

| animal's hair (pelage) | pels | [pɛls] |
| pelt (hide) | vel | [fəl] |

222. Actions of animals

to fly (vi)	**vlieg**	[flix]
to fly in circles	**sirkel**	[sirkəl]
to fly away	**wegvlieg**	[veꭓflix]
to flap (~ the wings)	**klapwiek**	[klapwik]
to peck (vi)	**pik**	[pik]
to sit on eggs	**broei**	[brui]
to hatch out (vi)	**uitbroei**	[œjtbræj]
to slither, to crawl	**seil**	[sæjl]
to sting, to bite (insect)	**steek**	[steək]
to bite (ab. animal)	**byt**	[bajt]
to sniff (vt)	**snuffel**	[snuffəl]
to bark (vi)	**blaf**	[blaf]
to hiss (snake)	**sis**	[sis]
to scare (vt)	**bang maak**	[baŋ māk]
to attack (vt)	**aanval**	[ānfal]
to gnaw (bone, etc.)	**knaag**	[knāꭓ]
to scratch (with claws)	**krap**	[krap]
to hide (vi)	**wegkruip**	[veꭓkrœip]
to play (kittens, etc.)	**speel**	[speəl]
to hunt (vi, vt)	**jag**	[jaꭓ]
to hibernate (vi)	**oorwinter**	[oərwintər]
to go extinct	**uitsterf**	[œitsterf]

223. Animals. Habitats

habitat	**habitat**	[habitat]
migration	**migrasie**	[miꭓrasi]
mountain	**berg**	[berꭓ]
reef	**rif**	[rif]
cliff	**rots**	[rots]
forest	**woud**	[væʊt]
jungle	**oerwoud**	[urwæʊt]
savanna	**veld**	[fɛlt]
tundra	**toendra**	[tundra]
steppe	**steppe**	[stɛppə]
desert	**woestyn**	[vustajn]
oasis	**oase**	[oasə]
sea	**see**	[seə]
lake	**meer**	[meər]

ocean	oseaan	[oseãn]
swamp (marshland)	moeras	[muras]
freshwater (adj)	varswater	[fars·vatər]
pond	dam	[dam]
river	rivier	[rifir]

den (bear's ~)	hol	[hol]
nest	nes	[nes]
hollow (in a tree)	holte	[holtə]
burrow (animal hole)	gat	[χat]
anthill	miershoop	[mirs·hoəp]

224. Animal care

| zoo | dieretuin | [dirə·tœin] |
| nature preserve | natuurreservaat | [natɪr·reserfãt] |

breeder (cattery, kennel, etc.)	teelplaas	[teəlplãs]
open-air cage	opelughok	[opeluχ·hok]
cage	kooi	[koj]
doghouse (kennel)	hondehok	[hondə·hok]

dovecot	duiwehok	[dœivə·hok]
aquarium (fish tank)	vistenk	[fis·tɛnk]
dolphinarium	dolfynpark	[dolfajn·park]

to breed (animals)	teel	[teəl]
brood, litter	werpsel	[verpsəl]
to tame (vt)	mak maak	[mak mãk]
to train (animals)	afrig	[afrəχ]
feed (fodder, etc.)	voer	[fur]
to feed (vt)	voer	[fur]

pet store	troeteldierwinkel	[truteldir·vinkəl]
muzzle (for dog)	muilkorf	[mœil·korf]
collar (e.g., dog ~)	halsband	[hals·bant]
name (of animal)	naam	[nãm]
pedigree (of dog)	stamboom	[stam·boəm]

225. Animals. Miscellaneous

pack (wolves)	trop	[trop]
flock (birds)	swerm	[swerm]
shoal, school (fish)	skool	[skoəl]
herd (horses)	trop	[trop]
male (n)	mannetjie	[mannəki]
female (n)	wyfie	[vajfi]

hungry (adj)	honger	[hoŋər]
wild (adj)	wild	[vilt]
dangerous (adj)	gevaarlik	[χefārlik]

226. Horses

| horse | perd | [pert] |
| breed (race) | ras | [ras] |

| foal | vulling | [fulliŋ] |
| mare | merrie | [merri] |

mustang	mustang	[mustaŋ]
pony	ponie	[poni]
draft horse	trekperd	[trek·pert]

| mane | maanhaar | [mānhār] |
| tail | stert | [stert] |

hoof	hoef	[huf]
horseshoe	hoefyster	[huf·ajstər]
to shoe (vt)	beslaan	[beslān]
blacksmith	grofsmid	[χrofsmit]

saddle	saal	[sāl]
stirrup	stiebeuel	[stibøəəl]
bridle	toom	[toəm]
reins	leisels	[læjscls]
whip (for riding)	peits	[pæjts]

rider	ruiter	[rœitər]
to saddle up (vt)	opsaal	[opsāl]
to mount a horse	bestyg	[bestajχ]

gallop	galop	[χalop]
to gallop (vi)	galoppeer	[χaloppeər]
trot (n)	draf	[draf]
to go at a trot	draf	[draf]

| racehorse | resiesperd | [resispert] |
| horse racing | perdewedren | [perdə·vedrən] |

stable	stal	[stal]
to feed (vt)	voer	[fur]
hay	hooi	[hoj]
to water (animals)	water gee	[vatər χee]
to wash (horse)	was	[vas]

| horse-drawn cart | perdekar | [perdə·kar] |
| to graze (vi) | wei | [væj] |

| to neigh (vi) | **runnik** | [runnik] |
| to kick (about horse) | **skop** | [skop] |

Flora

227. Trees

tree	**boom**	[boəm]
deciduous (adj)	**bladwisselend**	[bladwisselent]
coniferous (adj)	**kegeldraend**	[keχɛldraent]
evergreen (adj)	**immergroen**	[immərχrun]
apple tree	**appelboom**	[appɛl·boəm]
pear tree	**peerboom**	[peər·boəm]
cherry tree	**kersieboom**	[kersi·boəm]
sweet cherry tree	**soetkersieboom**	[sutkersi·boəm]
sour cherry tree	**suurkersieboom**	[sɪrkersi·boəm]
plum tree	**pruimeboom**	[prœimə·boəm]
birch	**berk**	[berk]
oak	**eik**	[æjk]
linden tree	**lindeboom**	[lində·boəm]
aspen	**trilpopulier**	[trilpopulir]
maple	**esdoring**	[ɛsdoriŋ]
spruce	**spar**	[spar]
pine	**denneboom**	[dɛnnə·boəm]
larch	**lorkeboom**	[lorkə·boəm]
fir tree	**den**	[den]
cedar	**seder**	[sedər]
poplar	**populier**	[populir]
rowan	**lysterbessie**	[lajstərbɛssi]
willow	**wilger**	[vilχər]
alder	**els**	[ɛls]
beech	**beuk**	[bøək]
elm	**olm**	[olm]
ash (tree)	**esboom**	[ɛs·boəm]
chestnut	**kastaiing**	[kastajiŋ]
magnolia	**magnolia**	[maχnolia]
palm tree	**palm**	[palm]
cypress	**sipres**	[sipres]
mangrove	**wortelboom**	[vortəl·boəm]
baobab	**kremetart**	[kremetart]
eucalyptus	**bloekom**	[blukom]
sequoia	**mammoetboom**	[mammut·boəm]

228. Shrubs

| bush | struik | [strœik] |
| shrub | bossie | [bossi] |

| grapevine | wingerdstok | [viŋerd·stok] |
| vineyard | wingerd | [viŋert] |

raspberry bush	framboosstruik	[framboəs·strœik]
blackcurrant bush	swartbessiestruik	[swartbɛssi·strœik]
redcurrant bush	rooi aalbessiestruik	[roj ālbɛssi·strœik]
gooseberry bush	appelliefiestruik	[appɛllifi·strœik]

acacia	akasia	[akasia]
barberry	suurbessie	[sɪr·bɛssi]
jasmine	jasmyn	[jasmajn]

juniper	jenewer	[jenevər]
rosebush	roosstruik	[roəs·strœik]
dog rose	hondsroos	[honds·roəs]

229. Mushrooms

mushroom	paddastoel	[paddastul]
edible mushroom	eetbare paddastoel	[eetbarə paddastul]
poisonous mushroom	giftige paddastoel	[xiftiχə paddastul]
cap (of mushroom)	hoed	[hut]
stipe (of mushroom)	steel	[steəl]

cep (Boletus edulis)	Eetbare boleet	[eetbarə boleet]
orange-cap boletus	rooihoed	[rojhut]
birch bolete	berkboleet	[berk·boleet]
chanterelle	dooierswam	[dojer·swam]
russula	russula	[russula]

morel	morielje	[morilje]
fly agaric	vlieëswam	[fliɛ·swam]
death cap	duiwelsbrood	[dœivɛls·broət]

230. Fruits. Berries

| fruit | vrug | [fruχ] |
| fruits | vrugte | [fruχtə] |

apple	appel	[appəl]
pear	peer	[peər]
plum	pruim	[prœim]

strawberry (garden ~)	aarbei	[ārbæj]
cherry	kersie	[kersi]
sour cherry	suurkersie	[sɪr·kersi]
sweet cherry	soetkersie	[sut·kersi]
grape	druif	[drœif]

raspberry	framboos	[framboəs]
blackcurrant	swartbessie	[swartbɛssi]
redcurrant	rooi aalbessie	[roj ālbɛssi]
gooseberry	appelliefie	[appɛllifi]
cranberry	bosbessie	[bosbɛssi]

orange	lemoen	[lemun]
mandarin	nartjie	[narki]
pineapple	pynappel	[pajnappəl]
banana	piesang	[pisaŋ]
date	dadel	[dadəl]

lemon	suurlemoen	[sɪr·lemun]
apricot	appelkoos	[appɛlkoəs]
peach	perske	[perskə]
kiwi	kiwi, kiwivrug	[kivi], [kivi·fruχ]
grapefruit	pomelo	[pomelo]

berry	bessie	[bɛssi]
berries	bessies	[bɛssis]
cowberry	pryselbessie	[prajsɛlbɛssi]
wild strawberry	wilde aarbei	[vildə ārbæj]
bilberry	bloubessie	[blæʊbɛssi]

231. Flowers. Plants

| flower | blom | [blom] |
| bouquet (of flowers) | boeket | [buket] |

rose (flower)	roos	[roəs]
tulip	tulp	[tulp]
carnation	angelier	[anχəlir]
gladiolus	swaardlelie	[swārd·leli]

cornflower	koringblom	[koriŋblom]
harebell	grasklokkie	[χras·klokki]
dandelion	perdeblom	[perdə·blom]
camomile	kamille	[kamillə]

aloe	aalwyn	[ālwajn]
cactus	kaktus	[kaktus]
rubber plant, ficus	rubberplant	[rubbər·plant]
lily	lelie	[leli]
geranium	malva	[malfa]

hyacinth	hiasint	[hiasint]
mimosa	mimosa	[mimosa]
narcissus	narsing	[narsiŋ]
nasturtium	kappertjie	[kapperki]

orchid	orgidee	[orχideə]
peony	pinksterroos	[pinkstər·roəs]
violet	viooltjie	[fioəlki]
pansy	gesiggie	[χesiχi]
forget-me-not	vergeet-my-nietjie	[ferχeet-maj-niki]
daisy	madeliefie	[madelifi]

poppy	papawer	[papavər]
hemp	hennep	[hɛnnəp]
mint	kruisement	[krœisəment]

| lily of the valley | dallelie | [dalleli] |
| snowdrop | sneeuklokkie | [sniʊ·klokki] |

nettle	brandnetel	[brant·netəl]
sorrel	veldsuring	[fɛltsuriŋ]
water lily	waterlelie	[vatər·leli]
fern	varing	[fariŋ]
lichen	korsmos	[korsmos]
greenhouse (tropical ~)	broeikas	[bruikas]
lawn	grasperk	[χras·perk]
flowerbed	blombed	[blom·bet]

plant	plant	[plant]
grass	gras	[χras]
blade of grass	grasspriet	[χras·sprit]

leaf	blaar	[blār]
petal	kroonblaar	[kroən·blār]
stem	stingel	[stiŋəl]
tuber	knol	[knol]

| young plant (shoot) | saailing | [sājliŋ] |
| thorn | doring | [doriŋ] |

to blossom (vi)	bloei	[blui]
to fade, to wither	verlep	[ferlep]
smell (odor)	reuk	[røək]
to cut (flowers)	sny	[snaj]
to pick (a flower)	pluk	[pluk]

232. Cereals, grains

| grain | graan | [χrān] |
| cereal crops | graangewasse | [χrān·χəwassə] |

ear (of barley, etc.)	aar	[ār]
wheat	koring	[koriŋ]
rye	rog	[roχ]
oats	hawer	[havər]
millet	gierst	[χirst]
barley	gars	[χars]

corn	mielie	[mili]
rice	rys	[rajs]
buckwheat	bokwiet	[bokwit]

pea plant	ertjie	[ɛrki]
kidney bean	nierboon	[nir·boən]
soy	soja	[soja]
lentil	lensie	[lɛŋsi]
beans (pulse crops)	boontjies	[boənkis]

233. Vegetables. Greens

| vegetables | groente | [χruntə] |
| greens | groente | [χruntə] |

tomato	tamatie	[tamati]
cucumber	komkommer	[komkommər]
carrot	wortel	[vortəl]
potato	aartappel	[ārtappəl]
onion	ui	[œi]
garlic	knoffel	[knoffəl]

cabbage	kool	[koəl]
cauliflower	blomkool	[blom·koəl]
Brussels sprouts	Brusselspruite	[brussɛl·sprœitə]
broccoli	broccoli	[brokoli]

beetroot	beet	[beət]
eggplant	eiervrug	[æjerfruχ]
zucchini	vingerskorsie	[fiŋər·skorsi]
pumpkin	pampoen	[pampun]
turnip	raap	[rāp]

parsley	pietersielie	[pitərsili]
dill	dille	[dillə]
lettuce	blaarslaai	[blārslāi]
celery	seldery	[selderaj]
asparagus	aspersie	[aspersi]
spinach	spinasie	[spinasi]

pea	ertjie	[ɛrki]
beans	boontjies	[boənkis]
corn (maize)	mielie	[mili]

kidney bean	**nierboon**	[nir·boən]
pepper	**peper**	[pepər]
radish	**radys**	[radajs]
artichoke	**artisjok**	[artiʃok]

REGIONAL GEOGRAPHY

Countries. Nationalities

234. Western Europe

Europe	Europa	[øəropa]
European Union	Europese Unie	[øəropesə uni]
European (n)	Europeaan	[øəropeān]
European (adj)	Europees	[øəropeəs]

Austria	Oostenryk	[oəstenrajk]
Austrian (masc.)	Oostenryker	[oəstenrajkər]
Austrian (fem.)	Oostenryker	[oəstenrajkər]
Austrian (adj)	Oostenryks	[oəstenrajks]

Great Britain	Groot-Brittanje	[χroət-brittanje]
England	Engeland	[ɛŋəlant]
British (masc.)	Engelsman	[ɛŋəlsman]
British (fem.)	Engelse dame	[ɛŋəlsə damə]
English, British (adj)	Engels	[ɛŋəls]

Belgium	België	[belχiɛ]
Belgian (masc.)	Belg	[belχ]
Belgian (fem.)	Belg	[belχ]
Belgian (adj)	Belgies	[belχis]

Germany	Duitsland	[dœitslant]
German (masc.)	Duitser	[dœitsər]
German (fem.)	Duitser	[dœitsər]
German (adj)	Duits	[dœits]

Netherlands	Nederland	[nedərlant]
Holland	Holland	[hollant]
Dutch (masc.)	Nederlander	[nedərlandər]
Dutch (fem.)	Nederlander	[nedərlandər]
Dutch (adj)	Nederlands	[nedərlands]

Greece	Griekeland	[χrikəlant]
Greek (masc.)	Griek	[χrik]
Greek (fem.)	Griek	[χrik]
Greek (adj)	Grieks	[χriks]

Denmark	Denemarke	[denemarkə]
Dane (masc.)	Deen	[deən]

Dane (fem.)	Deen	[deən]
Danish (adj)	Deens	[deɛŋs]
Ireland	Ierland	[irlant]
Irish (masc.)	Ier	[ir]
Irish (fem.)	Ier	[ir]
Irish (adj)	Iers	[irs]
Iceland	Ysland	[ajslant]
Icelander (masc.)	Yslander	[ajslandər]
Icelander (fem.)	Yslander	[ajslandər]
Icelandic (adj)	Yslandse	[ajslandsə]
Spain	Spanje	[spanje]
Spaniard (masc.)	Spanjaard	[spanjãrt]
Spaniard (fem.)	Spaanjaard	[spānjãrt]
Spanish (adj)	Spaans	[spãŋs]
Italy	Italië	[italiɛ]
Italian (masc.)	Italianer	[italianər]
Italian (fem.)	Italianer	[italianər]
Italian (adj)	Italiaans	[italiãŋs]
Cyprus	Ciprus	[siprus]
Cypriot (masc.)	Ciprioot	[siprioət]
Cypriot (fem.)	Ciprioot	[siprioət]
Cypriot (adj)	Cipries	[sipris]
Malta	Malta	[malta]
Maltese (masc.)	Maltees	[malteəs]
Maltese (fem.)	Maltees	[malteəs]
Maltese (adj)	Maltees	[malteəs]
Norway	Noorweë	[noərweɛ]
Norwegian (masc.)	Noor	[noər]
Norwegian (fem.)	Noor	[noər]
Norwegian (adj)	Noors	[noərs]
Portugal	Portugal	[portuχal]
Portuguese (masc.)	Portugees	[portuχeəs]
Portuguese (fem.)	Portugees	[portuχeəs]
Portuguese (adj)	Portugees	[portuχeəs]
Finland	Finland	[finlant]
Finn (masc.)	Fin	[fin]
Finn (fem.)	Fin	[fin]
Finnish (adj)	Fins	[fins]
France	Frankryk	[frankrajk]
French (masc.)	Fransman	[fraŋsman]
French (fem.)	Franse dame	[fraŋsə damə]
French (adj)	Frans	[fraŋs]

Sweden	Swede	[swedə]
Swede (masc.)	Sweed	[sweət]
Swede (fem.)	Sweed	[sweət]
Swedish (adj)	Sweeds	[sweəds]

Switzerland	Switserland	[switsərlant]
Swiss (masc.)	Switser	[switsər]
Swiss (fem.)	Switser	[switsər]
Swiss (adj)	Switser	[switsər]

Scotland	Skotland	[skotlant]
Scottish (masc.)	Skot	[skot]
Scottish (fem.)	Skot	[skot]
Scottish (adj)	Skots	[skots]

Vatican	Vatikaan	[fatikān]
Liechtenstein	Lichtenstein	[liχtɛŋstejn]
Luxembourg	Luksemburg	[luksemburχ]
Monaco	Monako	[monako]

<h2>235. Central and Eastern Europe</h2>

Albania	Albanië	[albaniɛ]
Albanian (masc.)	Albaniër	[albaniɛr]
Albanian (fem.)	Albaniër	[albaniɛr]
Albanian (adj)	Albanies	[albanis]

Bulgaria	Bulgarye	[bulχaraje]
Bulgarian (masc.)	Bulgaar	[bulχār]
Bulgarian (fem.)	Bulgaar	[bulχār]
Bulgarian (adj)	Bulgaars	[bulχārs]

Hungary	Hongarye	[honχaraje]
Hungarian (masc.)	Hongaar	[honχār]
Hungarian (fem.)	Hongaar	[honχār]
Hungarian (adj)	Hongaars	[honχārs]

Latvia	Letland	[letlant]
Latvian (masc.)	Let	[let]
Latvian (fem.)	Let	[let]
Latvian (adj)	Lets	[lets]

Lithuania	Litoue	[litæʊə]
Lithuanian (masc.)	Litouer	[litæʊər]
Lithuanian (fem.)	Litouer	[litæʊər]
Lithuanian (adj)	Litous	[litæʊs]

Poland	Pole	[polə]
Pole (masc.)	Pool	[poəl]
Pole (fem.)	Pool	[poəl]

Polish (adj)	Pools	[poəls]
Romania	Roemenië	[rumeniɛ]
Romanian (masc.)	Roemeen	[rumeən]
Romanian (fem.)	Roemeen	[rumeən]
Romanian (adj)	Roemeens	[rumeəŋs]

Serbia	Serwië	[serwiɛ]
Serbian (masc.)	Serwiër	[serwiɛr]
Serbian (fem.)	Serwiër	[serwiɛr]
Serbian (adj)	Servies	[serfis]

Slovakia	Slowakye	[slovakaje]
Slovak (masc.)	Slowaak	[slovāk]
Slovak (fem.)	Slowaak	[slovāk]
Slovak (adj)	Slowaaks	[slovāks]

Croatia	Kroasië	[kroasiɛ]
Croatian (masc.)	Kroaat	[kroāt]
Croatian (fem.)	Kroaat	[kroāt]
Croatian (adj)	Kroaties	[kroatis]

Czech Republic	Tjeggië	[tʃeχiɛ]
Czech (masc.)	Tjeg	[tʃeχ]
Czech (fem.)	Tjeg	[tʃeχ]
Czech (adj)	Tjegies	[tʃeχis]

Estonia	Estland	[ɛstlant]
Estonian (masc.)	Estlander	[ɛstlandər]
Estonian (fem.)	Estlander	[ɛstlandər]
Estonian (adj)	Estlands	[ɛstlands]

Bosnia and Herzegovina	Bosnië & Herzegowina	[bosniɛ en hersegovina]
Macedonia (Republic of ~)	Masedonië	[masedoniɛ]
Slovenia	Slovenië	[slofeniɛ]
Montenegro	Montenegro	[montənegro]

236. Former USSR countries

Azerbaijan	Azerbeidjan	[azerbæjdjan]
Azerbaijani (masc.)	Azerbeidjanner	[azerbæjdjannər]
Azerbaijani (fem.)	Azerbeidjanner	[azerbæjdjannər]
Azerbaijani, Azeri (adj)	Azerbeidjans	[azerbæjdjaŋs]

Armenia	Armenië	[armeniɛ]
Armenian (masc.)	Armeniër	[armeniɛr]
Armenian (fem.)	Armeniër	[armeniɛr]
Armenian (adj)	Armeens	[armeɛŋs]

| Belarus | Belarus | [belarus] |
| Belarusian (masc.) | Belarus | [belarus] |

| Belarusian (fem.) | **Belarus** | [belarus] |
| Belarusian (adj) | **Belarussies** | [belarussis] |

Georgia	**Georgië**	[χeorχiɛ]
Georgian (masc.)	**Georgiër**	[χeorχiɛr]
Georgian (fem.)	**Georgiër**	[χeorχiɛr]
Georgian (adj)	**Georgies**	[χeorχis]
Kazakhstan	**Kazakstan**	[kasakstan]
Kazakh (masc.)	**Kasak**	[kasak]
Kazakh (fem.)	**Kasak**	[kasak]
Kazakh (adj)	**Kasaks**	[kasaks]

Kirghizia	**Kirgisië**	[kirχisiɛ]
Kirghiz (masc.)	**Kirgisiër**	[kirχisiɛr]
Kirghiz (fem.)	**Kirgisiër**	[kirχisiɛr]
Kirghiz (adj)	**Kirgisies**	[kirχisis]

Moldova, Moldavia	**Moldawië**	[moldaviɛ]
Moldavian (masc.)	**Moldawiër**	[moldaviɛr]
Moldavian (fem.)	**Moldawiër**	[moldaviɛr]
Moldavian (adj)	**Moldawies**	[moldavis]
Russia	**Rusland**	[ruslant]
Russian (masc.)	**Rus**	[rus]
Russian (fem.)	**Rus**	[rus]
Russian (adj)	**Russies**	[russis]

Tajikistan	**Tadjikistan**	[tadʒikistan]
Tajik (masc.)	**Tadjik**	[tadʒik]
Tajik (fem.)	**Tadjik**	[tadʒik]
Tajik (adj)	**Tadjiks**	[tadʒiks]

Turkmenistan	**Turkmenistan**	[turkmenistan]
Turkmen (masc.)	**Turkmeen**	[turkmeən]
Turkmen (fem.)	**Turkmeen**	[turkmeən]
Turkmenian (adj)	**Turkmeens**	[turkmeəŋs]

Uzbekistan	**Oezbekistan**	[uzbekistan]
Uzbek (masc.)	**Oezbeek**	[uzbeək]
Uzbek (fem.)	**Oezbeek**	[uzbeək]
Uzbek (adj)	**Oezbekies**	[uzbekis]

Ukraine	**Oekraïne**	[ukraïnə]
Ukrainian (masc.)	**Oekraïner**	[ukraïnər]
Ukrainian (fem.)	**Oekraïner**	[ukraïnər]
Ukrainian (adj)	**Oekraïns**	[ukraïns]

237. Asia

| Asia | **Asië** | [asiɛ] |
| Asian (adj) | **Asiaties** | [asiatis] |

Vietnam	Viëtnam	[viɛtnam]
Vietnamese (masc.)	Viëtnamees	[viɛtnameəs]
Vietnamese (fem.)	Viëtnamees	[viɛtnameəs]
Vietnamese (adj)	Viëtnamees	[viɛtnameəs]

India	Indië	[indiɛ]
Indian (masc.)	Indiër	[indiɛr]
Indian (fem.)	Indiër	[indiɛr]
Indian (adj)	Indies	[indis]

Israel	Israel	[israəl]
Israeli (masc.)	Israeli	[israeli]
Israeli (fem.)	Israeli	[israeli]
Israeli (adj)	Israelies	[israelis]

Jew (n)	Jood	[joət]
Jewess (n)	Jodin	[jodin]
Jewish (adj)	Joods	[joəds]

China	Sjina	[ʃina]
Chinese (masc.)	Sjinees	[ʃineəs]
Chinese (fem.)	Sjinees	[ʃineəs]
Chinese (adj)	Sjinees	[ʃineəs]

Korean (masc.)	Koreaan	[koreãn]
Korean (fem.)	Koreaan	[koreãn]
Korean (adj)	Koreaans	[koreãŋs]

Lebanon	Libanon	[libanon]
Lebanese (masc.)	Libanees	[libaneəs]
Lebanese (fem.)	Libanees	[libaneəs]
Lebanese (adj)	Libanees	[libaneəs]

Mongolia	Mongolië	[monχoliɛ]
Mongolian (masc.)	Mongool	[monχoəl]
Mongolian (fem.)	Mongool	[monχoəl]
Mongolian (adj)	Mongools	[monχoəls]

Malaysia	Maleisië	[malæjsiɛ]
Malaysian (masc.)	Maleisiër	[malæjsiɛr]
Malaysian (fem.)	Maleisiër	[malæjsiɛr]
Malaysian (adj)	Maleisies	[malæjsis]

Pakistan	Pakistan	[pakistan]
Pakistani (masc.)	Pakistani	[pakistani]
Pakistani (fem.)	Pakistani	[pakistani]
Pakistani (adj)	Pakistans	[pakistaŋs]

Saudi Arabia	Saoedi-Arabië	[saudi-arabiɛ]
Arab (masc.)	Arabier	[arabir]
Arab (fem.)	Arabier	[arabir]
Arab, Arabic (adj)	Arabiese	[arabisə]

Thailand	Thailand	[tajlant]
Thai (masc.)	Thailander	[tajlandər]
Thai (fem.)	Thailander	[tajlandər]
Thai (adj)	Thais	[tajs]

Taiwan	Taiwan	[tajvan]
Taiwanese (masc.)	Taiwannees	[tajvanneəs]
Taiwanese (fem.)	Taiwannees	[tajvanneəs]
Taiwanese (adj)	Taiwannees	[tajvanneəs]

Turkey	Turkye	[turkaje]
Turk (masc.)	Turk	[turk]
Turk (fem.)	Turk	[turk]
Turkish (adj)	Turks	[turks]

Japan	Japan	[japan]
Japanese (masc.)	Japannees, Japanner	[japanneəs], [japannər]
Japanese (fem.)	Japannees, Japanner	[japanneəs], [japannər]
Japanese (adj)	Japannees, Japans	[japanneəs], [japaŋs]

Afghanistan	Afghanistan	[afχanistan]
Bangladesh	Bangladesj	[bangladeʃ]
Indonesia	Indonesië	[indonesiɛ]
Jordan	Jordanië	[jordaniɛ]

Iraq	Irak	[irak]
Iran	Iran	[iran]
Cambodia	Kambodja	[kambodja]
Kuwait	Kuwait	[kuvajt]

Laos	Laos	[laos]
Myanmar	Myanmar	[mjanmar]
Nepal	Nepal	[nepal]
United Arab Emirates	Verenigde Arabiese Emirate	[ferenixdə arabisə emiratə]

Syria	Sirië	[siriɛ]
Palestine	Palestina	[palestina]
South Korea	Suid-Korea	[sœid-korea]
North Korea	Noord-Korea	[noərd-korea]

238. North America

United States of America	Verenigde State van Amerika	[ferenixdə statə fan amerika]
American (masc.)	Amerikaan	[amerikān]
American (fem.)	Amerikaan	[amerikān]
American (adj)	Amerikaans	[amerikāŋs]
Canada	Kanada	[kanada]
Canadian (masc.)	Kanadees	[kanadeəs]

| Canadian (fem.) | Kanadees | [kanadees] |
| Canadian (adj) | Kanadees | [kanadees] |

Mexico	Meksiko	[meksiko]
Mexican (masc.)	Meksikaan	[meksikān]
Mexican (fem.)	Meksikaan	[meksikān]
Mexican (adj)	Meksikaans	[meksikāŋs]

239. Central and South America

Argentina	Argentinië	[arχentiniɛ]
Argentinian (masc.)	Argentyn	[arχentajn]
Argentinian (fem.)	Argentyn	[arχentajn]
Argentinian (adj)	Argentyns	[arχentajns]

Brazil	Brasilië	[brasiliɛ]
Brazilian (masc.)	Brasiliaan	[brasiliān]
Brazilian (fem.)	Brasiliaan	[brasiliān]
Brazilian (adj)	Brasiliaans	[brasiliāŋs]

Colombia	Colombia, Kolombië	[kolombia], [kolombiɛ]
Colombian (masc.)	Colombiaan	[kolombiān]
Colombian (fem.)	Colombiaan	[kolombiān]
Colombian (adj)	Colombiaans	[kolombiāŋs]

Cuba	Kuba	[kuba]
Cuban (masc.)	Kubaan	[kubān]
Cuban (fem.)	Kubaan	[kubān]
Cuban (adj)	Kubaans	[kubāŋs]

Chile	Chili	[tʃili]
Chilean (masc.)	Chileen	[tʃileen]
Chilean (fem.)	Chileen	[tʃileen]
Chilean (adj)	Chileens	[tʃileɛŋs]

| Bolivia | Bolivië | [boliviɛ] |
| Venezuela | Venezuela | [fenesuela] |

| Paraguay | Paraguay | [paragwaj] |
| Peru | Peru | [peru] |

Suriname	Suriname	[surinamə]
Uruguay	Uruguay	[urugwaj]
Ecuador	Ecuador	[ɛkuador]

The Bahamas	die Bahamas	[di bahamas]
Haiti	Haïti	[haïti]
Dominican Republic	Dominikaanse Republiek	[dominikāŋsə republik]
Panama	Panama	[panama]
Jamaica	Jamaika	[jamajka]

240. Africa

Egypt	Egipte	[εχiptə]
Egyptian (masc.)	Egiptenaar	[εχiptenār]
Egyptian (fem.)	Egiptenaar	[εχiptenār]
Egyptian (adj)	Egipties	[εχiptis]

Morocco	Marokko	[marokko]
Moroccan (masc.)	Marokkaan	[marokkān]
Moroccan (fem.)	Marokkaan	[marokkān]
Moroccan (adj)	Marokkaans	[marokkāŋs]

Tunisia	Tunisië	[tunisiε]
Tunisian (masc.)	Tunisiër	[tunisiεr]
Tunisian (fem.)	Tunisiër	[tunisiεr]
Tunisian (adj)	Tunisies	[tunisis]

Ghana	Ghana	[χana]
Zanzibar	Zanzibar	[zanzibar]
Kenya	Kenia	[kenia]

| Libya | Libië | [libiε] |
| Madagascar | Madagaskar | [madaχaskar] |

Namibia	Namibië	[namibiε]
Senegal	Senegal	[seneχal]
Tanzania	Tanzanië	[tansaniε]
South Africa	Suid-Afrika	[sœid-afrika]

African (masc.)	Afrikaan	[afrikān]
African (fem.)	Afrikaan	[afrikān]
African (adj)	Afrika-	[afrika-]

241. Australia. Oceania

| Australia | Australië | [ɔustraliε] |
| Australian (masc.) | Australiër | [ɔustraliεr] |

| Australian (fem.) | Australiër | [ɔustraliεr] |
| Australian (adj) | Australies | [ɔustralis] |

| New Zealand | Nieu-Seeland | [niu-seəlant] |
| New Zealander (masc.) | Nieu-Seelander | [niu-seəlandər] |

| New Zealander (fem.) | Nieu-Seelander | [niu-seəlandər] |
| New Zealand (as adj) | Nieu-Seelands | [niu-seəlants] |

| Tasmania | Tasmanië | [tasmaniε] |
| French Polynesia | Frans-Polinesië | [fraŋs-polinesiε] |

242. Cities

Amsterdam	**Amsterdam**	[amsterdam]
Ankara	**Ankara**	[ankara]
Athens	**Athene**	[atenə]
Baghdad	**Bagdad**	[baχdat]
Bangkok	**Bangkok**	[baŋkok]
Barcelona	**Barcelona**	[barselona]
Beijing	**Beijing**	[bæjdʒiŋ]
Beirut	**Beiroet**	[bæjrut]
Berlin	**Berlyn**	[berlæjn]
Mumbai (Bombay)	**Moembai**	[mumbaj]
Bonn	**Bonn**	[bonn]
Bordeaux	**Bordeaux**	[bordo:]
Bratislava	**Bratislava**	[bratislava]
Brussels	**Brussel**	[brussəl]
Bucharest	**Boekarest**	[bukarest]
Budapest	**Boedapest**	[budapest]
Cairo	**Cairo**	[kajro]
Kolkata (Calcutta)	**Kalkutta**	[kalkutta]
Chicago	**Chicago**	[ʃikago]
Copenhagen	**Kopenhagen**	[kopənχagen]
Dar-es-Salaam	**Dar-es-Salaam**	[dar-es-salãm]
Delhi	**Delhi**	[deli]
Dubai	**Dubai**	[dubaj]
Dublin	**Dublin**	[dablin]
Düsseldorf	**Dusseldorf**	[dussɛldorf]
Florence	**Florence**	[florɛŋs]
Frankfurt	**Frankfurt**	[frankfurt]
Geneva	**Genève**	[dʒənɛ:v]
The Hague	**Den Haag**	[den hãχ]
Hamburg	**Hamburg**	[hamburχ]
Hanoi	**Hanoi**	[hanoj]
Havana	**Havana**	[havana]
Helsinki	**Helsinki**	[hɛlsinki]
Hiroshima	**Hiroshima**	[hiroʃima]
Hong Kong	**Hongkong**	[hoŋkoŋ]
Istanbul	**Istanbul**	[istanbul]
Jerusalem	**Jerusalem**	[jerusalem]
Kyiv	**Kiëf**	[kiɛf]
Kuala Lumpur	**Kuala Lumpur**	[kuala lumpur]
Lisbon	**Lissabon**	[lissabon]
London	**Londen**	[londen]
Los Angeles	**Los Angeles**	[los andʒəles]

Lyons	Lyon	[lioŋ]
Madrid	Madrid	[madrit]
Marseille	Marseille	[marsæj]
Mexico City	Meksiko Stad	[meksiko stat]
Miami	Miami	[majami]
Montreal	Montreal	[montreal]
Moscow	Moskou	[moskæʊ]
Munich	München	[mønchen]

Nairobi	Nairobi	[najrobi]
Naples	Napels	[napɛls]
New York	New York	[nju jork]
Nice	Nice	[nis]
Oslo	Oslo	[oslo]
Ottawa	Ottawa	[ottava]

Paris	Parys	[parajs]
Prague	Praag	[prāχ]
Rio de Janeiro	Rio de Janeiro	[rio də janæjro]
Rome	Rome	[romə]

Saint Petersburg	Sint-Petersburg	[sint-petersburg]
Seoul	Seoel	[seul]
Shanghai	Shanghai	[ʃangaj]
Singapore	Singapore	[singaporə]
Stockholm	Stockholm	[stokχolm]
Sydney	Sydney	[sidni]

Taipei	Taipei	[tæjpæj]
Tokyo	Tokio	[tokio]
Toronto	Toronto	[toronto]

Venice	Venesië	[fenesiɛ]
Vienna	Wene	[venə]
Warsaw	Warskou	[varskæʊ]
Washington	Washington	[vaʃington]

243. Politics. Government. Part 1

politics	politiek	[politik]
political (adj)	politieke	[politikə]
politician	politikus	[politikus]

state (country)	staat	[stāt]
citizen	burger	[burgər]
citizenship	burgerskap	[burgərskap]

national emblem	nasionale wapen	[naʃionalə vapen]
national anthem	volkslied	[folkslit]
government	regering	[reχeriŋ]

head of state	staatshoof	[stāts·hoəf]
parliament	parlement	[parlement]
party	partij	[partij]
capitalism	kapitalisme	[kapitalismə]
capitalist (adj)	kapitalis	[kapitalis]
socialism	sosialisme	[soʃialisme]
socialist (adj)	sosialis	[soʃialis]
communism	kommunisme	[kommunismə]
communist (adj)	kommunis	[kommunis]
communist (n)	kommunis	[kommunis]
democracy	demokrasie	[demokrasi]
democrat	demokraat	[demokrāt]
democratic (adj)	demokraties	[demokratis]
Democratic party	Demokratiese party	[demokratisə partaj]
liberal (n)	liberaal	[liberāl]
liberal (adj)	liberaal	[liberāl]
conservative (n)	konservatief	[kɔŋserfatif]
conservative (adj)	konservatief	[kɔŋserfatif]
republic (n)	republiek	[republik]
republican (n)	republikein	[republikæjn]
Republican party	Republikeinse Party	[republikæjnsə partaj]
elections	verkiesings	[ferkisiŋs]
to elect (vt)	verkies	[ferkis]
elector, voter	kieser	[kisər]
election campaign	verkiesingskampanje	[ferkisiŋs·kampanje]
voting (n)	stemming	[stɛmmiŋ]
to vote (vi)	stem	[stem]
suffrage, right to vote	stemreg	[stem·reχ]
candidate	kandidaat	[kandidāt]
campaign	kampanje	[kampanje]
opposition (as adj)	opposisie	[opposisi]
opposition (n)	opposisie	[opposisi]
visit	besoek	[besuk]
official visit	amptelike besoek	[amptelikə besuk]
international (adj)	internasionaal	[internaʃionāl]
negotiations	onderhandelinge	[ondərhandeliŋə]
to negotiate (vi)	onderhandel	[ondərhandəl]

244. Politics. Government. Part 2

society	samelewing	[sameleviŋ]
constitution	grondwet	[χront·wet]
power (political control)	mag	[maχ]
corruption	korrupsie	[korrupsi]
law (justice)	wet	[vet]
legal (legitimate)	wetlik	[vetlik]
justice (fairness)	geregtigheid	[χereχtiχæjt]
just (fair)	regverdig	[reχferdəχ]
committee	komitee	[komiteə]
bill (draft law)	wetsontwerp	[vetsontwerp]
budget	begroting	[beχrotiŋ]
policy	beleid	[belæjt]
reform	hervorming	[herformiŋ]
radical (adj)	radikaal	[radikāl]
power (strength, force)	mag	[maχ]
powerful (adj)	magtig	[maχtəχ]
supporter	ondersteuner	[ondərstøənər]
influence	invloed	[influt]
regime (e.g., military ~)	bewind	[bevint]
conflict	konflik	[konflik]
conspiracy (plot)	sameswering	[samesweriŋ]
provocation	uitdaging	[œitdaχiŋ]
to overthrow (regime, etc.)	omvergooi	[omferχoj]
overthrow (of government)	omvergooi	[omferχoj]
revolution	revolusie	[refolusi]
coup d'état	staatsgreep	[stāts·χreəp]
military coup	militêre staatsgreep	[militærə stātsχreəp]
crisis	krisis	[krisis]
economic recession	ekonomiese agteruitgang	[ɛkonomisə aχtər·œitχaŋ]
demonstrator (protester)	betoër	[betoɛr]
demonstration	demonstrasie	[demoŋstrasi]
martial law	krygswet	[krajχs·wet]
military base	militêre basis	[militærə basis]
stability	stabiliteit	[stabilitæjt]
stable (adj)	stabiel	[stabil]
exploitation	uitbuiting	[œitbœitiŋ]
to exploit (workers)	uitbuit	[œitbœit]
racism	rassisme	[rassimə]

racist	**rassis**	[rassis]
fascism	**fascisme**	[faʃismə]
fascist	**fascis**	[faʃis]

245. Countries. Miscellaneous

foreigner	**vreemdeling**	[freəmdeliŋ]
foreign (adj)	**vreemd**	[freəmt]
abroad	**in die buiteland**	[in di bœitəlant]
(in a foreign country)		

emigrant	**emigrant**	[ɛmiχrant]
emigration	**emigrasie**	[ɛmiχrasi]
to emigrate (vi)	**emigreer**	[ɛmiχreər]

the West	**die Weste**	[di vestə]
the East	**die Ooste**	[di oəstə]
the Far East	**die Verre Ooste**	[di ferrə oəstə]

civilization	**beskawing**	[beskaviŋ]
humanity (mankind)	**mensdom**	[mɛŋsdom]
the world (earth)	**die wêreld**	[di værəlt]
peace	**vrede**	[fredə]
worldwide (adj)	**wêreldwyd**	[værəlt·wajt]

homeland	**vaderland**	[fadər·lant]
people (population)	**volk**	[folk]
population	**bevolking**	[befolkiŋ]
people (a lot of ~)	**mense**	[mɛŋsə]
nation (people)	**nasie**	[nasi]
generation	**generasie**	[χenerasi]

territory (area)	**gebied**	[χebit]
region	**streek**	[streək]
state (part of a country)	**staat**	[stãt]

tradition	**tradisie**	[tradisi]
custom (tradition)	**gebruik**	[χebrœik]
ecology	**ekologie**	[ɛkoloχi]

Indian (Native American)	**Indiaan**	[indiãn]
Gypsy (masc.)	**Sigeuner**	[siχøənər]
Gypsy (fem.)	**Sigeunerin**	[siχøənərin]
Gypsy (adj)	**sigeuner-**	[siχøənər-]

empire	**rijk**	[rijk]
colony	**kolonie**	[koloni]
slavery	**slawerny**	[slavərnaj]
invasion	**invasie**	[infasi]
famine	**hongersnood**	[hoŋərsnoət]

246. Major religious groups. Confessions

religion	**godsdiens**	[χodsdiŋs]
religious (adj)	**godsdienstig**	[χodsdiŋstəχ]
faith, belief	**geloof**	[χeloəf]
to believe (in God)	**glo**	[χlo]
believer	**gelowige**	[χeloviχə]
atheism	**ateïsme**	[ateïsmə]
atheist	**ateïs**	[ateïs]
Christianity	**Christendom**	[χristəndom]
Christian (n)	**Christen**	[χristən]
Christian (adj)	**Christelik**	[χristəlik]
Catholicism	**Katolisisme**	[katolisismə]
Catholic (n)	**Katoliek**	[katolik]
Catholic (adj)	**katoliek**	[katolik]
Protestantism	**Protestantisme**	[protestantismə]
Protestant Church	**Protestantse Kerk**	[protestantsə kerk]
Protestant (n)	**Protestant**	[protestant]
Orthodoxy	**Ortodoksie**	[ortodoksi]
Orthodox Church	**Ortodokse Kerk**	[ortodoksə kerk]
Orthodox (n)	**Ortodoks**	[ortodoks]
Presbyterianism	**Presbiterianisme**	[presbiterianismə]
Presbyterian Church	**Presbiteriaanse Kerk**	[presbiteriãŋsə kerk]
Presbyterian (n)	**Presbiteriaan**	[presbiteriãn]
Lutheranism	**Lutheranisme**	[luteranismə]
Lutheran (n)	**Lutheraan**	[lutərãn]
Baptist Church	**Baptistiese Kerk**	[baptistisə kerk]
Baptist (n)	**Baptis**	[baptis]
Anglican Church	**Anglikaanse Kerk**	[anχlikãŋsə kerk]
Anglican (n)	**Anglikaan**	[anχlikãn]
Mormonism	**Mormonisme**	[mormonismə]
Mormon (n)	**Mormoon**	[mormoən]
Judaism	**Jodendom**	[jodɛndom]
Jew (n)	**Jood**	[joət]
Buddhism	**Boeddhisme**	[buddismə]
Buddhist (n)	**Boeddhis**	[buddis]
Hinduism	**Hindoeïsme**	[hinduïsmə]
Hindu (n)	**Hindoe**	[hindu]

Islam	Islam	[islam]
Muslim (n)	Islamiet	[islamit]
Muslim (adj)	Islamities	[islamitis]

Shiah Islam	Sjia Islam	[ʃia islam]
Shiite (n)	Sjïït	[ʃiït]

Sunni Islam	Sunni Islam	[sunni islam]
Sunnite (n)	Sunniet	[sunnit]

247. Religions. Priests

priest	priester	[pristər]
the Pope	die Pous	[di pæʊs]

monk, friar	monnik	[monnik]
nun	non	[non]
pastor	pastoor	[pastoər]

abbot	ab	[ap]
vicar (parish priest)	priester	[pristər]
bishop	biskop	[biskop]
cardinal	kardinaal	[kardinãl]

preacher	predikant	[predikant]
preaching	preek	[preək]
parishioners	kerkgangers	[kerk·χaŋərs]

believer	gelowige	[χeloviχə]
atheist	ateïs	[ateïs]

248. Faith. Christianity. Islam

Adam	Adam	[adam]
Eve	Eva	[efa]

God	God	[χot]
the Lord	die Here	[di herə]
the Almighty	die Almagtige	[di almaχtiχə]

sin	sonde	[sondə]
to sin (vi)	sondig	[sondəχ]
sinner (masc.)	sondaar	[sondãr]
sinner (fem.)	sondares	[sondares]

hell	hel	[həl]
paradise	paradys	[paradajs]
Jesus	Jesus	[jesus]

Jesus Christ	**Jesus Christus**	[jesus χristus]
the Holy Spirit	**die Heilige Gees**	[di hæjliχə χeəs]
the Savior	**die Verlosser**	[di ferlossər]
the Virgin Mary	**die Maagd Maria**	[di māχt maria]
the Devil	**die duiwel**	[di dœivəl]
devil's (adj)	**duiwels**	[dœivɛls]
Satan	**Satan**	[satan]
satanic (adj)	**satanies**	[satanis]
angel	**engel**	[ɛŋəl]
guardian angel	**beskermengel**	[beskerm·eŋəl]
angelic (adj)	**engelagtig**	[ɛŋəlaχtəχ]
apostle	**apostel**	[apostəl]
archangel	**aartsengel**	[ārtseŋəl]
the Antichrist	**die antichris**	[di antiχris]
Church	**Kerk**	[kerk]
Bible	**Bybel**	[bajbəl]
biblical (adj)	**bybels**	[bajbəls]
Old Testament	**Ou Testament**	[æʊ testament]
New Testament	**Nuwe Testament**	[nuvə testament]
Gospel	**evangelie**	[ɛfanχəli]
Holy Scripture	**Heilige Skrif**	[hæjliχə skrif]
Heaven	**hemel**	[heməl]
Commandment	**gebod**	[χebot]
prophet	**profeet**	[profeət]
prophecy	**profesie**	[profesi]
Allah	**Allah**	[allah]
Mohammed	**Mohammed**	[mohammet]
the Koran	**die Koran**	[di koran]
mosque	**moskee**	[moskeə]
mullah	**moella**	[mulla]
prayer	**gebed**	[χebet]
to pray (vi, vt)	**bid**	[bit]
pilgrimage	**pelgrimstog**	[pɛlχrimstoχ]
pilgrim	**pelgrim**	[pɛlχrim]
Mecca	**Mecca**	[mɛkka]
church	**kerk**	[kerk]
temple	**tempel**	[tempəl]
cathedral	**katedraal**	[katedrāl]
Gothic (adj)	**Goties**	[χotis]
synagogue	**sinagoge**	[sinaχoχə]
mosque	**moskee**	[moskeə]
chapel	**kapel**	[kapəl]

abbey	**abdy**	[abdaj]
convent	**klooster**	[kloəstər]
monastery	**klooster**	[kloəstər]
bell (church ~s)	**klok**	[klok]
bell tower	**kloktoring**	[klok·toriŋ]
to ring (ab. bells)	**lui**	[lœi]
cross	**kruis**	[krœis]
cupola (roof)	**koepel**	[kupəl]
icon	**ikoon**	[ikoən]
soul	**siel**	[sil]
fate (destiny)	**noodlot**	[noədlot]
evil (n)	**die bose**	[di bosə]
good (n)	**goed**	[χut]
vampire	**vampier**	[fampir]
witch (evil ~)	**heks**	[heks]
demon	**demoon**	[demoən]
spirit	**gees**	[χeəs]
redemption (giving us ~)	**versoening**	[fersuniŋ]
to redeem (vt)	**verlos**	[ferlos]
church service, mass	**kerkdies**	[kerkdis]
to say mass	**die mis opdra**	[di mis opdra]
confession	**bieg**	[biχ]
to confess (vi)	**bieg**	[biχ]
saint (n)	**heilige**	[hæjliχə]
sacred (holy)	**heilig**	[hæjləχ]
holy water	**wywater**	[vaj·vatər]
ritual (n)	**ritueel**	[ritueəl]
ritual (adj)	**ritueel**	[ritueəl]
sacrifice	**offerande**	[offerandə]
superstition	**bygeloof**	[bajχəloəf]
superstitious (adj)	**bygelowig**	[bajχəlovəχ]
afterlife	**hiernamaals**	[hirna·māls]
eternal life	**ewige lewe**	[εviχə levə]

MISCELLANEOUS

249. Various useful words

background (green ~)	**agtergrond**	[aχtərχront]
balance (of situation)	**balans**	[balaŋs]
barrier (obstacle)	**hindernis**	[hindərnis]
base (basis)	**basis**	[basis]
beginning	**begin**	[beχin]
category	**kategorie**	[kateχori]
cause (reason)	**rede**	[redə]
choice	**keuse**	[køəsə]
coincidence	**toeval**	[tufal]
comfortable (~ chair)	**gemaklik**	[χemaklik]
comparison	**vergelyking**	[ferχelajkiŋ]
compensation	**kompensasie**	[kompɛnsasi]
degree (extent, amount)	**graad**	[χrãt]
development	**ontwikkeling**	[ontwikkeliŋ]
difference	**verskil**	[ferskil]
effect (e.g., of drugs)	**effek**	[ɛffek]
effort (exertion)	**inspanning**	[inspanniŋ]
element	**element**	[ɛlement]
end (finish)	**einde**	[æjndə]
example (illustration)	**voorbeeld**	[foərbeəlt]
fact	**feit**	[fæjt]
frequent (adj)	**gereeld**	[χereəlt]
growth (development)	**groei**	[χrui]
help	**hulp**	[hulp]
ideal	**ideaal**	[ideãl]
kind (sort, type)	**soort**	[soərt]
labyrinth	**labirint**	[labirint]
mistake, error	**fout**	[fæʊt]
moment	**moment**	[moment]
object (thing)	**objek**	[objek]
obstacle	**hinderpaal**	[hindərpãl]
original (original copy)	**origineel**	[oriχineəl]
part (~ of sth)	**deel**	[deəl]
particle, small part	**deeltjie**	[deəlki]
pause (break)	**pouse**	[pæʊsə]

position	**posisie**	[posisi]
principle	**beginsel**	[beχinsəl]
problem	**probleem**	[probleəm]

process	**proses**	[proses]
progress	**vooruitgang**	[foərœitχaŋ]
property (quality)	**eienskap**	[æjeŋskap]
reaction	**reaksie**	[reaksi]
risk	**risiko**	[risiko]

secret	**geheim**	[χəhæjm]
series	**reeks**	[reəks]
shape (outer form)	**vorm**	[form]
situation	**toestand**	[tustant]
solution	**oplossing**	[oplossiŋ]

standard (adj)	**standaard**	[standārt]
standard (level of quality)	**standaard**	[standārt]
stop (pause)	**pouse**	[pæʊsə]
style	**styl**	[stajl]

system	**sisteem**	[sisteəm]
table (chart)	**tabel**	[tabəl]
tempo, rate	**tempo**	[tempo]
term (word, expression)	**term**	[term]

thing (object, item)	**ding**	[diŋ]
truth (e.g., moment of ~)	**waarheid**	[vārhæjt]
turn (please wait your ~)	**beurt**	[bøərt]
type (sort, kind)	**tipe**	[tipə]
urgent (adj)	**dringend**	[driŋən]

urgently (adv)	**dringend**	[driŋən]
utility (usefulness)	**nut**	[nut]
variant (alternative)	**variant**	[fariant]
way (means, method)	**manier**	[manir]
zone	**sone**	[sonə]

250. Modifiers. Adjectives. Part 1

additional (adj)	**addisioneel**	[addiʃioneəl]
ancient (~ civilization)	**antiek**	[antik]
artificial (adj)	**kunsmatig**	[kunsmatəχ]
back, rear (adj)	**agter-**	[aχtər-]
bad (adj)	**sleg**	[sleχ]

beautiful (~ palace)	**pragtig**	[praχtəχ]
beautiful (person)	**pragtig**	[praχtəχ]
big (in size)	**groot**	[χroət]

bitter (taste)	**bitter**	[bittər]
blind (sightless)	**blind**	[blint]
calm, quiet (adj)	**kalm**	[kalm]
careless (negligent)	**nalatig**	[nalatəχ]
caring (~ father)	**sorgsaam**	[sorχsām]
central (adj)	**sentraal**	[sentrāl]
cheap (low-priced)	**goedkoop**	[χudkoəp]
cheerful (adj)	**opgewek**	[opχevek]
children's (adj)	**kinder-**	[kindər-]
civil (~ law)	**burgerlik**	[burgerlik]
clandestine (secret)	**agterbaks**	[aχtərbaks]
clean (free from dirt)	**skoon**	[skoən]
clear (explanation, etc.)	**duidelik**	[dœidelik]
clever (smart)	**slim**	[slim]
close (near in space)	**digby**	[diχbaj]
closed (adj)	**gesluit**	[χeslœit]
cloudless (sky)	**wolkloos**	[volkloəs]
cold (drink, weather)	**koud**	[kæʊt]
compatible (adj)	**verenigbaar**	[fereniχbār]
contented (satisfied)	**tevrede**	[tefredə]
continuous (uninterrupted)	**onophoudelik**	[onophæʊdelik]
cool (weather)	**koel**	[kul]
dangerous (adj)	**gevaarlik**	[χefārlik]
dark (room)	**donker**	[donkər]
dead (not alive)	**dood**	[doət]
dense (fog, smoke)	**dig**	[diχ]
destitute (extremely poor)	**brandarm**	[brandarm]
different (not the same)	**verskillend**	[ferskillent]
difficult (decision)	**moeilik**	[muilik]
difficult (problem, task)	**moeilik**	[muilik]
dim, faint (light)	**dof**	[dof]
dirty (not clean)	**vuil**	[fœil]
distant (in space)	**ver**	[fer]
dry (clothes, etc.)	**droog**	[droəχ]
easy (not difficult)	**maklik**	[maklik]
empty (glass, room)	**leeg**	[leəχ]
even (e.g., ~ surface)	**gelyk**	[χelajk]
exact (amount)	**juis**	[jœis]
excellent (adj)	**uitstekend**	[œitstekent]
excessive (adj)	**oormatig**	[oərmatəχ]
expensive (adj)	**duur**	[dɪr]
exterior (adj)	**buite-**	[bœite-]
far (the ~ East)	**ver**	[fer]

fast (quick)	vinnig	[finnəχ]
fatty (food)	vettig	[fɛttəχ]
fertile (land, soil)	vrugbaar	[fruχbār]

flat (~ panel display)	plat	[plat]
foreign (adj)	buitelands	[bœitəlands]
fragile (china, glass)	breekbaar	[breəkbār]
free (at no cost)	gratis	[χratis]
free (unrestricted)	gratis	[χratis]

fresh (~ water)	vars	[fars]
fresh (e.g., ~ bread)	vars	[fars]
frozen (food)	gevries	[χefris]
full (completely filled)	vol	[fol]
gloomy (house, forecast)	somber	[sombər]

good (book, etc.)	goed	[χut]
good, kind (kindhearted)	vriendelik	[frindəlik]
grateful (adj)	dankbaar	[dankbār]
happy (adj)	gelukkig	[χelukkəχ]
hard (not soft)	hard	[hart]

heavy (in weight)	swaar	[swār]
hostile (adj)	vyandig	[fajandəχ]
hot (adj)	warm	[varm]
huge (adj)	kolossaal	[kolossāl]

humid (adj)	bedompig	[bedompəχ]
hungry (adj)	honger	[hoŋər]
ill (sick, unwell)	siek	[sik]
immobile (adj)	doodstil	[doədstil]

important (adj)	belangrik	[belaŋrik]
impossible (adj)	onmoontlik	[onmoentlik]
incomprehensible	onverstaanbaar	[onferstānbār]
indispensable (adj)	onontbeerlik	[onontbeərlik]

inexperienced (adj)	onervare	[onerfarə]
insignificant (adj)	onbelangrik	[onbelaŋrik]
interior (adj)	binne-	[binne-]
joint (~ decision)	gesamentlik	[χesamentlik]
last (e.g., ~ week)	laas-	[lās-]

last (final)	laaste	[lāstə]
left (e.g., ~ side)	linker-	[linkər-]
legal (legitimate)	wetlik	[vetlik]
light (in weight)	lig	[liχ]
light (pale color)	lig-	[liχ-]

limited (adj)	beperk	[beperk]
liquid (fluid)	vloeibaar	[fluibār]
long (e.g., ~ hair)	lang	[laŋ]

| loud (voice, etc.) | hard | [hart] |
| low (voice) | sag | [saχ] |

251. Modifiers. Adjectives. Part 2

main (principal)	hoof-	[hoəf-]
matt, matte	mat	[mat]
meticulous (job)	akkuraat	[akkurāt]
mysterious (adj)	raaiselagtig	[rājselaχtəχ]
narrow (street, etc.)	smal	[smal]
native (~ country)	geboorte-	[χeboərtə-]
nearby (adj)	naby	[nabaj]
nearsighted (adj)	bysiende	[bajsində]
needed (necessary)	nodig	[nodəχ]
negative (~ response)	negatief	[neχatif]
neighboring (adj)	naburig	[naburəχ]
nervous (adj)	senuweeagtig	[senuveə·aχtəχ]
new (adj)	nuut	[nɪt]
next (e.g., ~ week)	volgend	[folχent]
nice (kind)	vriendelik	[frindəlik]
nice (voice)	mooi	[moj]
normal (adj)	normaal	[normāl]
not big (adj)	nie groot nie	[ni χroət ni]
not difficult (adj)	nie moeilik nie	[ni muilik ni]
obligatory (adj)	verplig	[ferpləχ]
old (house)	ou	[æʊ]
open (adj)	oop	[oəp]
opposite (adj)	teenoorgestel	[teənoərχestəl]
ordinary (usual)	gewoon	[χevoən]
original (unusual)	oorspronklik	[oərspronklik]
past (recent)	laas-	[lās-]
permanent (adj)	permanent	[permanent]
personal (adj)	persoonlik	[persoənlik]
polite (adj)	beleefd	[beleəft]
poor (not rich)	arm	[arm]
possible (adj)	moontlik	[moəntlik]
present (current)	huidig	[hœidəχ]
previous (adj)	vorig	[forəχ]
principal (main)	vernaamste	[fernāmstə]
private (~ jet)	privaat	[prifāt]
probable (adj)	waarskynlik	[vārskajnlik]
prolonged (e.g., ~ applause)	langdurig	[laŋdurəχ]

public (open to all)	openbaar	[openbãr]
punctual (person)	stip	[stip]
quiet (tranquil)	rustig	[rustəχ]
rare (adj)	seldsaam	[sɛldsãm]
raw (uncooked)	rou	[ræʊ]
right (not left)	regter	[reχtər]

right, correct (adj)	reg	[reχ]
ripe (fruit)	ryp	[rajp]
risky (adj)	riskant	[riskant]
sad (~ look)	droewig	[druvəχ]

sad (depressing)	droewig	[druvəχ]
safe (not dangerous)	veilig	[fæjləχ]
salty (food)	sout	[sæʊt]
satisfied (customer)	tevrede	[tefredə]

second hand (adj)	gebruik	[χebrœik]
shallow (water)	vlak	[flak]
sharp (blade, etc.)	skerp	[skerp]
short (in length)	kort	[kort]

short, short-lived (adj)	kort	[kort]
significant (notable)	beduidend	[bedœident]
similar (adj)	eenders	[eənders]
simple (easy)	eenvoudig	[eənfæʊdəχ]
skinny	brandmaer	[brandmaər]

small (in size)	klein	[klæjn]
smooth (surface)	glad	[χlat]
soft (~ toys)	sag	[saχ]
solid (~ wall)	stewig	[stevəχ]

sour (flavor, taste)	suur	[sɪr]
spacious (house, etc.)	ruim	[rœim]
special (adj)	spesiaal	[spesiãl]
straight (line, road)	reg	[reχ]
strong (person)	sterk	[sterk]

stupid (foolish)	dom	[dom]
suitable (e.g., ~ for drinking)	geskik	[χeskik]
sunny (day)	sonnig	[sonnəχ]
superb, perfect (adj)	uitstekend	[œitstekent]
swarthy (adj)	blas	[blas]

sweet (sugary)	soet	[sut]
tan (adj)	bruingebrand	[brœiŋəbrant]
tasty (delicious)	smaaklik	[smãklik]
tender (affectionate)	teer	[teər]
the highest (adj)	hoogste	[hoəχstə]
the most important	belangrikste	[belaŋrikstə]

the nearest	naaste	[nãstə]
the same, equal (adj)	dieselfde	[disɛlfdə]
thick (e.g., ~ fog)	dig	[diχ]
thick (wall, slice)	dik	[dik]

thin (person)	maer	[maər]
tight (~ shoes)	strak	[strak]
tired (exhausted)	moeg	[muχ]
tiring (adj)	vermoeiend	[fermujent]

transparent (adj)	deursigtig	[døərsiχtəχ]
unclear (adj)	onduidelik	[ondœidelik]
unique (exceptional)	uniek	[unik]
various (adj)	verskillend	[ferskillent]

warm (moderately hot)	louwarm	[læuvarm]
wet (e.g., ~ clothes)	nat	[nat]
whole (entire, complete)	heel	[heəl]
wide (e.g., ~ road)	breed	[breət]
young (adj)	jong	[joŋ]

MAIN 500 VERBS

252. Verbs A-C

to accompany (vt)	begelei	[beχelæj]
to accuse (vt)	beskuldig	[beskuldəχ]
to acknowledge (admit)	erken	[ɛrken]
to act (take action)	optree	[optreə]
to add (supplement)	byvoeg	[bajfuχ]
to address (speak to)	toespreek	[tuspreək]
to admire (vi)	bewonder	[bevondər]
to advertise (vt)	adverteer	[adferteər]
to advise (vt)	aanraai	[ānrāi]
to affirm (assert)	beweer	[beveər]
to agree (say yes)	saamstem	[sāmstem]
to aim (to point a weapon)	mik op	[mik op]
to allow (sb to do sth)	toelaat	[tulāt]
to amputate (vt)	amputeer	[amputeər]
to answer (vi, vt)	antwoord	[antwoərt]
to apologize (vi)	verskoning vra	[ferskoniŋ fra]
to appear (come into view)	verskyn	[ferskajn]
to applaud (vi, vt)	apploudisseer	[applæʊdisseər]
to appoint (assign)	aanstel	[āŋstəl]
to approach (come closer)	nader	[nadər]
to arrive (ab. train)	aankom	[ānkom]
to ask (~ sb to do sth)	vra	[fra]
to aspire to ...	streef	[streəf]
to assist (help)	assisteer	[assisteər]
to attack (mil.)	aanval	[ānfal]
to attain (objectives)	bereik	[beræjk]
to avenge (get revenge)	wreek	[vreək]
to avoid (danger, task)	vermy	[fermaj]
to award (give medal to)	toeken	[tuken]
to battle (vi)	stry	[straj]
to be (vi)	wees	[veəs]
to be a cause of ...	veroorsaak ...	[feroərsāk ...]
to be afraid	bang wees	[baŋ veəs]
to be angry (with ...)	kwaad wees ...	[kwāt veəs ...]

to be at war	oorlog voer	[oərloχ fur]
to be based (on …)	gebaseer wees op	[χebaseer veəs op]
to be bored	verveeld wees	[ferveəlt veəs]
to be convinced	oortuig wees	[oərtœiχ veəs]
to be enough	genoeg wees	[χenuχ veəs]
to be envious	jaloers wees	[jalurs veəs]
to be indignant	verontwaardig wees	[ferontwārdəχ veəs]
to be interested in …	belangstel in …	[belaŋstəl in …]
to be lost in thought	peins	[pæjns]
to be lying (~ on the table)	lê	[lɛ:]
to be needed	nodig wees	[nodəχ veəs]
to be perplexed (puzzled)	verbouereerd wees	[ferbæʋereərt veəs]
to be preserved	bewaar wees	[bevār veəs]
to be required	nodig wees	[nodəχ veəs]
to be surprised	verbaas wees	[ferbās veəs]
to be worried	bekommerd wees	[bekommərt veəs]
to beat (to hit)	slaan	[slān]
to become (e.g., ~ old)	word	[vort]
to behave (vi)	jou gedra	[jæʋ χedra]
to believe (think)	glo	[χlo]
to belong to …	behoort aan …	[behoərt ān …]
to berth (moor)	vasmeer	[fasmeər]
to blind (other drivers)	verblind	[ferblint]
to blow (wind)	waai	[vāi]
to blush (vi)	bloos	[bloəs]
to boast (vi)	spog	[spoχ]
to borrow (money)	leen	[leən]
to break (branch, toy, etc.)	breek	[breək]
to breathe (vi)	asemhaal	[asemhāl]
to bring (sth)	bring	[briŋ]
to burn (paper, logs)	verbrand	[ferbrant]
to buy (purchase)	koop	[koəp]
to call (~ for help)	roep	[rup]
to call (yell for sb)	roep	[rup]
to calm down (vt)	kalmeer	[kalmeər]
can (v aux)	kan	[kan]
to cancel (call off)	kanselleer	[kaŋsɛlleər]
to cast off (of a boat or ship)	vertrek	[fertrek]
to catch (e.g., ~ a ball)	vang	[faŋ]
to change (~ one's opinion)	verander	[ferandər]
to change (exchange)	wissel	[vissəl]
to charm (vt)	sjarmeer	[ʃarmeər]
to choose (select)	kies	[kis]

to chop off (with an ax)	afkap	[afkap]
to clean (e.g., kettle from scale)	skoonmaak	[skoənmāk]
to clean (shoes, etc.)	skoonmaak	[skoənmāk]
to clean up (tidy)	skoonmaak	[skoənmāk]
to close (vt)	sluit	[slœit]
to comb one's hair	hare kam	[harə kam]
to come down (the stairs)	afkom	[afkom]
to come out (book)	verskyn	[ferskajn]
to compare (vt)	vergelyk	[ferχəlajk]
to compensate (vt)	vergoed	[ferχut]
to compete (vi)	kompeteer	[kompeteər]
to compile (~ a list)	saamstel	[sāmstəl]
to complain (vi, vt)	kla	[kla]
to complicate (vt)	bemoeilik	[bemuilik]
to compose (music, etc.)	komponeer	[komponeər]
to compromise (reputation)	kompromitteer	[kompromitteər]
to concentrate (vi)	konsentreer	[kɔŋsentreər]
to confess (criminal)	beken	[beken]
to confuse (mix up)	verwar	[ferwar]
to congratulate (vt)	gelukwens	[χelukwɛŋs]
to consult (doctor, expert)	konsulteer	[kɔŋsulteər]
to continue (~ to do sth)	vervolg	[ferfolχ]
to control (vt)	kontroleer	[kontroleər]
to convince (vt)	oortuig	[oərtœəχ]
to cooperate (vi)	saamwerk	[sāmwerk]
to coordinate (vt)	koördineer	[koordineər]
to correct (an error)	korrigeer	[korriχeər]
to cost (vt)	kos	[kos]
to count (money, etc.)	tel	[təl]
to count on ...	reken op ...	[reken op ...]
to crack (ceiling, wall)	kraak	[krāk]
to create (vt)	skep	[skep]
to crush, to squash (~ a bug)	verpletter	[ferplɛttər]
to cry (weep)	huil	[hœil]
to cut off (with a knife)	afsny	[afsnaj]

253. Verbs D-G

| to dare (~ to do sth) | durf | [durf] |
| to date from ... | dateer van ... | [dateər fan ...] |

| to deceive (vi, vt) | bedrieg | [bedrəχ] |
| to decide (~ to do sth) | beslis | [beslis] |

to decorate (tree, street)	versier	[fersir]
to dedicate (book, etc.)	opdra	[opdra]
to defend (a country, etc.)	verdedig	[ferdedəχ]
to defend oneself	jouself verdedig	[jæusɛlf ferdedəχ]

to demand (request firmly)	eis	[æjs]
to denounce (vt)	aankla	[ānkla]
to deny (vt)	ontken	[ontken]
to depend on ...	afhang van ...	[afhaŋ fan ...]

to deprive (vt)	ontneem	[ontneəm]
to deserve (vt)	verdien	[ferdin]
to design (machine, etc.)	ontwerp	[ontwerp]
to desire (want, wish)	wens	[vɛŋs]

to despise (vt)	minag	[minaχ]
to destroy (documents, etc.)	vernietig	[fernitəχ]
to differ (from sth)	verskil	[ferskil]
to dig (tunnel, etc.)	grawe	[χravə]
to direct (point the way)	die pad wys	[di pat vajs]

to disappear (vi)	verdwyn	[ferdwajn]
to discover (new land, etc.)	ontdek	[ontdek]
to discuss (vt)	bespreek	[bespreək]
to distribute (leaflets, etc.)	versprei	[ferspræj]

to disturb (vt)	steur	[støər]
to dive (vi)	duik	[dœik]
to divide (math)	deel	[deəl]
to do (vt)	doen	[dun]

to do the laundry	die wasgoed was	[di vasχut vas]
to double (increase)	verdubbel	[ferdubbəl]
to doubt (have doubts)	twyfel	[twajfəl]

to dream (daydream)	droom	[droəm]
to dream (in sleep)	droom	[droəm]
to drink (vi, vt)	drink	[drink]

to drive away (scare away)	wegry	[veχraj]
to drop (let fall)	laat val	[lāt fal]
to drown (ab. person)	verdrink	[ferdrink]
to dry (clothes, hair)	droog	[droəχ]

to eat (vi, vt)	eet	[eət]
to eavesdrop (vi)	afluister	[aflœeistər]
to emit (diffuse - odor, etc.)	versprei	[ferspræj]

to enjoy oneself	jouself geniet	[jæʊsɛlf χenit]
to enter (on the list)	byvoeg	[bajfuχ]
to enter (room, house, etc.)	binnegaan	[binnəχān]
to entertain (amuse)	amuseer	[amuseər]
to equip (fit out)	toerus	[turus]

to examine (proposal)	ondersoek	[ondərsuk]
to exchange (sth)	uitruil	[œitrajl]
to excuse (forgive)	verskoon	[ferskoən]
to exist (vi)	bestaan	[bestān]

to expect (anticipate)	verwag	[ferwaχ]
to expect (foresee)	voorsien	[foərsin]
to expel (from school, etc.)	uitsit	[œitsit]
to explain (vt)	verklaar	[ferklār]

to express (vt)	uitdruk	[œitdruk]
to extinguish (a fire)	blus	[blus]
to fall in love (with ...)	verlief raak	[ferlif rāk]
to feed (provide food)	voer	[fur]

to fight (against the enemy)	veg	[feχ]
to fight (vi)	veg	[feχ]
to fill (glass, bottle)	vul	[ful]
to find (~ lost items)	vind	[fint]

to finish (vt)	klaarmaak	[klārmāk]
to fish (angle)	visvang	[fisfaŋ]
to fit (ab. dress, etc.)	pas	[pas]
to flatter (vt)	vlei	[flæj]

to fly (bird, plane)	vlieg	[fliχ]
to follow ... (come after)	volg ...	[folχ ...]
to forbid (vt)	verbied	[ferbit]
to force (compel)	verplig	[ferpləχ]

to forget (vi, vt)	vergeet	[ferχeət]
to forgive (pardon)	vergewe	[ferχevə]
to form (constitute)	vorm	[form]
to get dirty (vi)	vuil word	[fœil vort]

to get infected (with ...)	besmet word met ...	[besmet vort met ...]
to get irritated	geïrriteerd raak	[χeïrriteərt rāk]
to get married	trou	[træʊ]
to get rid of ...	ontslae raak van ...	[ontslaə rāk fan ...]

to get tired	moeg word	[muχ vort]
to get up (arise from bed)	opstaan	[opstān]
to give (vt)	gee	[χeə]
to give a bath (to bath)	bad	[bat]

to give a hug, to hug (vt)	**omhels**	[omhɛls]
to give in (yield to)	**toegee**	[tuχeə]
to glimpse (vt)	**skrams raaksien**	[skrams rāksin]
to go (by car, etc.)	**gaan**	[χān]
to go (on foot)	**gaan**	[χān]
to go for a swim	**gaan swem**	[χān swem]
to go out (for dinner, etc.)	**uitgaan**	[œitχān]
to go to bed (go to sleep)	**gaan slaap**	[χān slāp]
to greet (vt)	**groet**	[χrut]
to grow (plants)	**kweek**	[kweək]
to guarantee (vt)	**waarborg**	[vārborχ]
to guess (the answer)	**raai**	[rāi]

254. Verbs H-M

to hand out (distribute)	**uitdeel**	[œitdeəl]
to hang (curtains, etc.)	**ophang**	[ophaŋ]
to have (vt)	**hê**	[hɛ:]
to have a try	**probeer**	[probeər]
to have breakfast	**ontbyt**	[ontbajt]
to have dinner	**aandete gebruik**	[āndetə χebrœik]
to have lunch	**gaan eet**	[χān eət]
to head (group, etc.)	**lei**	[læj]
to hear (vt)	**hoor**	[hoər]
to heat (vt)	**verwarm**	[ferwarm]
to help (vt)	**help**	[hɛlp]
to hide (vt)	**wegsteek**	[veχsteək]
to hire (e.g., ~ a boat)	**huur**	[hɪr]
to hire (staff)	**huur**	[hɪr]
to hope (vi, vt)	**hoop**	[hoəp]
to hunt (for food, sport)	**jag**	[jaχ]
to hurry (vi)	**opskud**	[opskut]
to imagine (to picture)	**verbeel**	[ferbeəl]
to imitate (vt)	**naboots**	[naboəts]
to implore (vt)	**smeek**	[smeək]
to import (vt)	**invoer**	[infur]
to increase (vi)	**toeneem**	[tuneəm]
to increase (vt)	**verhoog**	[ferhoəχ]
to infect (vt)	**besmet**	[besmet]
to influence (vt)	**beïnvloed**	[beïnflut]
to inform (e.g., ~ the police about)	**in kennis stel**	[in kɛnnis stəl]
to inform (vt)	**in kennis stel**	[in kɛnnis stəl]

| to inherit (vt) | erf | [ɛrf] |
| to inquire (about …) | navraag doen | [nafrāχ dun] |

to insert (put in)	insteek	[insteək]
to insinuate (imply)	sinspeel	[sinspeəl]
to insist (vi, vt)	aandring	[āndriŋ]
to inspire (vt)	inspireer	[inspireər]
to instruct (teach)	leer	[leər]

to insult (offend)	beledig	[beledəχ]
to interest (vt)	interesseer	[interesseər]
to intervene (vi)	tussenbeide tree	[tussenbæjdə treə]
to introduce (sb to sb)	voorstel	[foərstəl]
to invent (machine, etc.)	uitvind	[œitfint]

to invite (vt)	uitnooi	[œitnoj]
to iron (clothes)	stryk	[strajk]
to irritate (annoy)	irriteer	[irriteər]
to isolate (vt)	isoleer	[isoleər]
to join (political party, etc.)	aansluit	[āŋslœit]

to joke (be kidding)	grappies maak	[χrappis māk]
to keep (old letters, etc.)	bewaar	[bevār]
to keep silent	stilbly	[stilblaj]
to kill (vt)	doodmaak	[doədmāk]
to knock (at the door)	klop	[klop]

to know (sb)	ken	[ken]
to know (sth)	weet	[veət]
to laugh (vi)	lag	[laχ]
to launch (start up)	van stapel stuur	[fan stapəl stɪr]

to leave (~ for Mexico)	vertrek	[fertrek]
to leave (forget sth)	vergeet	[ferχeət]
to leave (spouse)	verlaat	[ferlāt]
to liberate (city, etc.)	bevry	[befraj]
to lie (~ on the floor)	lê	[lɛ:]

to lie (tell untruth)	lieg	[liχ]
to light (campfire, etc.)	aansteek	[āŋsteək]
to light up (illuminate)	verlig	[ferləχ]
to like (I like …)	hou van	[hæʊ fan]
to limit (vt)	beperk	[beperk]

to listen (vi)	luister	[lœistər]
to live (~ in France)	woon	[voən]
to live (exist)	leef	[leəf]
to load (gun)	laai	[lāi]
to load (vehicle, etc.)	laai	[lāi]

| to look (I'm just ~ing) | kyk | [kajk] |
| to look for … (search) | soek … | [suk …] |

to look like (resemble)	lyk	[lajk]
to lose (umbrella, etc.)	verloor	[ferloər]
to love (e.g., ~ dancing)	hou van	[hæʊ fan]

to love (sb)	liefhê	[lifhɛ:]
to lower (blind, head)	laat sak	[lāt sak]
to make (~ dinner)	maak	[māk]
to make angry	kwaad maak	[kwāt māk]

to make easier	makliker maak	[maklikər māk]
to make multiple copies	aantal kopieë maak	[āntal kopiɛ māk]
to make the acquaintance	kennismaak	[kɛnnismāk]
to make use (of ...)	gebruik ...	[xebrœik ...]
to manage, to run	beheer	[beheər]

to mark (make a mark)	merk	[merk]
to mean (signify)	beteken	[betekən]
to memorize (vt)	van buite leer	[fan bœitə leər]
to mention (talk about)	verwys na	[ferwajs na]
to miss (school, etc.)	bank	[bank]

to mix (combine, blend)	meng	[meŋ]
to mock (make fun of)	terg	[terχ]
to move (to shift)	skuif	[skœif]
to multiply (math)	vermenigvuldig	[fermeniχ·fuldəχ]
must (v aux)	moet	[mut]

255. Verbs N-R

to name, to call (vt)	noem	[num]
to negotiate (vi)	onderhandel	[ondərhandəl]
to note (write down)	noteer	[noteər]
to notice (see)	raaksien	[rāksin]

to obey (vi, vt)	gehoorsaam	[xehoərsām]
to object (vi, vt)	beswaar maak	[beswār māk]
to observe (see)	waarneem	[vārneəm]
to offend (vt)	beledig	[beledəχ]
to omit (word, phrase)	weglaat	[veχlāt]

to open (vt)	oopmaak	[oəpmāk]
to order (in restaurant)	bestel	[bestəl]
to order (mil.)	beveel	[befeəl]
to organize (concert, party)	organiseer	[orχaniseər]
to overestimate (vt)	oorskat	[oərskat]

to own (possess)	besit	[besit]
to participate (vi)	deelneem	[deəlneəm]
to pass through (by car, etc.)	ry deur	[raj døər]

to pay (vi, vt)	**betaal**	[betāl]
to peep, spy on	**loer**	[lur]
to penetrate (vt)	**deurdring**	[døərdriŋ]
to permit (vt)	**toelaat**	[tulāt]
to pick (flowers)	**pluk**	[pluk]
to place (put, set)	**sit**	[sit]
to plan (~ to do sth)	**beplan**	[beplan]
to play (actor)	**speel**	[speəl]
to play (children)	**speel**	[speəl]
to point (~ the way)	**wys**	[vajs]
to pour (liquid)	**skink**	[skink]
to pray (vi, vt)	**bid**	[bit]
to prefer (vt)	**verkies**	[ferkis]
to prepare (~ a plan)	**voorberei**	[foərberæj]
to present (sb to sb)	**voorstel**	[foərstəl]
to preserve (peace, life)	**bewaar**	[bevār]
to prevail (vt)	**oorheers**	[oərheərs]
to progress (move forward)	**vorder**	[fordər]
to promise (vt)	**beloof**	[beloəf]
to pronounce (vt)	**uitspreek**	[œitspreək]
to propose (vt)	**voorstel**	[foərstəl]
to protect (e.g., ~ nature)	**beskerm**	[beskerm]
to protest (vi)	**protesteer**	[protesteər]
to prove (vt)	**bewys**	[bevajs]
to provoke (vt)	**uittart**	[œittart]
to pull (~ the rope)	**trek**	[trek]
to punish (vt)	**straf**	[straf]
to push (~ the door)	**stoot**	[stoət]
to put away (vt)	**bêre**	[bærə]
to put in order	**aan kant maak**	[ān kant māk]
to put, to place	**plaas**	[plās]
to quote (cite)	**aanhaal**	[ānhāl]
to reach (arrive at)	**bereik**	[beræjk]
to read (vi, vt)	**lees**	[lees]
to realize (a dream)	**verwesenlik**	[ferwesenlik]
to recognize (identify sb)	**herken**	[herken]
to recommend (vt)	**aanbeveel**	[ānbefeəl]
to recover (~ from flu)	**herstel**	[herstəl]
to redo (do again)	**oordoen**	[oərdun]
to reduce (speed, etc.)	**verminder**	[fermindər]
to refuse (~ sb)	**weier**	[væjer]
to regret (be sorry)	**jammer wees**	[jammər veəs]

to reinforce (vt)	**versterk**	[fersterk]
to remember (Do you ~ me?)	**herinner**	[herinnər]
to remember (I can't ~ her name)	**onthou**	[onthæʊ]
to remind of ...	**laat onthou ...**	[lāt onthæʊ ...]
to remove (~ a stain)	**verwyder**	[ferwajdər]
to remove (~ an obstacle)	**verwyder**	[ferwajdər]
to rent (sth from sb)	**huur**	[hɪr]
to repair (mend)	**herstel**	[herstəl]
to repeat (say again)	**herhaal**	[herhāl]
to report (make a report)	**rapporteer**	[rapporteər]
to reproach (vt)	**verwyt**	[ferwajt]
to reserve, to book	**bespreek**	[bespreək]
to restrain (hold back)	**in bedwang hou**	[in bedwaŋ hæʊ]
to return (come back)	**terugkeer**	[teruχkeər]
to risk, to take a risk	**waag**	[vāχ]
to rub out (erase)	**uitvee**	[œitfeə]
to run (move fast)	**hardloop**	[hardloəp]
to rush (hurry sb)	**aanjaag**	[ānjāχ]

256. Verbs S-W

to satisfy (please)	**bevredig**	[befredəχ]
to save (rescue)	**red**	[ret]
to say (~ thank you)	**sê**	[sɛː]
to scold (vt)	**uitvaar teen**	[œitfār teən]
to scratch (with claws)	**krap**	[krap]
to select (to pick)	**selekteer**	[selekteər]
to sell (goods)	**verkoop**	[ferkoəp]
to send (a letter)	**stuur**	[stɪr]
to send back (vt)	**terugstuur**	[teruχstɪr]
to sense (~ danger)	**aanvoel**	[ānful]
to sentence (vt)	**veroordeel**	[feroərdeəl]
to serve (in restaurant)	**bedien**	[bedin]
to settle (a conflict)	**besleg**	[besleχ]
to shake (vt)	**skommel**	[skommel]
to shave (vi)	**skeer**	[skeər]
to shine (gleam)	**blink**	[blink]
to shiver (with cold)	**ril**	[ril]
to shoot (vi)	**skiet**	[skit]
to shout (vi)	**skreeu**	[skriʊ]

to show (to display)	wys	[vajs]
to shudder (vi)	huiwer	[hœivər]
to sigh (vi)	sug	[suχ]
to sign (document)	teken	[tekən]
to signify (mean)	beteken	[betekən]

to simplify (vt)	vereenvoudig	[fereənfæʊdəχ]
to sin (vi)	sondig	[sondəχ]
to sit (be sitting)	sit	[sit]
to sit down (vi)	gaan sit	[χān sit]

to smell (emit an odor)	ruik	[rœik]
to smell (inhale the odor)	ruik	[rœik]
to smile (vi)	glimlag	[χlimlaχ]
to snap (vi, ab. rope)	breek	[breək]
to solve (problem)	oplos	[oplos]

to sow (seed, crop)	saai	[sāi]
to spill (liquid)	mors	[mors]
to spill out, scatter (flour, etc.)	laat val	[lāt fal]
to spit (vi)	spoeg	[spuχ]

to stand (toothache, cold)	verdra	[ferdra]
to start (begin)	begin	[beχin]
to steal (money, etc.)	steel	[steəl]
to stop (for pause, etc.)	stilhou	[stilhæʊ]

to stop (please ~ calling me)	ophou	[ophæʊ]
to stop talking	ophou praat	[ophæʊ prāt]
to stroke (caress)	streel	[streəl]
to study (vt)	studeer	[studeər]

to suffer (feel pain)	ly	[laj]
to support (cause, idea)	steun	[støən]
to suppose (assume)	veronderstel	[feronderstəl]
to surface (ab. submarine)	opduik	[opdœik]

to surprise (amaze)	verras	[ferras]
to suspect (vt)	verdink	[ferdink]
to swim (vi)	swem	[swem]
to take (get hold of)	vat	[fat]

to take a bath	bad	[bat]
to take a rest	rus	[rus]
to take away (e.g., about waiter)	wegvat	[veχfat]

| to take off (airplane) | opstyg | [opstajχ] |
| to take off (painting, curtains, etc.) | afneem | [afneəm] |

to take pictures	fotografeer	[fotoχrafeər]
to talk to ...	praat met ...	[prāt met ...]
to teach (give lessons)	leer	[leər]

to tear off, to rip off (vt)	afskeur	[afskøər]
to tell (story, joke)	vertel	[fertəl]
to thank (vt)	dank	[dank]
to think (believe)	glo	[χlo]

to think (vi, vt)	dink	[dink]
to threaten (vt)	dreig	[dræjχ]
to throw (stone, etc.)	gooi	[χoj]
to tie to ...	vasbind aan ...	[fasbint ān ...]

to tie up (prisoner)	vasbind	[fasbint]
to tire (make tired)	vermoei	[fermui]
to touch (one's arm, etc.)	aanraak	[ānrāk]
to tower (over ...)	uitstyg bo	[œitstajχ boə]

to train (animals)	afrig	[afrəχ]
to train (sb)	afrig	[afrəχ]
to train (vi)	oefen	[ufen]
to transform (vt)	transformeer	[traŋsformeər]

to translate (vt)	vertaal	[fertāl]
to treat (illness)	behandel	[behandəl]
to trust (vt)	vertrou	[fertræʊ]
to try (attempt)	probeer	[probeər]

to turn (e.g., ~ left)	draai	[drāi]
to turn away (vi)	wegdraai	[veχdrāi]
to turn off (the light)	afskakel	[afskakəl]
to turn on (computer, etc.)	aanskakel	[āŋskakəl]
to turn over (stone, etc.)	omkeer	[omkeər]

to underestimate (vt)	onderskat	[ondərskat]
to underline (vt)	onderstreep	[ondərstreəp]
to understand (vt)	verstaan	[ferstān]
to undertake (vt)	onderneem	[ondərneəm]

to unite (vt)	verenig	[ferenəχ]
to untie (vt)	losmaak	[losmāk]
to use (phrase, word)	gebruik	[χebrœik]
to vaccinate (vt)	inent	[inɛnt]

to vote (vi)	stem	[stem]
to wait (vt)	wag	[vaχ]
to wake (sb)	wakker maak	[vakkər māk]
to want (wish, desire)	wil	[vil]

| to warn (of the danger) | waarsku | [vārsku] |
| to wash (clean) | was | [vas] |

| to water (plants) | nat gooi | [nat χoj] |
| to wave (the hand) | wuif | [vœif] |

to weigh (have weight)	weeg	[veəχ]
to work (vi)	werk	[verk]
to worry (make anxious)	bekommerd maak	[bekommərt māk]
to worry (vi)	bekommer	[bekommər]

to wrap (parcel, etc.)	inpak	[inpak]
to wrestle (sport)	worstel	[vorstəl]
to write (vt)	skryf	[skrajf]
to write down	opskryf	[opskrajf]

CPSIA information can be obtained
at www.ICGtesting.com
Printed in the USA
BVHW041254160621
609733BV00013B/313